Bumpings and Blessings

❧ GRANNY'S REMEMBERING BOOK ❧

Helen Cole Littleton

CROSSBOOKS
PUBLISHING

CrossBooks™
A Division of LifeWay
1663 Liberty Drive
Bloomington, IN 47403
www.crossbooks.com
Phone: 1-866-879-0502

First published by CrossBooks 11/05/2012

ISBN: 978-1-4627-1941-9 (sc)
ISBN: 978-1-4627-1940-2 (hc)
ISBN: 978-1-4627-1942-6 (e)

Library of Congress Control Number: 2012910764

Printed in the United States of America

This book is printed on acid-free paper.

Preface

During the summer of 1981, Daddy Lit and I attended an Elderhostel at Yavapai College in Prescott, Arizona. One of the courses offered was Creative Writing. From this stems this collection of memories of people, events and occasions.

Julia Day, our instructor, repeatedly begged us to write such a book, else when we died our memories would die with us. According to her, you, our children, grandchildren and great grandchildren would like to know more about what we did, what we thought, how we worked and how we played.

If it sounds crude and "corny," that is just because your granny could never be anything else. But it is because of the love she has for life and for you that she would dare attempt to write a collection of memories.

If you enjoy this or find it interesting, all I ask of you is to start your own Remembering Book.

Helen M. Littleton

Introduction

by William David Downs, Jr.

I never met Helen Marie Cole, (1914-1994), the author of *"Bumpings and Blessings,"* but I wish I had. Subtitled "Granny's Remembering Book," her exquisitely detailed 437-page handwritten autobiography was presented to Vera and me as an expression of the Cole family's appreciation for how I had portrayed the life and death of Lt. Merrill Cole, Helen's husband, in *"The Fighting Tigers,"* the stories of the thirty-six Ouachita Baptist University students who had given their lives during World War II.

While I was working on another project, the manuscript languished in *"The Fighting Tigers"* file cabinet until late in 2011. It was then that out of the blue, Vera asked me to retrieve the manuscript. For the next few weeks, whatever I was doing was almost constantly interrupted, when laughing or choking back tears or both, she would cry, *"You've got to hear this!"*

I did—*and did and did!*—until I began to recognize what I was hearing—these were touching and unforgettable stories of being raised in the poverty of Arkansas, of her storybook romance with Merrill and how they succeeded in raising five children during the depths of the Great Depression.

"It was a simple life," she recalled, "but a good one. The Depression may have denied us some of the things we would have liked and really needed, but it didn't keep us from being happy." She recalls falling in love:

I can remember the admiration I had always felt for [Merrill]. He was something like a hero to me. Here was a prince saying to me, 'I love you.' It seemed like a fairy tale. I had such a peculiar feeling, but as the days, weeks and months went on, I knew I was not dreaming. This guy really loved me.

Written to *express* rather than to impress, the hallmark of effective writing, Helen Marie's touching stories of faith, hope, love, happiness, sadness, courage and everyday life ring with heartfelt sincerity that must be shared with others as in *"You've got to hear this!"* With that in mind, Vera transcribed the original work just as it had been written. *"Bumpings and Blessings"* contains stories of universal and timeless appeal in that they invite us to share in the everyday lives of the Cole family. For example, here is how Helen described the typical content of "three square meals a day":

We had breakfast, dinner and supper. For breakfast we had home-cured bacon or ham, gravy, eggs, oatmeal and biscuits. For dinner we had vegetables, some meat, either pork or chicken, and corn bread. Often we had fruit cobbler, cake or cookies of some sort. I remember especially the molasses cookies. Supper was a lighter meal, often left-over corn bread and milk. Sometimes Granny made hot mush to eat with our 'sweet milk.' We had sweet milk, buttermilk, clabber milk, skim milk—but never just 'milk.'

In these pages, readers will discover that in April 1956, twelve years after Merrill's death, Helen married James W. Littleton, an event that was whole-heartedly approved by the extended Cole family, who lovingly referred to him as "Daddy Lit."

In the summer of 1981, he and Helen attended an Elderhostel in Prescott, Ariz. "One of the courses offered," she said, was Creative writing," in which the instructor encouraged them to write a collection of memories of the people, events and occasion of their lives. I consider this to be some very good advice for all of us who hope to be remembered well long after we are gone.

"You may wonder why I named the book *'Bumpings and Blessings,'* she said. "Life for me became full of them. War bumped me into widowhood, blessings were ahead. God did not forget me. Rather, He used family and friends to minister to me, and I want to tell you how."

Helen Marie Cole was surely "The wife of noble character" spoken of in Proverbs 31:

She is worth more than rubies. Her husband has full confidence in her and lacks nothing of value. She brings him good, not harm, all the days of her life. She opens her arms to the poor and extends her hands to the needy. When it snows, she has no fear for her household; for all of them are clothed in scarlet. She makes coverings for her bed; she is clothed in fine linen and purple. Her husband is respected at the city gate. . .She is clothed with strength and dignity; she can laugh at the days to come. . .She speaks with wisdom, and faithful instruction is on her tongue. . .She watches over the affairs of her household and does not eat the bread of idleness. . .Charm is deceptive, and beauty is fleeting; but a woman who fears the Lord is to be praised.

Enjoy!

William D. Downs Jr., Ph.D.
Professor Emeritus – Mass Communications
Ouachita Baptist University • Arkadelphia, Arkansas

November 6, 2011

Dedicated to my "Granny," Nancy Catherine Hudson

Part 1: 1914-1930

Bumpings and Blessings

Along side Crooked Creek in Boone County, Arkansas, there stood a beautiful southern home. One morning in March, 1914, St. Patrick's Day to be exact, Grandpa Hudson, Christopher Columbus Hudson, was out in the garden planting Irish potatoes. His wife, Nancy Catherine, whom I called Granny, was helping him when suddenly they were called into the house. Their potato planting was stopped abruptly because Mattie was having a baby. This came as a surprise since they had not ever suspected that their daughter was pregnant, so Granny told me. But soon a tiny, tiny baby girl was born. She was named Helen Marie, a name "Miss Mattie" had picked out of a story she had once read.

She was truthfully "Miss Mattie," as her students called her, because my mother had never been married. She had graduated from Bellefonte High School in 1910 and continued to live with Grandpa and Granny and taught in the neighborhood schools, and she was known in the community as "Miss Mattie."

Mother said I was so small they could put a teacup over my head. I made it without a thought of being placed in an incubator. Of course,

Baby picture of Helen Marie

there were none available in the Ozark Mountains. I weighed four pounds when I was six weeks old.

I do not know what happened during my first two years of life as mother never talked about my birth or the circumstances around it. I was loved and cared for and that was the most important thing, after all. In those days you didn't talk about such things. I am thankful to her for giving me life and to my grandparents for allowing Mother and me to make our home with them. Thirty-one years later, Granny died while living with me, still watching after me.

By the time I was two, we had moved to the 60-acre farm I remember as my home.

The farmhouse

This was just about a mile or so from my birthplace and five and one half miles south of Harrison, Arkansas. The gray clapboard house with two dormer windows on the roof stood in a grove of black-walnut trees.

I remember often seeing Granny and Mother cracking walnuts. The fireplace in one room of the house was the center of activity. There were two double beds in this room and my earliest recollection perhaps was the time I crawled out of bed and sat down on a cocklebur. I was going to sit in my little red chair and put on my shoes in front of the fire. It must have made a real impression on me.

The fireplace was where they boiled the clothes in the wintertime. I can remember the big black iron pot that would barely go inside the fireplace. The smell of the homemade lye soap had an odor all its own as Mother punched the clothes with a big stick. Cracking walnuts on a back stick that was placed on the hearth was Granny's main winter's occupation. The kernels were sold or mailed to kinfolks as far away as California. It was here I heard Granny tell lots of tales about our ancestors.

On January seventeenth, in this bedroom my Grandpa Hudson died. The only thing I remember about his death is going to the burial at Bellefonte Cemetery about four miles away. The coffin was in a wagon and since my grandfather was a Mason, men on horseback hurried ahead of the wagon to be at each turn of the road. There they would form an arch with their spears and the wagon bearing the corpse would pass underneath it. Then the horsemen would go ahead to the next corner. I love the epitaph on his tomb-stone, "A smile hath passed which filled our home with light. A soul whose beauty made that smile so bright."

Grandpa and Granny Hudson

Granny is buried beside him. It is one of the most peaceful spots I know. It overlooks a green meadow with a pond at the bottom of the hill. You can watch the cattle gently grazing or drinking from the pond. I have often thought what a beautiful spot to wait for the Lord to come again.

I can't remember much about Grandpa Hudson. I do remember hearing him say on my second birthday, "You are two years old and not as big as a cake of soap after a hard day's washing." I heard Granny tell of him many times. On January thirty-first, she would always say to me, "This is your Grandpa's birthday." For twenty-seven years she said this to me so I have never gotten away from connecting Grandpa with this date. Granny always told me that she and Grandpa never had a cross word. I found her to be an honest woman, but I always wondered about her memory. She thought he was a pretty great man and I guess the local historians did too. This is a portion of an article★ I found about him at the Little Rock library in a book titled "A Reminiscent History of the Ozark Region." ★ *See at www.hearthstonelegacy.com/ozark.*

As you see, my mother came from a long line of pioneers. We can trace her father's family, the Hudsons, back to the 1700's. A recorded affidavit tells of my great, great, great grandfather Edward Hudson's service in the Revolutionary War. After the war, he lived in South Carolina for eight or ten years before moving to Tennessee. He was married to Mary Ann Wheat and they were parents of ten children. After nearly thirty years, he moved to Randolph County, Arkansas. It was at the age of eighty that he filed the affidavit and signed his mark. He and his wife were described as follows:

"They are poor old decrippled. He has no land or money from the government. He knows no person now alive by whom he can prove his services (his discharge was lost in moving to the West by accident in getting wet). He relinquishes all claims to any and all pay pension, land or money. He has a mare, two colts, six head of cattle and a few hogs. Owing to poverty, old age and decrepitude he has abandoned keeping house and lives with his son-in-law."

He died in 1845 and is buried at Ravendon Springs, Arkansas.

Edward's oldest son, Jon, born in 1773, is my great-great grandfather. He also died in 1845 and is buried in Bellar Cemetery near Harrison, Arkansas.

My great grandfather, Samuel Hudson, was born in Tennessee and came with his brother, Andrew Jackson, to Newton County and homesteaded land along the Little Buffalo River between Jasper and Parthenon. Many stories are told about these brave pioneers. One was about the time they chased a bear into a cave and following it inside they discovered the large Diamond Cave, a long-time attraction in Newton County. Time was when descendants of the two brothers were admitted free to tour the cave, but no longer. Many times I took advantage of the free pass and was thrilled as the guide told of the courage of those mountain men and pointed out the room named in their honor. Some of the family's log cabins have been moved to the cave and preserved in the park for thousands to see.

Granny loved to point out the bullet holes in the cabin walls made during the Civil War. Her tales of the Civil War were always hair-raising to me. She told of living in a log cabin near the cave at Parthenon. One day soldiers came by and Aunt Jane (now who Aunt Jane was, I don't know) answered the rap on the door. They wanted money. Aunt Jane went to the back room and got two or three purses. One had all the money they had in it, the other two had a little. She handed the two to the man and said, "There's our money. Now this one is full of old buttons. If you want it, you can have it." The men refused the "buttons" and their money was saved.

The tale I will never forget was when soldiers came again asking for money. When they were refused, they seized one of the old men of the family and stood him on red-hot coals of fire in the front yard to try to obtain money. The old man danced on the coals until he fell to his knees. Then the soldier pulled him off the coals and left! She said the family took the old man to a cave in a bluff along the river near Jasper where he remained during the remainder of the war. Members of the family would lower food to him from the top of the bluff. This hole was often pointed out to me as we passed along the road following the river, first in a wagon, then in a surrey and later in a car making fifty miles an hour.

My mother, Miss Mattie, continued to teach school and that left Granny and me together all day long. So I would beg her to tell me tales of my grandfathers over and over again. She talked a lot about her church. She told me about washing feet. The church she attended was some kind of Baptist Church other than Southern Baptist. I can remember seeing her baptized in Crooked Creek near the old Union Church when she joined the Southern Baptist Church. The minister would lead the "candidates" out into the water and cover their nose with his handkerchief, say a few words and baptize them. A member would take their hand and lead them out of the water. She was not a new Christian, just changing churches. This was odd to me but I'm sure it didn't bother Granny. She was a stickler for the discipline of the church.

She scolded me years later when I took the Lord's Supper in the First Baptist Church at Conway when I wasn't a member of that church. She strongly believed in "closed" communion. She also believed that cards, picture shows and dancing were sins and so was working on Sundays. She always told me that was why the man was in the moon—"he burned brush on Sunday."

Granny's faith in God was an inspiration to all who knew her. She attended church regularly as long as her health permitted and always insisted that everyone in the household attend. We knew in her later years that her first question on our return from church would be "What was the preacher's text?" So, we listened at least long enough to get that. Reading the Bible and studying her Sunday school lesson took priority in her life. As I look back I picture her with a pan full of apples in her lap and her Bible by her side. As soon as she finished eating her apples she would have her quiet time with her Lord.

Back to our home place, one thing those walnut trees did was teach me a lot of things Granny and Mother intended me to know. They used "keen cuts," which were the small switches left when the leaves were stripped off the stem. They really were keen. I don't recall being cut but if one hit hard enough it could bring the blood. I remember the feeling I had when I saw a hand reach up and pull off a keen cut and start de-leafing it.

Mother and Granny had to work hard in order to keep the farm after Grandpa died. Mother was the type of person who was determined to help herself and Granny was a person to whom an obstacle was only something to be overcome. She used to say, "I can't never did do nothing." And she proved that anyone could do anything if they tried.

She was little and stooped. Her body was bent and her ankles turned but that didn't mean she was handicapped. She was a bundle of energy and had a twinkle in her eye that made everyone know she enjoyed living.

It was fun to do things with her. For instance, she would let me churn. I remember learning to count that way. Every time the dash went up and down, I counted. I also learned some churning rhymes like:

Churn, butter, churn.
Helen Marie wants a pat of butter.

World War I came along about the time I was four years old. I remember going with Mother to Harrison and watching a troop train leave out. The old Missouri North Arkansas railroad ran through Harrison then. We were at the depot and people rolled up pieces of paper and made megaphones. I can still see the arms waving out the windows of the train as it rounded the bend and went out of sight as the onlookers waved their handkerchiefs and shouted their goodbyes. I would like to know if Jeff White was on that train, but I never asked my mother. Perhaps that was our reason for being there, because later this World War I veteran became my stepfather. But the word "step" never was heard, said or thought. He was always "Daddy" to me and a more wonderful dad could never have been found. He was the kindest man I have ever seen.

Mother and Granny washed on a rub board outside the back of the house and I remember seeing them stop their washing to look at the *Boone County Headlight*, our weekly newspaper. They would scan the paper for the casualty list. I would watch them brush a tear back when they would see a name they recognized. But, if they didn't know anyone listed, I would hear a sigh of relief and back to the rub board they went.

Our postman, Mr. Hawk Hudson, delivered the mail. What a daily happening that was. He drove a little square buggy. It was painted dark green and he sat up there on the black leather seat in what looked exactly like a box. I loved to watch for him to come and I would be at the mailbox waiting for any mail he might bring. If the Sears Roebuck or Montgomery Ward catalogs came it was like Christmas. It would take days to thumb through all those pages and look at everything. We would see something we wished for and often Granny would say, "Wish in one hand and spit in the other and see which will get full first." The old catalogs were carried to the outdoor toilet to be used for toilet paper.

Mother often read stories to me. One I shall never forget was about a large white water bird that had been injured and was forced to the ground while flying south for the winter. The children on the farm where the large bird fell were delighted. It was the most beautiful bird they had ever seen, so they mended its broken wing and nursed it until it was completely healed. It became a great pet. The children named him Dicky Daddles. For a year they were constant pals. Then in the early fall they were out in the barnyard when suddenly Dicky Daddles cocked his head to one side and looked up into the sky. The kids looked, too. There was a flock of birds in the shape of a V flying south. They could hear a honking sound. Dicky Daddles flapped his wings and he began to fly. He honked as he rose in the sky, higher and higher he went as the children watched. He seemed to turn his head as if to say, "Thank you" to the children. The children knew Dicky Daddles was joining his kind. Tears came to their eyes but they began to cheer as the beautiful bird got nearer and nearer to the large flock. They watched and waved until the birds were completely out of sight. Every time I heard that story I had to cry. It was such a sweet, sad story.

We always had cows to milk and one evening Mother was milking and she had me sitting on the milk shelf built on top of a big gatepost of the barn lot. I was to shoo the flies away from the milk. I remember looking down the road and seeing a soldier in uniform coming toward our house. He came right up to the gate and said hello to me. I couldn't believe my eyes or my ears. This was the first time I ever saw my daddy,

Mother and Daddy

Columbus Jefferson White. He had just returned from World War I where he was a member of the German Occupation Team.

A few months later Mother and my daddy were married on the fourth of July. Daddy came to live with us on the farm.

He never wanted to talk about his war experiences. Fighting those bloody battles was a thing to be forgotten and not relived. I remember his description of war very well, "War is hell." To be left the only living man on the battlefield and to lie deathly still while the enemy stalked around to see if all were dead would be enough to make one feel that it was hell. He managed to escape with only a small shrapnel wound in his heel. One thing I remember him telling was how he spit his last chew of tobacco out in the ocean on his way home.

Our farm consisted of sixty acres of land. A large portion was in apple orchards and we sold apples in the fall. There were Jonathan apples that got ripe first. These were good to eat and to cook with. I remember some apples called Ben Davis were only good when cooked. They were delicious baked and made good applesauce or pies. There were the Commerce and Champion apples that shipped well. We never ate them. Mother had two trees of Arkansas Blacks, one York Imperial and two or three Delicious. Spraying the orchards and harvesting the apples are farm chores I remember well.

There were large picksacks made of striped bed ticking. One would probably hold a bushel of apples. This made fewer trips up and down the ladder for them.

We made apple cider and always there was the vinegar barrel in the cellar, along with many bins for apples. One thing that still burns me up is how Granny always wanted me to eat the rotten spotted apples. She would sit down with a half dozen in a pan and peel them and eat the good part. I always wanted to choose a good apple to eat but she would say, "No, those will last all winter." I can still see the apple in my lunch pail with brown spots where the rot had been removed.

In back of our house was a new orchard with apples and peaches in it. There was one kind of peach I especially liked. Mother called it "Capp's White Cling." It was a large white peach.

Across the road from our house were several acres of pastureland. Along the fence row at the back of the pasture the blackberries grew thick on every vine. We picked and canned lots of blackberries and made blackberry jelly. The fourth of July was our measuring stick. We should have our berries for the winter by the fourth.

Granny raised turkeys. Sometimes she had white ones but usually they were black. She would raise about 100 and sell them just before Thanksgiving. And another thing that bugs me is we never ate a turkey–

chickens, yes, lots of them but Granny sold every turkey she ever raised. I remember what fun it was to help Granny drive the turkeys in when a cloud was approaching. She had long sticks handy, and we would pick up one and head out across the road to the large pasture with a huge oak tree in the middle of it. Granny would do her turkey call and the turkeys would all gather around her. Then with the sticks we would herd them toward the barn into the upper shed. It was fun to hear the gobbles of the toms and the strange clucking of the hens. Granny would close the gate to the shed and we would hurry on to the next thing that had to be done before it rained. The zinc tubs had to be put under the drip of the house. Clothes had to be gathered off the line. The stove wood box had to be filled and there just might be a hen and chickens to look after. Granny always managed to find enough to do to keep her out long enough to get wet.

Mother had a white Leghorn chicken and sold eggs. She had an incubator and each spring she filled it with eggs. During the three weeks of incubation she turned the eggs and kept the temperature just right. Then one day the darling little chickens would hatch. Watching them peck a hole in the shell and peep out was a thrill. From the incubator they would be moved to the brooder shed.

The brooder shed was one end of the hen house. In the other part were nests and roosts for the laying hens. In the brooder shed there was a round tin awning around a little stove. This awning was about a foot off the floor and served as the mother hen hovering over her chickens. Further out in the room were the watering jars, a glass jar with a metal pan fitted over it. Mother would fill the jar with water and add a few drops of medicine, screw on the pan then turn it upside down. The water would trickle out and keep a small amount of water available for the baby chicks to drink. There were also feeding troughs. These were long zinc trays with covers. The covers had several holes about the size of a quarter placed about an inch apart so the chicks could eat without wasting feed. Their chirping sounds were another sound of the farm that I loved to hear.

When the chicks grew up their gender determined their destiny. The little roosters would have their necks wrung when they got to be frying size. Often we had fried chicken for breakfast. It was a "must" for company—fried chicken and "light bread." Now why we didn't have good hot biscuits when we had company, I'll never figure out but light bread was the bread for company. The female chickens were kept for laying hens. Gathering the eggs at the end of every day was one of my happy jobs. They were beautiful white eggs and this experience has caused me to always choose white eggs over red ones.

One job around the chicken house I never wanted to do was clean out from under the roost. But Mother and Granny didn't seem to mind. They carried the manure to the garden for fertilizer.

Another thing Mother sold was cream. We had a cream separator. I remember large cans for the cream placed on the roadside to be picked up and carried into town. We also sold butter. This had to be molded and carried into town to be sold.

As you see, the little farm produced some income for us. But my dad decided to get a civil service job to supplement the money. He took an examination and was offered a part-time job at the Harrison post office five miles away. For several years our faithful horse, Old Dan, pulled our buggy into town for Dad every morning. Once I was with him and the horse fell down. What a frightening thing that was, but he got up and trotted on to town. Later Dad drove a Model T to work. The people along the road said they could set their clocks by the time Dad blew the horn when he approached a blind corner.

I had to have my tonsils removed when I was about four years old. Mother took me into town and Uncle James, Granny's brother who was Dr. Blackwood and one of the very best, did the surgery in his office. I screamed and screamed while I was under the anesthetic and Mother said someone came off the square up to his office, which was over a store, to see what was happening. About the middle of the afternoon, the doctor let Mother take me home. We had to make the trip in a buggy. He had said I could not have water until so many hours had passed after surgery. That time came before we reached home. I was so thirsty and begged so hard for water that Mother stopped at Mr. Burns' house to get me a drink. I could only have one or two tablespoons full but that was the best water I ever tasted.

I started to school when I was five years old.

Helen Marie at school age

I walked one and one-half miles to the one-room schoolhouse that sat near the little church in the beloved spot we called Union. Granny had taught me to read and write so I started in the second grade. We only had three months of school.

We must have had a different teacher every year because I can remember three. There were some Taylor boys who tried to run every teacher off. I recall one day the teacher, Ransom Williams, was trying to punish Ray Taylor and he pulled a knife on him. Mr. Williams told me to run up to Mr. Wes Hudson's and ask him to come to the school. Mr. Hudson was one of the school directors. I ran as fast as I could to his house a quarter of a mile away. Mrs. Hudson said he was in the field. I took off for the field because this was an emergency. Mr. Hudson tied up the horse and plow and went back to the school with me, only to find Mr. Williams had let Ray go home. I still wonder why he did that.

I have a lot of memories of my school days at Union. During my first year I had my first experience with death that I can remember. Mary Casey, my seatmate, died. Oh, she was a pretty little girl. I couldn't understand why she died but Mother told me she had diphtheria and that nearly always meant death.

Walking to school with other kids was full of experiences. Most of the kids were older than I. One of the bigger girls I loved was Agnes

Burns. She stopped by for me almost every morning. One morning she was holding a snake right in the middle of the back and it was writhing and curling, a very lively snake. My mother was on the front porch hollering for me to not touch that snake. Agnes whispered, "It isn't real, it is a toy. You take it and see what your mother will do." I did—and you can imagine her reaction!

In the winter when we were going to school, Agnes and I would stop by a pond and skate on the way. How Mother knew it, I'll never know. But, one day she said, "Helen Marie, don't you ever go by that pond again." I didn't for a day or two, then one morning Agnes said, "Oh, let's go by the pond and skate a little, Miss Mattie will never know it." Sounded good to me but wouldn't you know after the first round or two, I fell flat and hit my head so hard that a goose egg rose up over my eye like you have never seen. And it didn't go down before school was out. When I went home Mother knew immediately what had happened and she went straight to the walnut tree.

One day Oliver Browning, a neighbor boy just older than I and who loved to pester me, grabbed my lunch box lid and threw it out in Noah Dearing's field. I had to crawl through the fence to get it. I cried and cried and when I got to school I told the teacher—and what do you think he did? He got a chalk box and turned the little end up, which was about four inches square, then he made Oliver and me sit on it until we became friends. I would have been sitting there till now, I guess, if the teacher had held out. He's the same teacher that let Roy Taylor go home that day. I wonder about him.

Another thing that teacher did to me was once at noon I saw some brown sugar lumps in my friend Monette Taylor's lunch box. She wouldn't give me a one, even though I begged her to. Well, when she went out to play at recess, I found an excuse to go back to the coatroom and just helped myself to a sugar lump. She caught me and told the teacher. He made me sit on the steps the remainder of the recess.

Leaving Mother to walk to school by myself was hard when I was very young. One morning, no one came by or else I was not ready when they did. All I remember is that I was walking by myself to school and suddenly I remembered I hadn't kissed Mother goodbye.

My conscience really hurt me. I kept feeling worse until finally I just turned around and started the half mile back to give her a kiss. She was peeling peaches out under the walnut tree in front of the house. When she saw me coming back, she dropped her knife and wiped the juice off her hands and reached up in that tree and got a keen cut and came to meet me. She wouldn't let me say a word, just said angrily, "You turn around there and get to school, young lady. You're gonna be late. Now you make steps." I turned around and didn't tell her until many years later why I turned back.

Another day I remember turning back. I was going along by myself again and was almost half way to school when I came over the top of a hill and I saw two people coming toward me. I took one look and turned on my heels and ran back home screaming. Mother heard me and came to see what had frightened me. I told her, "I saw an old witch and Santa Claus coming up the road." She said she would walk with me to see. With Mother beside me, I felt braver. We topped the hill and there they were—but they looked different—for some reason they even looked familiar. And sure enough, as you may have guessed, they were friends of ours. It was Grandma Redden in her big black blousy dress and bonnet that she always wore and Elizabeth Taylor all dressed up in a bright red suit. Was I ever embarrassed! But, how was I to know with the sun shining right in my eyes? Guess I have always been a "fraidy cat."

But, let me tell you about Grandma Redden—that is what everyone in the neighborhood called her. She was a dear old lady with a heart as big as all outdoors. Mother used to take me over to her house to visit and she would always stuff me with food. On the kitchen table she had all kinds of good things to eat, covered with a large cloth. She would lift the cloth and give me whatever I chose. One day on our way over there, Mother said, "Now Helen Marie, you are not supposed to eat when you go to someone's house. You have had your lunch so you just say, 'No, thank you,' when Grandma Redden offers you something or you will be in trouble." When we got there, I sat still a little while and listened to them talk. I became restless and got up to wander around. This was a cue to Grandma Redden. "That child must be hungry," she thought, so into the kitchen she went with me behind her. But this time was different. All I would say was "No, thank you" to everything she offered me. Finally she asked, "Why do you keep saying that?" When I told her the truth, Mother was the one in trouble and I had myself another feast.

One morning when I was six years old, Daddy came to my bed before daylight and said, "Helen Marie, wake up! Your mother is sick and the doctor is coming. I'm going to take you over to Mr. Bryan's where you can sleep and you stay there until I call you to come home." This all seemed very strange to me, but I trusted my daddy and didn't ask a question. Before noon, the telephone rang. I listened. It was the Bryan's ring all right—a long and a short and a long. You see we were all on a party line with different rings. And you only answered your ring. Ours was a long and three shorts. Of course, I'll admit sometimes we gently raised the receiver and eavesdropped.

Mrs. Bryan answered, then said to me, "OK, Helen Marie, you may go home now." I raced as fast as my legs could take me. I had to see about my mother. She had never been sick like this before so I bounded into the room and jumped up on the bed. Mother said, "Watch out, be careful, you'll get on little sister." Little sister? What was she saying? Then she gently turned the cover back and there lay a tiny baby girl. I couldn't believe my eyes. "What's her name?" I asked. "Una Ruth," Mother said. Granny fixed me something for my lunch then they suggested I go over to Pearl Dozier's house and play that afternoon. We had a good time but I was anxious to go back home at four o'clock so I could see about my new sister. I never could get her off my mind.

My sister was very dear to me and I played with her like a doll. Once I remember we had the flu. There was an epidemic. I was in one bed in the fireplace room hot with fever and so sick I could die! I still remember the screams of my baby sister as my mother wrapped her in sheets that had been dipped into a tub of ice water that was sitting on the floor between our beds. Ruth had pneumonia with fever so high it took this to get it down. Mother told me later when we talked about it that she kept a thermometer under her arm to be certain her fever did not get too low. I remember another time I panicked when my sister toddled too near the fireplace and fell into the fire burning her hair off one side of her head.

Three years passed and one July day Dad woke me up again and said, "Helen Marie, we want you to go to school early this morning. You can go up to Mr. Hudson's and wait until Mr. Pfeifer (the teacher) gets to school." So off I went in the early dawn, but this time a wiser kid. I said to myself, "I bet there's going to be another baby there when I get home." And sure enough, there was! My new baby brother was named James Carl. He was a pitiful looking little baby, so thin. My mother said she cried when she first saw him. But he was such a sweet baby and added much joy to our family. Daddy would bounce Ruth and Jim on his knee and say, "Got me a pig and a pup." Ruth was his pig and Jim was his pup.

One of the best things the Lord did for me as a child was placing us on a farm that joined the Bryan farm. Mr. and Mrs. Witt Bryan lived just a little ways beyond our barn. Our families were very close and I kept the road hot running back and forth.

There was Lena, their oldest daughter, who was my ideal. She brushed my hair and played with me like I was her doll. Jeff was the oldest son and J. W. the second. He was my age and playmate. He later married Jane Dearing and we have been close friends throughout the years.

Esther Dell was the next child. I can remember once J. W. and I held her down and gave her a dose of castor oil. It is a good thing Mrs. Bryan never knew or she would have whipped us. We made a playhouse between our houses and this was a source of hours of play—lots of fun and great creativity. I remember making pies out of the shorts—food for hogs—and we would color the mixture blue with bluing used for whitening clothes when washing.

Anything that one family had the other was welcome to borrow. I learned a lesson once when returning a pair of scissors Mother had borrowed. Old Ned, the Bryan's dog, was lying near the path in their yard asleep. Guess I had never heard the saying, "Let sleeping dogs lie," because I pointed the scissors at Old Ned and said, "Boo!" Well, he jumped at me and grabbed my arm, leaving tooth prints all around. So, I learned a new lesson, "Never frighten a sleeping dog."

Their third daughter was named Grace and she was my sister's "twin," as there were only nine days difference in their ages. A few years later their youngest child was born. I can remember exactly where I was sitting in the gymnasium at Harrison watching a basket ball game when someone came and told me the Bryans had a new baby girl named Essie Fay. I felt a thrill just as if she were my sister.

The Bryans were great to include me in their family activities. I remember especially the times they took me to the circus. What a day! We got up early and were there in time to see the parade with all the elephants, tigers and clowns. Then we went to the big tent set up on the banks of Crooked Creek in the outskirts of Harrison. Once I remember the elephants came running around the ring and almost ran over Era Hudson, a friend of mine. Her folks grabbed her out of their path just in time. The time I remember best was one time when the circus was over and Mrs. Bryan told me, "Sit right here and don't you move." She and Mr. Bryan left with Jeff, J. W. and Esther Dell. I watched them all the way to the exit. I looked across the way and men were beginning to take the tent down. The crowd was about out of the huge tent. What was I to do? Fear rose within me. I wanted to run but Mrs. Bryan said "Sit" and I knew to always mind Mrs. Bryan. Suddenly someone tapped me on the shoulder from behind and said, "Come on Helen Marie, let's go." There was Lena. No doubt the plan all the time was for Lena to take care of me, but I didn't know that and I felt abandoned.

A child never feels as helpless as when they are lost, I don't believe. I can remember going to town with Mother shopping. Harrison has a square built around the court house. It was a small town but large enough for a child to get lost. I remember once I looked around and couldn't see Mother, so I panicked. I don't know what I did except cry, but I do remember where I found her. She was in a hat shop on the north side of the square. I probably was tagging along behind looking in a store window when she turned into the store and when I looked she was out of sight. But the feeling of being lost then found is not like any other.

When I was about seven years old a new friend came on the scene. As I walked to school I passed the Dearing's house. I saw a strange boy, twelve years old out in the barn lot helping with the cattle. (I didn't know then that this skinny kid would someday be my husband and the father of my children.) I asked Mother who that boy was because we very seldom had a stranger in our community. She told me that she had heard that this little boy's mother had died when he was a baby and he had come to live with his Aunt Jane, his mother's sister, and he was going to help Noah, his cousin, on the farm. The grimness of this story was not told to me until years later when Merrill told me himself.

Ida Francis Moore Cole had died when he was nine months old. She died of typhoid fever. Her brother, Uncle Willie Moore, told him that his father, Orin Cole, loved her so much that he could not stand to see her thirst for water. She was not permitted to have it on doctor's orders. When she continued to cry and beg for just a sip of water, he would slip her a drink and she continued to worsen until she died. She left four little children, three boys and one girl. Cassie, who was twelve, quickly assumed the role of mother, housekeeper, cook, nurse and whatever else her father and brothers needed. The neighbors and relatives helped some with the laundry and sewing, but it was mostly Cassie's responsibility.

Merrill, Cassie and two siblings

For a few years Cassie worked hard caring for the family. But the time came when she fell in love and married a young college professor and it was necessary for her to move to Kansas City, Kansas to be with him. She could not bear to leave little Merrill, as the other boys were working. They had found jobs at the Coca-Cola Co. In fact, Lonnie said he cut his teeth on a Coke bottle. Dad Cole was working away from home most of the time and couldn't take care of a young child. So off to Kansas City Cassie went, taking her brother with her.

A short time passed and she had two children of her own, Eugene and Martina. Merrill felt like they were his brother and sister. All went well for three or four years, then suddenly the father failed to come home. He completely disappeared. The food supply grew shorter and shorter and their money faded away. Soon Cassie gave up. There was nothing to do but go back to Harrison and live with her dad. She bought train tickets with money she had borrowed and with few belongings returned to Harrison.

It was not long until Cassie remarried—this time to Louis Bradwell. She moved back to Kansas City. Merrill stayed with his father this time as he was large enough to look after himself. There was not much family life. His dad and brothers were gone all day and into the night. Merrill would play in the neighborhood until dark, then he would slip into the dark house, remove his overalls and go to bed. Often he was hungry, sometimes having only syrup and bread to eat. He changed his clothes once a week. On Saturday, he put on a clean shirt and overalls. He never knew who washed their clothes; perhaps it was a neighbor.

He got a job shining shoes, perhaps bought a shoeshine kit and was self employed. This gave him a little spending money, ten cents a day or so.

One day when he was twelve years old, he got so hungry he decided he was going to go out to his Aunt Jane's because he

The Orin Cole family, 1912

had been there and knew how well she fed her family. Since he didn't see much of his dad those days, he just walked off, leaving a note that he had gone to Aunt Jane's. She was his mother's sister.

Aunt Jane and Uncle George Dearing lived on Crooked Creek near Union and just down the creek a little ways from where I was born. Merrill set out on foot for Aunt Jane's. It was more than six miles but his stomach urged him on. Along the way, when he needed something for energy, he would sit down under a walnut tree and crack some walnuts and eat them. With "second wind," he would trudge on. Finally, he arrived at the white farmhouse. There he saw the large pails of milk cooling in the springhouse. There were bowls of fresh churned butter that had rocks placed on the lids to keep them upright. All this looked so good.

Aunt Jane received him with open arms. She was a large "bosomy" lady with beautiful white hair and a face of angelic tenderness. She held her dead sister's little boy in her arms and vowed he would never be hungry again. There were some words between her and his father before it was agreed that he could stay with Noah and work on the farm for room and board.

Their son, Noah, had married Myrtle Eoff and they lived nearby in a beautiful stone house and they had a big red barn. They had one little girl, Jane, a beautiful brown-haired, brown-eyed child. Noah needed a farm boy and Merrill became one of the family. He was fed, clothed and loved just like a son. He started to school at Union. He was a very shy boy. I can remember how quiet and lonely he seemed. He was older than the others in his class and was a very good student.

School at Union didn't escape the storms of nature. We had no warnings, except as the teacher watched the clouds, but I can remember being herded into the bell room, where there were no windows, to wait until the storm passed.

Let me tell you about the bell room. It was a room between the two little entrance halls where the lunch boxes sat on shelves above the coat racks. The only thing in the bell room was the bell rope. When it was time for school to start or the end of recess or the noon hour, the teacher would go into the room or send one of the older boys to ring the bell. The rope would be pulled three or four times and we would all hurry to get in line, boys at one entrance and girls at the other. When all were in line and the pushing stopped, the teacher gave the signal and we would march inside and quietly find our desks and classes would begin. Grades one through eight each recited everything from reading to arithmetic. It was hard to concentrate on penmanship when someone was saying the multiplication tables. Then there was the fun time. I believe it must have been a special Friday afternoon activity when we would have spelling matches. Even though I couldn't spell the big words, I had my favorites in the match and got a thrill out of spelling a word correctly.

Back to the storms, we stayed in the bell room until it was over. We could see through the door and out a window. One day it was terrible. I was able to watch the old willow trees being blown around. Mr. Pfeifer had tied his old mule that he rode to school under a willow tree. I remember how excited that mule got with the limbs breaking all around him and the thunder and lightning having a ball.

There was one time during the year when the kids turned the tables on the teachers. The last day of school the big boys got there early bringing planks, hammers and nails. They boarded up the doors, thus locking the teachers out. I remember how frustrating it was to the teachers to try to break down the barricade so they could have some control over the day.

We had no inside bathroom facilities. There was an old "four-holer" outhouse up the fence from the schoolhouse. That was one way of getting out of the schoolroom. You raised your hand and waited for a nod from the teacher before you could go. The rule was that only one leaves the room at a time. Sometimes we vied for the opportunity.

Usually our teachers were men, but one teacher I had was a lady, Cora Dozier. The thing I remember about her is one time Daddy had to go to Fayetteville to take a postal examination. Mother asked Miss Cora to ride with us. We went across the mountains through Huntsville and Hindsville. It was quite a trip. I remember as we approached Fayetteville Miss Cora said, "Helen Marie, how lucky we are. Not many people get to go to their university city." I felt like I was truly a great traveler.

Death hit our school again. Norman Eoff, a boy in my class, was kicked by a horse and died. I had the strangest feeling this time. I could not believe he was dead. His father was a Baptist minister and Brother Troy, as we called him, had many, many friends. I remember going to the graveyard and passing by the casket and seeing the still form of my friend. I guess I cried for days about this. It really was the first time I felt the pangs of losing someone I loved in death. And the question, "Why? Why?" kept coming to my mind.

I have talked a lot about school, so let me tell you memories I have of the church. The church house was also a one-room building with a small entrance hall where the church bell rope hung. Both the schoolhouse and church house were white clapboard buildings. It was in this church I was expected to learn one of life's most important lessons: the art of keeping still. We went to Sunday school and church with no intermissions, so it was the natural thing to become restless. Once when I was very small, I seated myself on the front row for church. During the sermon, I decided to go back where my mother was sitting. I got up and started slowly and quietly down the aisle. A neighbor, Frank Burns, thinking he would scare me back to my seat, felt in his hip pocket and said, "Where is my knife? I'll cut that little girl's ears off." I began screaming to the top of my voice. He learned a lesson as well as I.

Years later a man, Loren Hudson, told my sister, Ruth, that if she didn't stay quiet and quit talking he was going to sew her mouth up. She believed he actually would do it and all it took was a look from him to shut her up. One time Ruth grew very restless during the sermon. She got down on the floor and started to take a walk down the aisle and came face to face with Loren Hudson. He started reaching for his pocket, she thought for a needle, so she let out a blood-curdling yell that really disturbed the congregation.

I can remember the little card class I went to back in the right hand corner of the church. There were four classes in our Sunday school, one for different age groups meeting in each corner of the church. Our teacher told us a Bible story, then gave us a card about 3" x 4" with a colored picture, perhaps of baby Moses in the bulrushes or David killing Goliath on one side and the story on the other. There was a memory verse or golden text at the top of the story and we were required to learn that verse. I will be forever grateful for the memory work I had in Sunday school. It was much later, many times, before I began to understand the true meaning of the words, but I can recall many verses I learned as a child. When I was old enough for the junior class, I moved over to the left side corner of the church. Merrill was our teacher.

My dad always led the singing at church. I can remember how he led with a closed fist, barely beating the time. I can hear him as he sang:

Send the Light, the blessed gospel Light
Let it shine, from shore to shore.
Send the Light, the blessed gospel Light,
Let it shine, forevermore.

I must tell you about my dad's conversion, the way it was told to me. Dad grew up in Newton County and he had some old cronies, as he called them, who loved to "take in" protracted meetings. Now, a protracted meeting was a revival meeting. Usually they were held in the summer with a visiting preacher and sometimes under a brush arbor. They were scheduled so one community's revival never went on at the same time as an adjoining community's, thus giving a chance for people to attend several in the course of a summer. These boys did that, going by horseback. They didn't ever go inside but hung around the windows on the outside. It was a real social occasion, a good place to meet their friends and maybe "catch a girl" and walk her home, leading their horse behind them.

One night Dad and his friends were on the outside when the invitation was given. There was no response and they heard the preacher say, "Now we will sing one more verse and if no one comes, this will close the revival." This posed a problem—their fun would be over because there was not another meeting coming up. So they hurriedly got their heads together and decided to save the day. If no one started up the aisle inside, they would come from the outside. The preacher would never know the difference. So they listened and watched. They came to the chorus, *"Come home, Come home, ye who are weary, come home."* Not a soul moved within the church. So they started up the steps and down the aisle toward the altar. But something happened to my dad after he got inside the church. Suddenly he felt pulled to the altar. He always compared his experience to Paul's on the Damascus Road when the Lord struck him down. He was in dead earnest by the time he got there and had a real "born again" experience then and there.

The church was always the center of community life. Often there was "dinner on the ground" after preaching on Sunday. The men would carry some seats out of the church, put the seats together in a long row and then the ladies would spread cloths on them. They would empty their baskets of all kinds of good things to eat. One summer we were having just this sort of happening when my sister, Ruth, was a toddler. The Ritchies from Kansas City were home for a visit, and to show off their new baby boy, the mother made a "pallet" out of a quilt near the table and laid her baby on it. All went well until Ruth came toddling along. She bent down over the baby to love it and instead she bit the baby's nose as hard as she could. The tooth prints were plainly visible to all the people who rushed up to see what had caused the baby's screams. Poor Mother was so embarrassed. Granny said to Ruth, "Now, I'd crawl off and stay there."

That wasn't the only time my sister disturbed the congregation. One night church was just about over. The preacher asked everyone to stand while Daddy dismissed the meeting with prayer. Daddy had Una Ruth cradled in his arms so he just stood up and began to pray. Soon we heard the "pit pat" of water hitting the floor. Poor Ruth—it was too late! Poor Daddy—he just kept on praying! And I should think he would. In an embarrassing time like that what better thing could one do than pray? Everyone else was in stitches, and I wouldn't be surprised if the Lord himself didn't laugh a bit.

Christmas time was a good time in those days. On Christmas Eve, everyone in the community went to the church where there was a huge cedar tree set up on the stage. All the family gifts were brought, unwrapped, and placed on the tree. Dolls were tied on the tree as were pop guns, shirts, sweaters, books and tea sets. One time we were on our way in our surrey when I spied a little doll buggy Aunt Angie, Dad's sister, was holding. I asked about it and was told it was for Billie Eoff, my good friend. Well, when it was tied on the tree, I couldn't keep my eyes off of it. When Santa Claus was taking the gifts off the tree and calling out the names, I watched him carefully cut the string and then he read the card and called out "Helen Marie White." What joy! This is the one Christmas present I remember. We hung our stockings by the fireplace for Santa Claus to fill. And on Christmas morning, we found oranges, candy, etc.

Going to church in the surrey was another experience. One Sunday Mother was driving, as Dad had to work at the post office most Sundays. We were about half way there when we met a couple of guys in a "bug," a little stripped down car much like a race car. This bug cut back into the road too soon and caught under the back axle of our surrey. It overturned enough to tip my sister Ruth out on the ground. Baby brother James Carl was pitched into the front wheel with his arms through the spokes. Granny was out on the bank and I was on the floor between the seats. Mother was across the dashboard. But our dear old horse was as steady as he could be. The surrey only moved enough for the wheel to run over my sister's leg but it was not broken, neither were the baby's arms. No one was seriously hurt. Granny picked herself up and blood was running down her face because sharp roots along the bank had cut her forehead. But she was determined she was going on to church. So everyone was brushed off, blood wiped away and we were on the road again, thankful for old Dan who had excellent "horse sense."

Trips in that surrey were fun. I can remember going over to Newton County to see Aunt Letha, Mother's sister and Granny's oldest child, when Ruth was a baby. There were five crossings of Buffalo River between Jasper and Parthenon. It must have been a hot day because the thing I remember about the trip is seeing Mother bathe Ruth in the river. There were huge gray bluffs along the opposite side of the river, and I can still see the scene.

It was such fun to go to Aunt Letha's. She and Uncle Levi had eight children, three boys and five girls. They lived three miles above Parthenon in the Ozark Mountains in a house way up on a hill. It wasn't an antebellum house with big white columns on the porch or anything like that, but it had lots of things I liked. There was an L-shaped back porch and the cistern was on one end next to the kitchen. Here they hung their milk. Aunt Letha would only allow the older kids to pull up the bucket of milk because, if even a little bit was spilled, it would ruin the cistern.

They had a large farm with upper fields, lower fields and all kinds of designated acres. But the thing I remember most is the cellar filled with canned fruit and the grapevine swings in the woods near the house.

One time I remember a little pig walked off the top step and fell into the cellar. I never laughed as much in my life as when the cousins and I chased that squealing pig until we caught him and lifted him out to safety.

We often walked down to Shop Creek and waded or swam. Sometimes we would find berries to pick or wild plums to eat. We never got enough playing until we had to start home and it was a long, long day's drive across the mountains. Uncle Levi and Aunt Letha and all the kids would see us off with, "Now, you all come back when you can."

They came to see us once in a while. I can remember eating supper on our back porch after the day's work was finished and occasionally we would hear a wagon rumbling in the distance. I would jump up and down for joy because that couldn't be anyone but Uncle Levi and Aunt Letha. As it came closer, I tried to guess who was with them. How many kids got to come? How long would they stay?, etc. We made pallets on the floor and had beds for as many as came. We played *Red Rover, Mother May I?, New Orleans, Hide and Seek, Ante-over* and all the fun games of the "good ol' days."

If time permitted, we would load up the wagon for a visit with Uncle Walter's family, my mother's brother who lived about ten miles away in Western Grove. Uncle Walter and Aunt Lou had seven kids so we could hardly wait to get with them. They would see the wagon when we got to the lane leading down to their house. By the time Uncle Levi got the gate opened and closed behind the wagon, the kids were running across the field to meet us. We would begin to yell, "Oh, there comes Pebble, and there's Esther!" Then we would see Lenora carrying Marcella in her arms. Alba, my age, would beat the girls and be the first to us. Homer, the oldest, was usually off plowing a field or gone into town for something. I don't remember him playing with us as he was older and *Farmer in the Dell* was much too childish for him to enjoy. But what a thrill it was to be picked for the wife or even the cat. We giggled and squealed and the whole countryside rang with joy. How Aunt Lou ever fixed enough food for all of us is a mystery to me now, but she knew how to make the best creamed corn and chicken and dumplings. All the girls helped in the kitchen and so that meant we were all under her feet. But we were fed and the dishes were done and I didn't realize she had a problem.

One time, Uncle Levi came to our house by himself. The wagon pulled up and the team stopped and only Uncle Levi was there. What a disappointment! He came in and Mother and Granny fixed something for supper. We all set down at the long table in the dining room with the kerosene lamp in the middle. Soon he began to talk. He had come to talk to us about the new Newton County Academy that the Arkansas Baptist Convention was establishing at Parthenon, three miles from their home. We had heard about it, or at least Daddy and Mother had. This school would be a nine-month school with grades one through twelve. The buildings were almost completed—a two-story school building made of grey stone to house all the grades and a frame dormitory with a porch around the front and one side for female boarding students.

Since I was ready for the fourth grade and his children needed more than three months of schooling, Uncle Levi suggested that he rent a house in Parthenon. Granny would go over and take me along, and he would move his seven kids down and we would all attend the Newton County Academy. And that's what happened. In the fall, Uncle Levi came back and loaded Granny's trunk, her little low chair, her feather bed, some quilts and our clothes. The next morning early, the old wagon rattled away down the road for the hard trip across the mountains. Leaving Mother and Dad was sad, but the anticipation of being with my cousins was quite an adventure.

we found the house Uncle Levi had rented. It was a weather-beaten old house about a half mile up the mountain from Parthenon. There was a well in the front yard and a porch across the front of the house. There were three rooms and a lean-to kitchen. We set up housekeeping with things Uncle Levi and Aunt Leatha had gathered up. It was very sparsely furnished. I remember most the long oak table that served as a dining table and a study table. After supper when the dishes were done, we all gathered around the table to do our homework.

I cannot remember as much about what I learned in school as I can the fun my cousins and I had. We could hardly wait for the last bell to ring so we could run home and play. We were a lively bunch. We spent many pleasant hours running up those hills and down the ravines, gathering wild flowers or wading mountain streams. I learned to love the mountains.

At Christmas, Granny and I would return home for a few days. I remember how hard it was to leave Mother and Daddy when we started back to school. I didn't cry or tell anyone how sad I felt as Mother tucked a quilt around me as I sat in the wagon seat ready for the long ride. Before many miles, the quilt began slipping off and Granny had to tuck it in again. She said, "Oh, your mother doesn't know how to do anything." It was all I could do to hold the tears back.

My cousins and I must have been a handful for Granny, but she seemed to enjoy it. I am afraid I felt like I had more strings on Granny than the other grandchildren because I remember one cold morning I wanted to sit in Granny's low chair in front of the fire to put on my shoes. Eula was in the chair and refused to get up and give it to me. Her oldest brother, Arvel, slapped her and told her to give it to me. I felt so bad. I didn't even want the chair then. I loved Eula. She was my favorite of the cousins. This is the only time I remember any trouble among us.

Ray only had one arm that he could use. The other arm hung limp at his side. When he was eight years old, he was climbing on a chicken coop and stepped on a rusty nail. He had tetanus—"lock-jaw"—they called it, and he almost died. For a time a large part of his body was paralyzed, but he recovered, except for his right arm. It grew in length but was withered. He must have done a good job rehabilitating himself because he was able to do anything anyone else could do and his left arm was much stronger than usual. I remember I thought it was great sport to try to take something out of his left hand. It made no difference how long I tried, I was never successful.

The scar I have over my left eye is a result of an uncouth race I had with my cousins. One day we were outside playing and I yelled, "The last one in the house is a 'rotten egg.'" I was leading the pack until I hit a loose board in the front porch and fell, striking my head against the door facing. We were miles and miles from a doctor, so there was no chance of having stitches to close the gash.

The worst thing we did, I guess, was smoke rabbit tobacco. There was some kind of plant that they called "rabbit tobacco" growing near the barn. We decided to smoke it as we had heard kids talk about smoking it. Guess we weren't too impressed because I don't recall trying it the second time. Perhaps it made us too sick!

The next year Uncle Levi bought a house on the corner of the school campus. This was a new house and we had more room. Uncle Levi moved their piano down to this house and all of us girls took piano lessons. A dear young lady from Little Rock came to teach piano. She was Evelyn Voyles and I loved her. She lived in the dormitory as did the school principal and his wife, Mr. and Mrs. Walter Burdine. Later Mrs. Burdine died with TB and Evelyn married Walter. Years later she became one of my closest friends when we lived in Conway.

We had to carry water from the Matlock spring but there were plenty of us to do it. Everyone had a job to do. One time, Granny sent me to the barn with Lura to milk. My job was to keep the geese out of the milk. Lura filled one bucket and set it aside. I watched it faithfully for a little while. My mind wandered off and so did my feet. When I remembered, it was too late. The geese had found the milk and there was all kinds of barnyard trash floating on top of the milk. Lura and I decided to dip off the trash and not say a word about it. Then we figured out when Granny would use the milk, we were going to drink water for that meal. She would skim the cream off and we would drink the milk for breakfast the next day. The next morning, we were just about finished with breakfast when we thought about the milk. My glass was almost empty. I said, "Oh, Lura, we forgot." Then Granny knew something was wrong because we absolutely could not keep a straight face. We had to confess and she thought the joke was on us—and hoped we would not all come down with typhoid fever.

We had the flu and other diseases, but the thing I remember the most was the pink eye. When we had that we were put in isolation, so to speak. The shades were drawn in one bedroom and all who had the pink eye had to stay in the darkened room until it cleared up. We were not sick, just gummy-eyed, so when there was more than one in the room it was great fun.

Aunt Letha had to come and help Granny when several of us were sick. I remember there were two double beds in one room. I was in one and Eula and Ava were in the other. Ava didn't want to take a pill Aunt Letha was trying to give her. In fact, it was hard to get a pill down any of us. Ava refused to open her mouth and was putting up a fight. Eula thought that was very funny. She started laughing real big and Aunt Letha, taking advantage of the situation, threw a pill down her throat, much to my enjoyment.

Our walls and ceilings were papered with newspaper. We had quite a game when we were in bed. One would find a word on the wall or ceiling and call it out. The first one to find it got to name the next word or phrase. There was no money for games or toys so we made our own.

I will tell you how to build a play house. Find a nice mossy place under some trees. Outline each room with small rocks. Build your furniture with rocks and scraps of wood, perhaps an old shingle for a sofa or table. Decide who will be the daddy, the mother and the kids, and then use your imagination. You can't believe how much fun you can have.

My Sunday school teacher was Mrs. Nora Henderson. The Henderson family was related to our family. Mr. Henderson's mother was Granny's sister. All the family meant a lot to me then. Mr. Henderson—William— was my school teacher and the four kids, Boyd, Berlin, Bertie and Kenneth, were good friends. My favorite was Berlin and he continued to be a part of my life for many years. Mrs. Henderson loved the little girls in her class and we loved her. It was a nice bunch of girls.

Each year, there was a revival. During one of these, I accepted Christ and joined the church. My experience was nothing like my dad's. I had been taught all my life that Jesus loved me. We were always at church every Sunday morning, Sunday night and Wednesday night. My love for Christ grew as I did. When Mrs. Henderson talked to Eula and me and asked us if we would like to meet with her and talk about making a profession of our faith, we were glad to go. I remember how we knelt and she prayed that we might accept Christ as our Savior. When the prayer was over and she said, "If you are willing to accept Christ, stand up," I immediately got up. I was more than willing. Perhaps I did not understand all about atonement and justification, but I did believe that Christ died for my sins and that forgiveness of sin was a gift and all I needed to do was accept it. That was not a problem for me. During the evening service, Eula and I both made a public profession and joined the church. We were baptized in Buffalo River along with other friends. This was a meaningful experience for me.

I was a bit anxious to follow the suggestion of the minister to tell others about Christ. One day I decided I would write a note to Carl Casey, a boy in my room. I didn't have enough nerve to talk to him, I guess. He was a good friend of mine but he never went to church, so I felt this was my first real mission field. I tried hard to write a good evangelistic letter, and then passed it to him in the classroom. Mr. Henderson, my teacher, saw me. Writing notes was taboo! So he took the note from Carl, opened it and read it, not aloud, thank goodness. Then he looked at me and said, "Helen Marie, there is a time for all things and this is not the time for this." So my venture was nipped in the bud—but I bet God knew I tried.

Mr. Henderson got me again one day. We had to go to an outdoor toilet. When I got permission to leave the room and I got out in the hall, I saw the high school girls' coats hanging there. For some unknown reason, I reached my hand in Jewel McFerin's coat pocket and found a lipstick. This was what the older girls did, why couldn't I? So I quickly took the top off and without a mirror put on some of the lipstick. I went on to the toilet feeling so grown up and the taste and smell made me feel dressed up. But when I got back into the room, Mr. Henderson took one look at me and then told me to get out of there and wash that lipstick off. We had no lavatory, so what was I to do? I thought of the snow on the ground. I was able to smear it around a little bit but I know it looked terrible.

You are right if you say, "Granny was something!" If you were to look at my resume', you would find many things that would shock you. I would never come out of a computer as being an ideal girl. Some things I did shock me now. For instance, when my dad's sister, Aunt Angie, came to see us from Kansas City, she appeared to be very rich, I thought. I opened her purse once and found a fifty-cent piece. I took it and saved it, hidden away, until we went in to Harrison. I slipped away long enough to go into the ice cream parlor on the square and I bought an ice cream sundae—just like the town girls did.

For three years, while I was in the fourth, fifth and sixth grades, Granny and I made the jaunt to Parthenon for the nine-month school. Along the road just before reaching Jasper, there was a big curve overlooking the Buffalo River. There was a large sign by the side of the road on which was printed, "*The Heavens declare the glory of God, the firmament showeth his handiwork.*" I never read the 19th Psalm that I don't see Newton County and the Buffalo River, now a National Park, with its bluffs and rippling water. Traveling in our wagon, I had time to observe the beauty and I pray it will forever remain in my mind.

Those were happy days. I remember the wild flowers, especially the wild honeysuckle, gathering flowers, hickory nuts and huckleberries. I remember digging May apple roots, which we sold for medicinal purposes. Anything to make a little money. I even picked cotton all day and made twelve cents. I loved the mountain streams and the swinging bridges.

Each one of my classmates was so very dear. The lovely lady, Annie McGraw, who led our Girl's Auxiliary, inspired us so much with exciting missionary stories. (I thought surely God wanted me to be a missionary to Japan.)

Living with my cousins, learning to play piano duets with Eula, eavesdropping on Lura and her boy friend and a thousand other things made these years very memorable.

When I was ready for the seventh grade, the district of Union consolidated with other small districts and the Valley Springs District was formed. This was a big step forward in education in Arkansas—and one of the first consolidated districts in Arkansas. The four districts near us were Red Oak, Elmwood, Highland and Union. There were other districts around Valley Springs in the consolidation. I can think of three, Overton, Olvey and Hog Creek. This meant scores of kids would get to attend a nine-month school. It also meant I could stay home, even though I would miss my friends at Newton County Academy.

This meant the first school buses for the state. We had two buses for those living in our area. One carried the Elmwood and Union students and the other the Highland and Red Oak kids. A bus driver, who was a high school student, boarded at Mr. Daniel's at the end of the line. All of us who did not live on the bus route walked to the nearest intersection. I had about a quarter of a mile to walk. Waiting on the bus was great fun even on cold days.

We had a white two-story school building that stood up on the hill overlooking the little town. It was six miles from our house to school. At one time I remember there were more children than our two Model-T buses could carry, so Mr. Dan Hole drove an old truck with a tarpaulin over it. We even liked that. I remember once Merrill broke his arm trying to crank it.

Middle-school bus kids

When this picture was made, the kids in our neighborhood were riding on the middle bus. I guess I did not go to school that day because I cannot find myself among my friends. The smallest girl on the front row is my sister, Ruth. I found Merrill and also my three cousins who were living with us. My mother's brother, Oliver, had divorced his wife and gained custody of his children. My dear mother and daddy took the children and kept them for him for three years. They were lovely children, not as much fun as my Parthenon cousins, but I guess they had good reason to be quieter. The little white haired boy, R. O., was so cute and he was the youngest. His sisters, Velma and Vera Dean, were beautiful blondes. Velma, the oldest, was my age. When they left our house they went to live with their mother in Oklahoma City.

Soon larger buses were brought in with straddle boards down the middle for smaller children to sit on. We carried our lunch usually wrapped in a newspaper and tied with a string. There was no plastic or aluminum foil in those days.

The Methodist church saw the need for mountain schools so they established the Valley Springs Training School for high school students. They built a beautiful gray stone building on the hill across town from the square frame school. This was a girls' dormitory and classroom combination, named Albright Hall.

Albright Hall

It was during these years that friends became so important to me. In this larger school I met many new friends. I remember my seatmate, Gladys Brazeal, from Highland District. She later married my dad's brother, Clyde, and has been very dear to me all these years. Then there was Clyde McMahon, whom I loved with all my heart. She lived on the other bus line, but we were together as soon as we got to school. Hazel

Ragland lived in Valley Springs. When the roads were icy, I could stay with Hazel and walk to school. Sometimes the winter weather caught me at home with no chance of getting to Valley Springs.

Daddy bought our first car about this time—a Model T Ford. The Bryans had had one for some time and our relatives from Kansas City had driven down in their Studebaker, so we felt right "up town" to have a car. It was a black two-seated touring car with running boards and tool box on one side. We had Isinglass curtains to put on to keep out the rain or cold. Dad taught me to drive even though I was much too young. Mother tried and tried to learn. I remember one day she drove us to Elmwood for a special day at the church. When she tried to get the car out of the grove of trees beside the church, she had such a time. She backed up, pulled forward, backed up, pulled forward over and over. Suddenly there was a crash. She had backed into the cistern. She gave up. This was the last drive she ever made. The running boards were fun to ride. When Mother and Dad would let us, me and my friends would stand on the running board and hold to the top and ride from church, or a short distance.

Our main social organization was 4-H Club. We met regularly, learned to hem tea towels (flour sacks) and do all kinds of "girl" things but what I liked best was raising beef calves. Every summer some of us would go to Farmers' Week at the University of Arkansas. Kids from all over the state would attend and this was a real exciting experience for me. My dad and mother were great to allow me this opportunity. J. W. Bryan always went, too. We went in the back of a pickup truck. If we did not have a full load, we stopped in Alpena and picked up more. This picture shows how small I was in 1927.

On the way to Farmers Week

We did lots of things at Farmers' Week but I remember most the songs we sang. For example: when it rained and we all gathered inside and auditorium we would sing:

Hail, hail, the gang's all here,
In spite of the weather, we're all together!
Hail, hail, the gang's all here,
What in the heck do we care now?

When we stood in line waiting for the dining hall to open, we would sing:

When do we eat?
When do we eat?
I'm so hungry, my mouth won't shut.
My stomach thinks my throat's been cut.
When do we eat?

Then there was the "chigger song." Chiggers were tiny red bugs that were plentiful in the mountains of Arkansas. The song tells the story quite well.

Oh, there was a little chigger,
And he wasn't any bigger
Than the point on a very small pin.
But the bump that it raises
Just itches like the blazes,
And that's where the rub comes in!

During the summer, I always got to go back to Parthenon and visit my cousins and my dear friend, Eileen Brasel. Eileen had a horse named Jeff. We rode that horse all over the pasture, round and round and round. I also visited Josephine Arbaugh in Jasper.

One of the fun things my cousins and I did was getting a group together to climb the mountain to Mr. Henson's place. Mr. Henson was an old mountaineer who claimed he could tell fortunes. We needed an egg and a quarter to get a look into the future. We would arrive at his house about dark. He would take one at a time into a side room where he would take their quarter and their egg, in that order. He would then break the egg and separate the white from the yolk. It was in the white that the fortune lay. He would put the white in a glass of water, shake it and read the findings. It seemed to me that the tiny bubbles indicated money, of course. The number of bubbles in one spot indicated the amount to expect.

One night when he had finished with the last person and collected the last quarter, we started outside for the trip home. One guy, blinded by the darkness, stepped off the porch into a tub of water. The tub had been placed under the "drip" to catch rain water from the roof. He was wet, embarrassed and angry at us for laughing.

There were so many things to do, so many rocks to climb and streams to wade, I was always sad when the day arrived for me to go home. In fact, we sometimes prayed that God would send a heavy rain upstream so the river would rise and it would be impossible to cross it to go home.

We always had visits from Dad's relatives during the summer. There were four brothers and two sisters.

The White family

In this picture from left to right seated is my dad, youngest sister, Angie (Brazeal), oldest sister Maude (Brasel), Clyde and William Carroll. Standing, left to right, Cyrus, Riley and a brother who died.) Only Clyde lived near us. Aunt Maude had four children, Beryl, Brice, Vance and Opal. I knew them because they went to Newton Count Academy when I did before they moved to Kansas City.

Uncle Cyrus taught in Indian schools. It was always interesting to have him and Aunt Murphy come with their four kids, Jim, Gerald, Emerson and Alden. The oldest brother, William Carol, lived in Kansas City. He, too, had four children, Lawrence, Lowell, Ardis and Angie Fae. They seldom visited us. When the children were large enough, they came but it seemed Uncle William Carrol seldom came.

Going to this house and visiting Grandpa and Grandma White was a treat. It was a very small house, not much room, but they had big hearts and we were always welcome. I can remember sleeping on pallets there, but what I remember most was the good food. Grandma White would make huge biscuits, bake them, pull them out of the oven, set them on the apron of the stove, and I cannot tell you how many I ate for breakfast. She would chuckle when I would ask for another one. She wore thick-lensed glasses and sat in a cane-bottomed chair and dipped snuff as we visited. I loved her.

Uncle Riley worked for the Corps of Engineers and lived in Memphis, Tennessee. He and Aunt Maud were the most fun. I always enjoyed their visits. She giggled like a little girl. I loved to hear her tell about how Uncle Riley came to Yardell to teach school. She came home the first day and told her mother that Mr. White, the new teacher, had the cutest nose. Must have been love at first sight. They were a happy couple and, having no children of their own at this time, they paid a lot of attention to me.

When I was twelve years old, they invited me to go to Kansas City with them to visit Uncle William Carroll, Aunt Maude and Aunt Angie and all the cousins. Of course, I was thrilled to go. I remember the surprise I had when we drove into Kansas City. I expected to see the skyline before we came to the city, like I had seen in geography books. I had never been to a city. Uncle Riley said as we drove down Prospect Avenue, "Well, Helen Marie, what do you think of Kansas?" I said, "I can't see it for the houses." He got a kick out of that! But it was true. I couldn't see the tall buildings.

One night, while there, Lowell, my cousin, took me to an amusement park. I had heard of the Giant Dipper, but I didn't know what it was. Lowell said we would ride it, so I was looking forward to it. As the bus we were riding approached the park (I believe it was a street car we were riding). Anyway, I looked out the window and saw tracks going over the tree tops. "What's that?" I asked. "Oh, that's the Giant Dipper," he answered. Well, my heart missed a beat or two. "Me ride that? Never! But, I can't let anyone call me chicken," I thought to myself. So, I rode it in spite of all the warnings on the walls outside the ticket window. It was "dangerous excitement," to borrow a statement from grandson Dan Watson.

We were in Kansas City at the time Lindbergh was being honored for his solo flight across the Atlantic, so we went down town for the big parade. To see this great hero riding on the back seat of a convertible was exciting to a little country girl.

Living in the country brought many experiences urban children never had. I remember helping Mother in the garden. She worked hard. I can see her now plowing the garden with a little garden plow with one wheel. Each spring we would set out plants and plant the seed. We would gather Burdock leaves, a large coarse leaf that grew close to the ground, and cover each plant with a leaf to protect it from the sun during the day. Then late in the afternoon, we would uncover the plants so they could breathe, then the next morning the shade would be put back on.

Mother and Granny did lots of canning and pickling. I remember seeing them make kraut. We had a large oblong wooden bread tray. This was filled with chunks of cabbage, then with a tin can they would chop it into fine bits. Can't remember the process they used but I know it was put into a large stone jar, about ten-gallon capacity, and a round piece of wood was put on top of the kraut and a clean stone on top of the wood to weigh it down. The process took several days before the kraut was actually canned and carried into the cellar and placed on the shelves with dozens of other cans of fruits and vegetables.

Let me tell you about the other things Mother had in the garden. There were rows of the usual vegetables and about four rows of grapevines. There was some rhubarb for rhubarb pies, sage for seasoning sausage and dressing. Along the fence next to the front yard was a bleeding heart, two or three peonies, a wisteria and some dahlias.

When winter came and the days began to get cold, Dad would say, "This is hog killing weather." He would ask two or three of the neighbor men to come over and help him kill hogs. There was a huge barrel full of water placed over a fire to heat the water. The barrel was tilted so the hog could be slid into it. This they called "scalding." The hog was killed and scalded then put on a table made with boards on saw horses. They proceeded to scrape the hair off of it. When this was done, a sharpened piece of wood was worked in to each hind foot and the hog was hoisted into the air by a chain over the limb of a tree. Then the butchering began. The meat for sausage was put in one dishpan, the fat for lard in another. The hams and shoulders were trimmed and ready to be smoked. The liver was put in a pan to be cooked soon. The spare ribs were carried into the kitchen for the next day's breakfast—this was my favorite thing. Granny would take some backbones and put them in a pot for supper. Oh, it was a busy, greasy day. The days that followed were busy, too. Lard had to be rendered. Mother made head cheese or souse out of the meat she got off the head and feet. After all of this was finished, Granny would make lye soap out of the "leavings."

My mother and grandmother worked so hard. There was never much leisure time. There was always something to be done. I have never felt like I could sit down and read for fun or "fiddle" away much time. The times I can relax and play and not feel that I must work are times when I am away from home. When I am home, I feel guilty if I am not working all the time.

Time came for me to enter high school. So I got off the school bus at the gray stone building called Albright Hall, named for Prof. Albright who was a famous pioneer in education in that area.

Mr. M. J. Russell was superintendent of the Training School. He and his wife lived in a large white frame house that stood on the hill over the spring a few yards from Albright Hall. This house had been remodeled for a boy's dormitory. Mr. Russell was a man of remarkable character and had almost unlimited ability and knowledge. He loved his students and taught us many things. He taught us how to depend on ourselves, play the game fairly, use reference books, enjoy history, music and literature and how to love and appreciate life and people.

It was fun to hear him read a poem or a bit from an author he loved. Uncle Remus tales were among his favorites. He had a great philosophy and wise outlook. I remember once when a favorite Methodist minister was transferred from the church in Valley Springs, we were so concerned because he taught our Bible class in school. Mr. Russell, seeing our frustration and concern, spoke about the situation in chapel service. He said, "Listen, the Lord never removes a Moses that he doesn't bring up a Joshua to take his place." This has been a reassurance to me ever since. Many of his students will testify by their words and their lives the value of his teaching.

Mrs. Russell taught piano and directed the Glee Club. I was her student for six years. It was sometimes a trial to undergo the severity of her criticism. She never stood for any foolishness and never hesitated to scold if she felt she should. One day I laughed when another student stumbled going to the stage. I remember she gently took me by the shoulder and reminded me that, "You don't laugh at other peoples' misfortunes."

I loved to play the piano but practicing scales and exercises was very boring. Mrs. Russell demanded that you count every measure out loud. This sounded ridiculous to me. Why couldn't I count under my breath? That didn't work so well. So it was "One, two, three, four, one, two, three, four," over and over and over. We had two recitals a year when we all performed.

The first year in high school, I had the cutest little girl for an English teacher. She was Maude Marvin Lindsey, the daughter of a well-known Methodist minister. She was under five feet tall but she stood ten feet tall among us. In Freshman English that fall she said in mid–September, "I want each of you to select a hill, a meadow or some particular spot where there are trees, and for the next few weeks, I want you to look at your trees every day. At the end of October I want you to tell me what you have seen." I picked out a hill on the way to school. Every morning as the bus went by I looked at my hill. For the first time in my life I saw Fall. It was a transformation I had never noticed. I shall be forever grateful to Miss Lindsey for this experience.

Mr. and Mrs. Russell: *This is a good picture of Mr. and Mrs. Russell. Back of them is Mr. Neff Hammons, the Principal of our school and professor of Math.*

I remember another thing she made me aware of—and that is foolish questions. "You hear them every day," so said the poem she read to us often about a man being asked where he was going. The man replied, "To so and so's funeral." The question then was, "Is he dead?" The man replied, "No, they are just having his funeral today, may be years before he dies. Foolish questions, you hear them every day." I can't remember the other examples in the poem but the idea comes back to me when I ask or hear a foolish question.

I took Expressions from Miss Lindsey. Mother and Daddy were giving me every opportunity the mountain school offered. They did not settle for an ordinary piano—somewhere, somehow, they found a Wing & Son piano, which was a much better instrument than the "run of the mill" brands. I don't think I was so talented, but Mother was so anxious for me to do the most I could with what I had.

My friend, Clyde McMahon, and I were together every chance we could get. She lived a few miles away and we would spend the night with each other often. Once I remember she was at my house on Sunday. After lunch Mother let us go for a drive in the surrey. We thought about driving to Valley Springs to see what boys we could see—but it was six miles away. Anyway, we took off and ran that horse every mile of the way. We got to Valley Springs, drove by the spring, by the post office, the store and the filling station. Not one boy could be seen. Disappointed, we turned for home, running Ol' Dan as fast as we could because Mother would be very angry if she discovered what we had done. We made it in time, even though Dan was wet with sweat, Mother never dreamed we had been all the way to Valley Springs.

Clyde's married sisters lived in Harrison, so we planned trips to Harrison for the County Fair, the Fourth of July, basketball tournaments, etc. We had lots of good times together. One time I remember begging Mother to let me do something with Clyde and she said, "No." I continued to nag and she said, "Ask your daddy!" I quickly snapped back, "He wouldn't let me go to save my life!" She calmly replied, "He might not let you go to save your soul." I didn't have a response to that.

We had Intramural contests in our high school. The Se-Fresh (seniors and freshmen) competed against the Ju-Sophs (juniors and sophomores). What competition that was!! I ran the 100-yard dash when I was a freshman and before the race was finished, my arch fell. No points for the Se-Fresh on that race.

We also had district meets at Harrison where all the high schools in our area competed. This was not only in track events but in academic subjects, speech, debate, piano and other arts. I remember going to the meet twice to compete for my school. I had been runner-up in the geometry tryouts. When the winner, Almond Potter, became sick and could not go, I was asked to take his place. I was a poor representative.

Another time I competed in speech. I remember well the night of the competition at Valley Springs. It was in the Methodist Church. I had prepared a reading and that was about all it amounted to until I overheard Miss Lindsey, my teacher, say something about Ruby Griffen being so great and no doubt would win. This made me green with envy and jealousy. "I would show her," I said to myself. So when my turn came to give my reading, I really put it on! It was a breathtaking story about a boy who attempted to climb the great Natural Bridge in Virginia. I had everyone on the edge of their seats and, when the boy was, at last, pulled to safety in his mother's arms, I could see the tears and feel the relief in the bodies of my audience. Never had I spoken with so much feeling. The house was loud with applause. And the judge gave me the decision. I had won! I had shown Ruby Griffen and Miss Lindsey! Then came the days of preparation for the district meet. Miss Lindsey, for some reason, decided that this reading was not the type for the meet. So she gave me another one. I memorized it, I went to the meet, I lost for my school and I felt guilty. Ruby Griffen probably would have won. I wasn't very proud of myself, and I felt embarrassed every time I was with Ruby after that.

In the fall of 1938, Mr. Corley, the Extension Agent for Boone County, took a group of 4-H Club members to the Arkansas State Fair in Little Rock to show their beef calves. I went along with my two young Herefords. Mr. Corley took the kids in his car and the calves went by truck. I was so proud of my calves. I had combed and groomed them for weeks trying to get them ready to show. Jeff and J. W. Bryan went, too.

This was a big trip for me. I remember the fairgrounds were where Fair Park is now. We were tented down near the large tents and ate at a special tent with all the other 4-H'ers. One day we were served something that made us all sick. I can remember the misery I felt standing in line for the toilet facilities.

The fair was fun, with its rides, its side shows and exhibits. But the biggest sight for this little country girl was the horse races. The track was on the fairgrounds and, of course, we took it all in. Time came for the judging. My calves were in different classifications. I won second prize on one and third prize on the other. I was so excited as I stood between my calves in my pink organdy dress for photographers to snap pictures. Newspaper reporters asked me questions and the next day an article was in the paper. Later an article came out in the Farm and Ranch paper or magazine entitled, *What a Girl Did with Two Calves.* There I stood with those two scrawny calves.

On the way to Little Rock, something happened that perhaps affected my life years later. I remember Mr. Corley had a flat tire before we got to Russellville. This was before Highway 65 was built. We had to come Highway 7 through the mountains. When we got to Russellville, Mr. Corley pulled into a service station to get the tire repaired. A black man was working on the tire. I heard Mr. Corley say, "Why don't you come up to Harrison and get a job?" The man answered, "I don't want to get thrown over the moon." I couldn't understand that answer. I thought we were pretty good folks. This kept bothering me and finally I discovered there were no blacks in Harrison. The only ones I ever saw were with the circus. I asked my mother some questions about this and she said, "They ran them out of Harrison several years ago." I kept on asking questions and learned about a lynching when they hanged a man under the bridge over Crooked Creek in the middle of Harrison. No one wanted to talk about it, but I did learn that no Negro dared let the sun go down on him in Harrison. I learned much more later on when I moved to Little Rock.

Well, I may have won ribbons with my calves, but I remember I flunked agriculture. Dad and Mother couldn't understand how a farm girl could flunk agriculture. I just didn't like it. I can remember where that class met in a small white house across the street from the Methodist church. As I told you, this was a Methodist school and the local church supported it all they could. They shared their buildings with us. We had classes in the church and in the little white house they owned across the street.

The church was an L-shaped frame building with a partition that could be pulled to make two sections. When Hoover and Smith were in their presidential campaign, they never realized what a hot campaign was on at Valley Springs Training School. There were pencils bearing the heads of the men so there was no getting away from it even in class. Either you had a pencil bearing Hoover's head or one with Smith's. I remember I was for Hoover. The only reason I was not for Smith was he was a Catholic. Hoover was a Quaker. We had some big arguments around the wood stove in the back section of the church. One day I remember some Smith supporter said, "I wouldn't want a president who had to depend on the Spirit to move him." I remember answering with the great statement, "I'd rather have a president depending on the Spirit than one depending on the Pope."

In that part of Arkansas, a Catholic or a Jew was about as welcome as a Negro. We had no understanding of or interest in either one. White Anglo-Saxons made up our communities, and other persons, even from northern states, were not welcome to move in. Folks with strange looks were feared—the slant of the eyes, the shape of the nose and the color of the skin pigeonholed everyone.

The love and concern these mountain folks had for their kind was shown in the neighborhood life. House raising, quilting, hog killing, hay making, sitting up with the sick or the dead, grave digging and all such things called for cooperation. When there was a neighborhood alert or announcement, someone would "ring the line." That is, ring seven long rings on the telephone. This brought all the phone holders on the line at one time. The news was given out. This was the most important thing that could happen on a winter evening. Mother always ran and took the receiver off the hook and listened while the family watched her face to see if the news was bad or if it was an uninteresting announcement.

We had some sad days on the farm. When the calves were fat enough to sell and the truck came to take them away, I always cried. But when a cow, a member of our family, went bad for some reason and had to be sold, it was like a funeral. Old Jersey, who had given us milk for so long and who was so gentle, her eyes so trusting—well, I could not bear to see her loaded or driven away. Then we had dogs that were dear to us. I remember Toy. This dog would bark its head off at every pedestrian who passed. Troy Paul often walked a mile around to keep from passing our house. When Toy died, we never had another dog on the farm.

Granny was the brave soul in our family.

One day Mr. Bryan's old bull got out of the pasture. This would have been a time for the men in the neighborhood to get pitchforks and together herd him into the right gate and back into his pasture. This day Granny saw him in the front of our house. She was in the garden. She walked over to the row of dried corn stalks and broke off one and here she went out the gate and came face to face with the bull. Mother and I were begging her to turn back. That only challenged her more. She said, "Shut your mouth!" She raised that corn stalk as if to strike the old bull. He turned as docile as a lamb and marched along in front of Granny

Granny

just like I did when she had a keen cut and was after me. She went in front of the huge animal and opened the gate and drove him in the pasture without a bit of trouble. Well, triumphantly she returned to her work in the garden. Her silence hurt even more than had she said, "Now don't you see! I did it!" Maybe that is why she and Grandpa never had a cross word.

Granny had her own way of doing things. She baked the best cornbread with a "pinch of salt and a pinch of soda." When she cooked oatmeal, she used a handful of oatmeal for every serving she wanted. I never saw her use a recipe. She had her own remedies, too. When we had a boil, it was bound up with a piece of fat meat to "bring it to a head." When we had an infection around our fingernails, a piece of a green black walnut hull was bound to it. A hot poultice was pinned inside our nightgown to relieve congestion in the chest and a flannel cloth, coated with salve, was pinned around our throat if it was sore. Onion or catnip tea was given to "break out" the measles or chicken pox. She made a concoction for cough syrup and it went something like this—"enough honey to make it sweet, enough vinegar to make it sour, enough butter to make it slick and enough alum to make it puckery." There was some preventive medicine practiced, too. I remember a dash of cold water, as the last rinse for your hair, closed the pores and you wouldn't catch cold. Sassafras tea in the spring was a good tonic (and I loved it). "Never wash clothes on Good Friday, because for every piece washed, you would have a boil."

My sophomore year in high school, Hazel Ragland and I were the only girls in our class. Some boys had come to stay in the dormitory, but no girls came until my junior year. I was not only small for my age but starting to school so young placed me with kids two years older than I. It didn't occur to me what a misfit I must have been.

Like my friends and classmates, the opposite sex began to play a big part in my life. My good friend, Clyde McMahon, had found a boy friend, Kent Askew. I had a crush on a boy, Billy Bumpers, who was a boarding student from Elaine, Arkansas. I guess as far as I ever got was to make a picture of him and Chink, a Chinese boy that attended our school.

There really was not much for kids to do in those days. In the early fall, we had a county fair—the rides, the stands, the parade, etc., all made it a fun time. Basketball games were the best times to get together with friends, especially tournaments. When frost came, we went out in the woods to hunt chinquapins, a tasty nut that grew in the mountains. This led to games of "hully-gull." A person would hide some chinquapins in his closed hand and hold his hand out to another and say, "Hully-gull. How many?" The person would try to guess how many nuts he had. If he guessed correctly, he got the nuts. If he guessed too many, he had to make up the difference.

Occasionally there would be a pie supper or a box supper at some church in the area. The girls baked a pie, dressed it all up fancy and it was auctioned off. Every girl gave her friend a hint so he could recognize her pie and bid on it. Sometimes a group got together and ran the price up so a guy had to pay a tremendous price to eat pie with his girl. The box suppers were the same idea except each box contained an entire supper.

I remember Rogers, Arkansas, had an Apple Blossom Festival every spring. When it was advertised on the radio, it sounded so wonderful. Lon Brazeal and Boyce Phifer got the idea of going and taking Clyde and me. It sounded so exciting. But, Mother and Dad said, "No!"

There was no telephoning between the sexes because everyone on the line could listen in. Mostly it was talking at school, writing notes, sitting together on the bus or at church. Walking home from church was about the most romantic thing to be done, but I was too young for that.

Something very important did happen that Christmas Eve. We went to Union church, as usual. When Santa Claus handed out the presents, I got a small box of chocolate-covered cherries from Merrill Cole. I couldn't believe it, but there was a card attached that said, "I love you." This was the first of many such cards I was to receive. Sometimes the card read, "*Amo te*," as we learned to say in Latin.

I thought Merrill was entirely unaware of my presence and not until soon after Christmas, when he slipped a note to me in a library book, did I learn his true feelings. He said he had been waiting for me to grow up so he could tell me he loved me. He was five years older than I. I can remember the admiration I had always felt for him. He was something like a hero to me. Here was a prince saying to me, "I love you." It seemed like a fairy tale. I had such a peculiar feeling, but as the days, weeks and months went on, I knew I was not dreaming. This guy really loved me.

We rode together on the bus—a six-mile ride from our house to Valley Springs. I only wished it had been farther. One day I remember he handed me a note when I started to get off the bus. J. W. saw it and he took the note from me. Off the bus jumped Merrill and a fight began. The bus driver waited until the note was retrieved and Merrill was back on the bus.

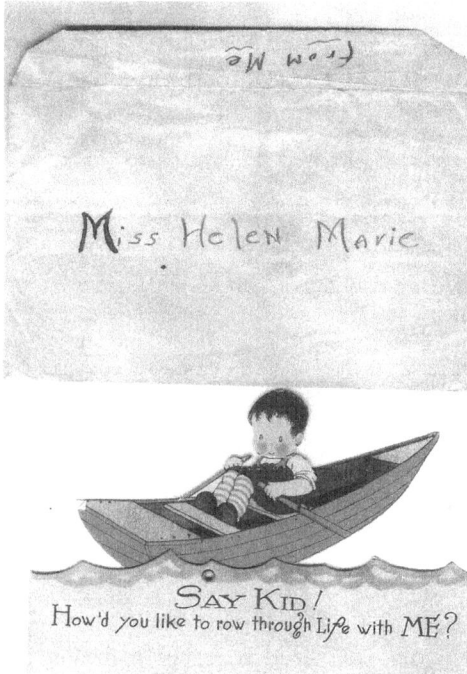

Card to Helen Marie from Merrill

We went together to the district meet. Merrill was so shy and quiet and I was so feisty, I guess. Anyway, he thought I was flirting with some of the other boys so he got him some cigarettes and smoked them and got as sick as a dog. He told me later that he wanted to get sick so he wouldn't care what I did.

That summer I remember going to Buffalo River at Pruitt to swim. One day I swam out into deep water and got frightened and almost drowned before Merrill saw I was in trouble and pulled me out. I never cared about swimming again.

Another summer activity was going to tent meetings—revivals, I expect they were. A large tent was set up by a Pentecostal group we called "Holy Rollers." We would walk over every evening to look on. They talked in tongues, and some other unusual things. One evening the crowd was unusually large and spring seats from wagons were brought in for extra seating. One spring seat was placed in the aisle. During the service, the preacher was telling about the battle of Jericho. Some of the listeners decided to portray it to the congregation, so they got up and started running around the tent. Round and round they went. Then two veered away and started running up the aisle, not realizing the people were seated there. There was not time to stop so they leaped over the people and on they went. This was good sport for us. I am sure our giggles must have been distracting for the worshippers.

Dad would let Merrill drive our car, so we went for rides on Sunday afternoon. Merrill had felt the call to be a minister and was approaching life with this in mind. He was studying his Bible and thinking of what the Lord would have him do. He was an excellent student. Having a late start in school, he was now nineteen years old. When school started in the fall, Merrill was a senior and he was elected president of his class. I was a junior.

I played basketball and made the team that year. You should see those big black bloomers we wore. I was running center. There were three divisions on the court with two girls playing in each division. I remember one time we went to Omaha to play on a cold icy winter night. Merrill drove our car and Mother and J. W. Bryan went with us. We played in the attic of a canning factory. I did not get to play a minute but I was on hand. On our return home, we were about a half mile out of Bellefonte when we ran out of gas. Merrill walked back to Bellefonte, woke someone up and got some gasoline. We were about frozen when we got home. Mother got a pan of water for Merrill to put his hands in as they were frost bitten.

Merrill was janitor at the little Union church. I can remember how it was his job to turn off all the lights and lock the doors. I hung around behind the family and others and waited for him in the little entrance at the top of the steps. He would lock the door, then steal a kiss before we went down the steps. Mother would never allow me to walk home with Merrill like the big girls did. I had to go home with the family, so Merrill rode along.

Our farmhouse had two front rooms. One was the bedroom with two beds and the fireplace. The other was the parlor. We sat in the parlor and listened to the "windup" Victrola. Dad bought us one of the new Edison models that played big thick records. We didn't have more than a dozen, so we played them over and over—didn't matter much anyway; we always had a lot to talk about.

One time when Aunt Letha and her girls were visiting us, Eula and I double dated with Jeff Bryan and Merrill. When we got home, Jeff said "goodnight" and left. Eula went on upstairs, leaving Merrill and me alone in the parlor. It wasn't long before I heard someone using the slop jar (upstairs over our head). The slop jar, or chamber pot, was necessary equipment for each bedroom because one didn't go outside to the toilet at night. Merrill soon left and I ran up the stairs and said, "Who used the slop jar over our heads?" Aunt Letha began to blush and giggle. She thought Merrill left with Jeff and she didn't want my dad to hear her, so she went to the other room.

After a year of close and delightful friendship, Merrill and I were married in the reception room of the boy's dormitory at Valley Springs on January 1, 1929.

Helen Marie and Merrill on their wedding day

Mr. and Mrs. Russell were present. Our Bible teacher and pastor of the Methodist Church, Ben T. Williams, married us. You may ask, "How could you get married so young?" Merrill was going to be leaving Noah's at the end of the school year. Noah knew how much he loved me. He told him he thought he better break up with me or marry me. Well, that was all he needed to hear, he wanted to marry. I was too young to realize all the responsibilities that came with marriage. I thought you married and lived happily ever afterwards. To love and be loved by Merrill was all I could wish for. Mother and Dad gave their consent—they thought I could never do better. They loved Merrill like their own and they welcomed him into the family.

We drove to Valley Springs that night in Dad's Model T Touring car. It was bitter cold and icy. We attended a watch party at school then went over to the dormitory for the secret ceremony. We intended to keep our marriage a secret until May when school would be out. After the wedding, Mr. and Mrs. Russell bade us farewell and we started home. The snap on the Isinglass curtains on the car flapped and flapped in the wind. They did not begin to keep the chill out and, of course, there was no such thing as a heater in the car in those days. I snuggled close to my new husband in my navy blue crepe de chine wedding dress. What I needed was "long handles" and long pants, but, after all, this was my wedding night and Mother had bought me a beautiful new dress to be married in. We decided before we reached home that Merrill should spend the night with me, then slip up before dawn and get to Noah's in time to do the chores.

He slipped up quietly, dressed in his Sunday suit, and started walking the one and one half miles to Noah's house. Who should he meet but one of the neighbors. Mr. Tucker said, "What are you doing out at this time of day?" Merrill said, "I'm looking for a cow that got out." Then Mr. Tucker looked him up and down but did not say a word. Merrill was not exactly dressed for hunting cows on an icy morning and he felt that Mr. Tucker knew he was lying.

Things had changed considerably in the Dearing home. On December nineteenth, a baby boy was born into their family. They named the darling baby Joe Bill. Now Jane was about ten years old. She and Ring had a new playmate. Merrill's duties on the farm became more domestic. Myrtle had taught him how to cook, clean house, do the laundry and help her during her pregnancy.

One of the funniest things he told me about his housekeeping was, one day when the family was away, he was cleaning the house. He heard chimney sweeps in the chimney. He thought he would have some fun, so he climbed up on top of the house and yelled, "Boo!" down the chimney. Well, the birds were frightened all right. What Merrill did not expect—they flew out into the living room and caused havoc before he could get them out. This was especially frustrating to him because the living and dining rooms were kept spotless and closed off; as the house was so large they were not used except for special occasions.

I continued to live at home and he lived down the road and we carefully guarded our secret. We were always glad for weekends to come when we would have a few hours together. After a few weeks, Merrill became ill. He had the flu and was very sick. Myrtle and Noah were very worried because they did not want Joe Bill, the new baby, to have the flu. Merrill was isolated in his little bedroom in the attic. I went over and sat with him and held his head and his hand. He was so sick! Noah brought his meals to the top of the stairs and Merrill would get up and get the tray. I begged him to go to our house so I could take care of him. Daddy and Mother wanted him to move to our house. He agreed, and so the secret was told. He moved and lived there the remainder of the time.

The days were trying in some respects as people had so much to say about me being so young to be married. I was a child bride, but I was content and happy and did not let the remarks and curiosity give me much worry. Merrill said he did not care. He told me he had heard the boys talking and laughing behind my back about me not having a father. He had once fought some of them because of their remarks. He said that was one reason he wanted to love me and protect me. So with his love, Mother and Dad's approval and willingness to help us, I went on to school serene and happy. Noah and Myrtle were always supportive. Jane was like a sister to Merrill and Joe Bill was getting to be so cute.

Merrill filled the pulpit on Sunday in some of the small churches in the Association. Since I was pianist at our church, I did not go with him very often. Our favorite church was at Gaither, the community where his mother grew up and where several of his cousins attended.

There were Cass and Everett Moore, sons of Uncle Wilburn, and the Adair cousins, Essie and Artie.

Merrill's grandmother Moore died just before we were married and I remember she had 114 grandchildren at the time of her death. Many of our paths never crossed. She had fourteen children. The oldest son was Uncle Wilson, a banker in Jasper. His son, Bynum, was a dentist there and sometimes Merrill and I went to him for treatment. Uncle Birchfield was a farmer near Harrison, and Jeff Bryan married his daughter, Mildred. Two of the uncles, Wilbur and Lon, had a grocery store in Harrison. My kids called Uncle Lon Moore "Grasscutter," and he loved it. Uncle Willie had the Boone County Telephone Co. and was a very good friend of Merrill. He watched after all of us until his death. The youngest brother, Uncle Arvin, had a barber shop in Harrison. His wife, Aunt Una, was very kind to me and invited me to their home occasionally.

Now for the aunts, Mrs. Coffman was killed in a train wreck while traveling to the West. I remember hearing the gory details of how this train derailed on a high trestle. The family felt she had a premonition as they found her rings in her purse where she had placed them before the accident. One of her sons, Troy, was a dentist, and another owned Coffman's Drug Store on the Northeast corner of the square. There was Aunt Rhoda Ratcliff, Aunt Vinnie Wasson, a Mrs. Shaddox, Mrs. Adair, Aunt Adeline Holt, mother of Frank, Jack, and a dozen others and, of course, our favorite, Aunt Jane Dearing. Fourteen in all.

All my family was very devoted to Merrill, especially Ruth and James Carl. One time Merrill preached at our church and Jim went to sleep. As we were going home, Mother said, "Well, son didn't get to hear Merrill's sermon." James Carl quickly replied, "Oh, yes I did, I left my ears open." No one could have been lovelier to each one of the family than Merrill was. He took on many of the chores, relieving Granny, Mother and Dad during the cold winter.

About this time Dad bought a Delco, a home generating plant, so we no longer had to use kerosene lamps and clean lamp globes and all the dirty things that entailed. Now we could reach up and turn a knob and have electric lights in every room. What a blessing! There were no fancy light fixtures, just a single bulb dropped down from the ceiling in the middle of the room. We had no electrical appliances at first. Soon Mother was able to have an electric iron to replace the "smoothin' irons" we heated on the stove or in front of the fireplace.

One day, Dad was putting some fresh oil in the motor of the generator that was housed in a small shed he had built in the back yard. James Carl was running around behind him, as he usually did. He decided to pull the lever to start the motor and, before Dad realized what was happening, black oil came flying up in his face and all over his clothes. I am sure Dad only said, "Son, mustn't do that," then whistled like he always did when things were a little "sticky."

One cold winter night, we were sitting around the fireplace. Granny was heating the old irons to carry to bed with her. This was a nightly routine. She had some pieces of old blankets she wrapped them in— one for her feet and one for her back. The telephone rang. This was a signal that something had happened. None of our neighbors called at night, except for an emergency. Dad answered the phone. It was a long distance call. We listened as Dad took the message. Granny's son, Mother's brother, Harvey, had died in Ft. Worth, Texas. Harvey had been Mother's pal. I had heard a lot about him but had never seen him but once. He never visited as he owned a grocery store in Ft. Worth and was always busy. I remember that his wife, Aunt Ethel, and their daughter, Marjorie Fay, came to see us one time when Ruth was a baby. But, Mother and Granny dearly loved Harvey. There were tears and a few words, but Granny continued to wrap her irons. Then she got up from her little chair and started toward the stairs. Her bedroom was upstairs. Dad walked over and said, "Let me carry your irons for you." She refused. I can see that dear little lady, grief stricken, heading for her bed where she would be alone with her God.

Merrill and I, along with Ruth, caught the bus to school every morning. This being Merrill's senior year, there was much for him to do. They had a senior play, called "Tea Toper Tavern." There were school picnics—each class had one before school was out. Autograph books were popular then and they were passed around for everyone to write a few lines. Some were very funny, such as, "May you and all your little Cole-ettes live happily," and "When you are married and spanking six, think of me between the licks."

There were spring recitals for piano students. Merrill participated in debates, etc. Our lives were very busy. His class built a post at the entrance of the gray stone building that still stands as a memorial to the Class of 1929. The class roll is on a marble slab built in with gray stone to match the building.

The junior class always had the task of decorating the church for the graduation exercises. It had been a tradition for the life of the school to have field daisies along the edge of the stage. So I went daisy picking. We filled gallon syrup buckets with daisies, wrapped the buckets with white paper and lined up about a dozen of them. It was beautiful and didn't cost a penny.

Merrill's graduation from Valley Springs Training School

The big day came. Merrill was valedictorian and delivered his speech in great style. Goodbyes were said with hugs, kisses and tears. Since several were boarding students and lived far away from Valley Springs, we felt the pangs of separation more.

The following summer was a time that affected our lives in more ways than one. Merrill had to make plans for the fall. He was going to college, but where?

Everybody was talking about a depression. It seemed something had happened to the government and no one knew what to do about it and hard times seemed to be all over the country. Farmers were hit hard as prices went down, down, down. President Hoover promised that prices would go up. I was not too concerned since we didn't sell much anyway—a little cream and a few eggs. We read a little about it in our weekly paper and heard people talking about it, but it seemed far, far away and I was happy in my little world. It's a good thing Dad had his job at the post office because, knowing that he could earn sixty-five cents an hour with no dread of unemployment made our family feel secure.

Merrill worked on our farm and "hired out" some. He helped the neighbors with their hay, helped Noah butcher beef and did anything else that would pay a little money. He tried selling Bibles in Harrison but, after he went to three or four houses and they turned him down, he gave that up as a bad investment.

To Granny, three square meals a day was the measure of success. Well, we had that. We had breakfast, dinner and supper. For breakfast we had home-cured bacon or ham, gravy, eggs, oatmeal and biscuits. For dinner we had vegetables, some meat, either pork or chicken, and corn bread. Often we had fruit cobbler, cake or cookies of some sort. I remember especially the molasses cookies. Supper was a lighter meal, often left over corn bread and milk. Sometimes Granny made hot mush to eat with our "sweet milk." We had sweet milk, buttermilk, clabber milk, skim milk—but never just "milk."

The only time we had lunch was when we went to school or on a picnic. Dad always carried a lunch to work at the post office. Speaking of picnics, about once a year our Sunday school class would go on a picnic. We usually went to Marble City Falls, where Dog Patch is today. This was a beautiful picnic area. We also went to Wilson Springs near Harrison or a spring on Crooked Creek, the name I have forgotten. But I always remember the tale Granny told about camping at that spring several years before. Grandpa had a dry goods store at Parthenon and once a year he made a trip in a wagon to buy stock for the store. This time Granny went with him. They bought the goods in Springfield, Missouri. This took about three or four days each way. Coming back home, they camped on the bank of Crooked Creek near a spring.

During the night, the creek got up and nearly washed them away before they realized what was happening. It had rained upstream but not in that area. She liked to tell of that narrow escape.

The family often went to Grandpa and Grandma White's near Sulphur Mountain and picnicked at Sulphur Springs nearby. Because the smell of the water was so bad, I never enjoyed those picnics. I held my nose and tried to drink the water but it was awful.

My favorite picnics were on the banks of the Buffalo River on Shop Creek when we went to the Casey's. We would fish, then cook our fish along with potatoes and onions. Aunt Letha usually had a gooseberry cobbler to carry along. Now that is good eating—and great fun.

Merrill made a trip to Arkadelphia early in the summer to see about entering Ouachita College, a Baptist institution. They said they had their quota of ministerial students and all the campus jobs were filled. He was disappointed. He came back by Hendrix College, a Methodist school at Conway. They would receive him with open arms. He came back home, but he was not satisfied about the situation. If he was to be a Baptist minister, he could not see taking advantage of the Methodist opportunity. He became a bit moody one day in late August. He stayed in our room upstairs all day. I tried several times to open the door, but it was locked. I called to him but no answer. I became worried. Finally he came out and he said, "Helen Marie, I have prayed it through. I have been praying all day for God to direct me and show me what I should do, and I have the answer. I am going to Ouachita when school opens and see what happens."

Our church at Union needed to be replaced. That summer an effort was made to raise the money. Someone took a wagon with chicken coops in it and drove all over our neighborhood and into adjoining neighborhoods, gathering up hens that people would give for the new church. These were sold and the money placed in the building fund. We also had pie suppers to raise more money. They asked each member to take a dollar and "invest" it some way and turn the earnings into the building fund. I remember taking my dollar and buying ingredients for cookies. I baked the cookies and Dad took them to the post office and sold them for me. The men and boys of the church picked up rocks from the creek bed and, with a little hired labor and a lot of volunteers, built the new church. Merrill painted the inside and the trim on the outside. He wrote in his diary, "Every stroke was a stroke of love."

Before time for school to open, Merrill was ordained a minister at our little church. Ministers and visitors came from all over the Association for the afternoon service. Merrill took his place on the rostrum and, during the service, one preacher said, "This young man is married to a girl who grew up in this church and plays the piano for services here." The nicely dressed lady from Harrison, sitting next to me, bent over and whispered, "Is his wife here?" I answered, "I'm his wife." She looked at me as if to say, "That can't be so."

I felt that all ministers were friends of mine. Mother and Dad always were hosts to visiting ministers. We had about two revivals a year in our church and that meant for two weeks they stayed with us. I loved every one of them, especially the ministers of music. We practiced for each service and often, just for fun, played and sang the old songs. I was looking forward to being a minister's wife.

Helen Marie

No one ever told us anything about birth control so, as you might guess, I got pregnant during the summer. I had early morning sickness and then came down with the summer flu. I can remember lying in our bed upstairs so sick I could die!

Merrill was planning a trip to Kansas City, Missouri for me to meet his folks. We were going on the train—the Missouri North Arkansas that ran through Harrison and up through Joplin, Missouri. Mother said I could not go unless my fever went down. I wanted to go, so I would get an ice cube and hold it in my mouth just before time for her to take my temperature. I managed to fool her and away I went. By the time the train reached Joplin, I wished I were back in my bed at home. It wasn't the fun I thought it would be. I could hardly hold my head up. I remember lying for hours it seems on the hard benches in the depot waiting for another train to come to carry us on to Kansas City.

Merrill's father lived with Lonnie in a small apartment overlooking the main street in Kansas City, Kansas. He did the housekeeping that was done and smoked his pipe and watched the people. Lex, the older brother, lived nearby with his wife and children. Both Lonnie and Lex worked at the Coca-Cola plant. Lonnie was superintendent. He told Merrill that he wanted him to come to Kansas City and work in the plant the next summer so he could make more money for school.

Most of our visit in Kansas City was with Cassie and Louis. They had two more children now. Of course, Merrill was so fond of Eugene and Martina, but we soon learned to love the other two. Cassie was so much like Aunt Jane. I loved her the first time I saw her. She took good care of me like I was her own child.

September came and Merrill packed his bags and took off. He reached Ouachita College and went into the Registrar's office. When the Registrar saw him, he said, "Did you not understand that we have no ministerial scholarships for you and all the campus jobs are filled?" Merrill answered, "Yes sir, I understood that, but I wanted to come and try once more. I thought something might open up for me." The man said, "Well, if you want to go to school that bad, I'll see what I can do for you."

Shortly he returned to the desk and told Merrill that a retired minister who lived in Arkadelphia would let him stay in his home until they could arrange other housing so he was admitted! He paid his fees and was given a green cap that identified him as a freshman at his beloved Ouachita. Before many days passed, he was in the dormitory and had a job waiting tables in the dining hall. He joined R.O.T.C. and became active on the campus.

Oh, how I missed him! Letters came almost every day, sometimes only a few lines, but they always brought me his love. Since I had gotten pregnant, I was not enrolled in high school. I stayed home and took on the jobs my grandmother and mother had done. I continued to study piano and practiced a lot. I cracked black walnuts, pieced quilts, helped with the turkeys and chickens, the canning, the cooking and other chores.

One thing Merrill did not like about college was the hazing by the upperclassmen. Because of this, he was often the brunt of an upperclassman's brutal licks. He would get off the walk and cut across the grass. Someone would always see him and call to him to come there. He refused to bend over when they ordered him to—so they would proceed to bend him and then he felt the sting of a board, a bat or a belt. One guy, whom he despised, was a football player called "Big Bob Moore." Years later I saw articles about him in the Arkansas Gazette, as he was Sheriff of a southern county in Arkansas.

In early November, word came that Ouachita would be coming to Hendrix College to play football on the weekend before Thanksgiving. Plans were made for us to meet Merrill at the game and he would ride back home with us for the Thanksgiving holidays. What excitement! I had never seen a football game, but that was not the most important thing. I would get to see Merrill after two months of absence.

We drove to Conway down Highway 65. It was not yet paved. We found Hendrix College and parked on the street by the side of the stadium. I was looking for Merrill among the crowd, and then I saw him coming toward the car in his R.O.T.C. uniform. How great he looked! We went into the game. All the color and excitement was surprising to me. The bands were playing and the cheerleaders were leading all the people in cheers. There were cheers for the Tigers coming from one side and cheers for the Warriors coming from the other. Banners were waving and spirits were high. But, my main interest was beside me. How had it been? Did he like it? Oh, there were thousands of questions. I had never seen a football game, so I had no idea what was going on on the field. Merrill told me they were trying to make a first down, ten yards, in four plays. Looked very rough to me. I watched halfheartedly, and was glad when time came for us to start back home, taking Merrill with us.

The holidays were much too short, and it was too soon that I was driving him down Highway 65 to meet his roommate, Gerald Berry who lived in Flippen, for the trip back to Arkadelphia. We waited at the intersection until the lights of the car approached. We held each other close for a minute, and then he got out of the car and was gone. I turned back toward home, recalling all the things we had said and all the things we had done. Christmas was not far away. I was looking forward to that as I drove those lonely miles. Dad had told Merrill he was going to buy a new Model-A car and we would drive down to Arkadelphia and pick him up for Christmas vacation. I could hardly wait. I was already counting the days.

Dad did buy a new car. The salesman took Mother, Granny, Ruth, Jim and I out for a drive before Dad closed the deal. He let me drive it. We all agreed that Dad had made a good choice. He told Dad I could drive the family home and so I did. For a week or more, I drove with Dad to work—he could not coordinate his hands and his feet and get it all together. But I didn't mind. I loved those minutes spent alone with Dad, just the two of us. He talked about how pleased he was that Merrill could go to school, how happy he was to have me stay with them and what a great future he saw for us.

I was unaware of what was going on in the United States economically. You see, I lived a real isolated life. There were no radios at our house. Noah had one, but very few people did. We took one paper, the *Boone County Headlight*, and it was a weekly paper with mostly local news. I had heard that businessmen in New York City were committing suicide because their businesses were going broke. But, that was far, far away—how could that bother me? I wasn't concerned.

So, it was a real shock when the day before we were to leave for Arkadelphia, the banks in Harrison closed. The depression had struck home! We had no money! My dad had thirty cents in his pocket, not even enough for a telephone call to tell Merrill we could not come for him. What was I to do? It was too late for a letter to reach him and he would have no way of knowing we were not coming. Then I thought of Uncle Willie Moore. Uncle Willie was Merrill's mother's brother and Ida, Merrill's mother, was the first one of the fourteen children to die. Uncle Willie had been interested in Merrill ever since—and he was sending him $10 each month now that he was in college. He owned the telephone company in Harrison, so I went to his office and told him my plight and asked him if he would call Merrill and let him know so he could hitchhike home. He was glad to do this and I was very grateful.

The thing I remember most about this Christmas is the present I got from Merrill. From the little bit he earned working in the dining hall, he had saved enough money to buy me something special—a small cedar chest. Now I would have a place for my quilt tops, pillowcases, tea towels and things I was making for our future home, especially for the clothes I was getting together for our new baby. It was due before the winter was over. I have found a list of the clothes I had ready for the baby: two wool sweaters, one wool cap, two nightingales, nine pairs of stockings, two pairs of booties, two pairs of silk shoes, two undershirts, three outing Gertrudes, three outing gowns, four long gowns, twelve bands, three kimonos, six slips, fifteen dresses, six bibs and three dozen Birdseye diapers.

When the holidays were over, Merrill went back to school. His funds were exhausted. In a couple of weeks fees for the second semester would have to be paid. His heart was heavy but he wasn't a quitter. When the day came to register and pay fees, he went into the office to see what kind of arrangements he could make to defer payments. Much to his surprise, they told him his fees had been paid. "That couldn't be so," he said, knowing he was broke and that my dad's assets all went with the foreclosure of the bank. When they looked into the situation, they found that Dr. Brown, his Bible professor, had come by and paid his tuition. This reassured us that God was opening the way for him to become a minister. He worked and studied harder than ever. Letters came every day but when there was a break, my dad knew he was out of stamps so he would buy a few and put them in the mail to him. The letters would pick up again.

The days would have been long for me but Mother kept encouraging me to take all the Bible study courses offered in our church and the First Baptist Church at Harrison. You see, if I were to be a minister's wife, I needed preparation, too. Also, I studied piano, going into Harrison for lessons from an old German, Mr. Kirkham, who would strike my hands with a ruler if I were not lifting my fingers just right or if I missed a rest or failed to pick up the tempo at the proper time. I was scared of the man, but he taught me a lot.

My dad drove into town every workday and parked his car behind the post office. This made good headquarters for me. I could leave my books or music there while I did a bit of shopping or visiting. In the car between the seats there were always half-gallon fruit jars, either full of whole milk or empty to be refilled the next day. My dad was a very compassionate man. We had more milk than we could use so he rose early and milked. Mother filled the fruit jars while he was dressing. Our Associational Missionary, Bro. Bow, would come by the post office and pick it up. I remember once someone in the family told Dad that was an awful lot of trouble and he said, "Well, I just figure sometime someone will share something with my kids—it will come back." How many times I remember those words when, through the hard years ahead, some good neighbors would give us a mess of beans or a gallon of molasses, etc. I would say to myself, "Here is some of Dad's milk coming back."

Being pregnant was a real experience for a young girl. I felt my body changing each day. The movement within me was almost alarming and yet I knew it was a product of love. It was our baby and so I waited. Mother took me to the doctor to be sure everything was all right. My doctor was Uncle James, Granny's brother. He took a specimen of urine and listened to my heart and lungs and felt my tummy. He told me how to expect the labor pains to start and told Mother to call him in time for him to get to our house which was five and one half miles out of town. Myrtle loaned me a big oval laundry basket to use for a bassinet. I lined it in pink and had it ready.

It was about midnight on Monday that the pains started. Mother waited and we counted the time between pains. About daybreak, she called Uncle James. He came right out, bringing his nurse, Mrs. Mary Goss, rubber sheets and all the paraphernalia that was needed for home delivery. I heard him tell Mother to put the teakettle on the stove. He would need some hot water. My labor continued and continued. The chloroform mask was put over my nose and occasionally a few drops would take me into unconsciousness and, oh, the joy to feel the pain subsiding, but not for long. Soon it would be increasing until it was so bad I was given another sniff and I faded out again. This ordeal went on and on. Finally, after thirty-six hours of labor, a beautiful baby boy was born at 12:10 p.m. on Wednesday, February 19, 1930. He weighed six pounds and was eighteen and three-fourths inches long. I was too weak to pay much attention to him that day but I was thankful for a perfect baby.

My dad got a telegram off to Merrill. It read, "Marie and the boy are all o.k." Signed, Jeff White, and the time stamped on the telegram was 2:33 p.m. Merrill responded with the following letter:

> Dear pals,
>
> Got your telegram just now. You can imagine how my hands trembled when I opened it. My! And the joy when I read, 'Marie and boy all okay.' Have someone write and tell me all about it. I'll be anxious to hear. Be sure and tell me what you named it.
>
> I was just reading the letter that you wrote yesterday. You closed with 'Maybe I'll have some more news tomorrow.' Well, you did, didn't you? Pal, I'm glad you are doing well. I know you are.
>
> There are so many emotions whirling around in my heart that I can hardly think.
>
> I love you both,
> Merrill

That day when school was out, my little brother, James Carl, came home and Mother met him to tell him the news. She announced, "Merrill and Helen Marie have a new baby boy." He ran to my bedside to see it. He saw the sweet little fellow and looked up and said, "Why can't it be yours and Daddy's and Helen Marie's and Merrill's, too?"

My brother and sister really loved that baby. He was such a cute little black-haired thing. They hung over his basket and watched his every move. The name for the baby was settled. His name would be Billie Jon. Jon was the Lindbergh's son's name, and I liked it.

The days that followed were so humiliating. Mother took care of me for fourteen days while I lay flat of my back in bed. This was what doctors required in 1930. I remember Myrtle came to help Mother. They had to give me an enema and that embarrassed me. But the most embarrassing thing happened when Mary Martin, a friend, came to see the baby. Mother discovered Bill had a dirty diaper so she took him out of his basket and put him across her knees in front of the fireplace and started to change him. Well, Bill wasn't finished. He drew up his face and strained and, lo and behold, the black soot on the back of the fireplace was sprayed in yellow. I wanted to crawl under the bed. I wished he could have waited until Mary was gone but, you know, it didn't bother him one bit.

I tried to relay to Merrill in letters the way the baby looked, how things were going and what it was like being a mother. He had to wait a few weeks before he could come home. He had been given a new job on campus. Now he was night watchman from midnight to six a.m. This meant he had to sleep, study and work all in one night, but he always found time to write us a letter. No one ever made a long-distance telephone call in those days, not in our community at least. Money was getting scarcer each month, so we lived on what we had and could raise on the farm.

The basketball season ended with a big tournament at Harrison. Some of my friends invited me to go with them one night and Mother insisted that I go, she thought I needed an outing. So I went, reluctantly. It was hard to leave Billie Jon but what hurt me most was the thirty-five cents I had to pay for admission. I kept thinking, "I could have bought a pair of socks for Billie Jon with that money," and my conscience hurt me.

Those of us who lived through the Depression can never enjoy wasting money. We never went hungry, but there sure were lots of things we had to do without. We never threw anything away either. Feed sacks made aprons, dresses, blouses, tea towels, etc. Mother sold the excess eggs and the cream from the milk. Mrs. Bryan made dresses for her younger children out of the older girls' clothes. Everyone was very thrifty. If you didn't need a scrap, leftover or discard, someone else would.

Bill grew and developed a real personality. We had lots of fun with him, especially Ruth and James Carl. Mother was eager to show him off and I enjoyed the daily care. We were at home most of the first four months of his life except for walks to the neighbors or a ride to some of the relatives or a trip into town. I remember quite well that I was waiting outside Hudson's Grocery on the southwest corner of the square with Ruth and James Carl while Mother was inside buying groceries. We didn't buy much because we had most everything we needed. But there was sugar, flour, cornmeal, salt, KC baking powder, soda, vanilla and a few things we had to buy. We always bought oatmeal—Mother's Oats it was called—and there was a piece of "depression" glass in each box This was one of the exciting times we had when the oatmeal box was opened and we found a different piece in every box.

But I was telling you about this day when I was waiting outside the store. Some other children gathered around to look at the darling baby. Ruth was holding him. He began to whimper and I said, "Come to Mother. Let Mother have him." This kid looked at me and said, "You aren't his Mother, are you?" I assured him I was. The child could not understand how such a little girl could be the mother of a baby. I knew then that I looked like a child.

Plans were being made for us to go to Kansas City during the summer so Merrill could work at the Coca-Cola plant. Lonnie, his brother, lived in an apartment with their father and they said we could live with them and that Merrill could keep all the money he made. If he could save enough money and I could can enough food for us, I would be able to go back to Arkadelphia with him in September. Big-hearted Mother and Dad wanted me to enter Ouachita that fall and let them take care of Bill. First, I would have to pass the entrance examination, since I had not finished high school. We heard that would not be difficult to do.

May came and, after a visit with our family and the Dearing's "ooh-ing and aah-ing" over Joe Bill and how much he had grown, we were soon packing our bags to go to Kansas City.

Mother, Ruth and Jim drove us over to Bergman to board the Missouri Pacific in order to avoid the layover at Joplin on the Missouri North Arkansas line that came through Harrison. The Missouri Pacific went directly to Kansas City. All the goodbyes were said. It was Billie Jon that they all loved and hugged and kissed. They were so fond of him.

They got back in the car and James Carl said, "Hurry and maybe we can see them in Harrison at the railroad crossing." When they drove back to the farm and went in the house, there was the empty bassinet. Jim walked over and looked in and said, "There's where his little head was."

In Kansas City, the apartment was over a store on the main street of downtown Kansas City, Kansas. Not much could be said for the furnishings. Cassie and her children lived close by and Billie Jon and I spent lots of days with them. We could walk over there.

One Sunday evening Merrill and I went to church and left Billie Jon with Grandpa Cole. Bill was asleep in the middle of the bed in the bedroom. Mr. Cole was sitting by the front window overlooking the street watching the traffic and smoking his pipe. This was his favorite pastime and he did it hour after hour. This particular evening his leisure was interrupted by a ghastly sound—like an explosion. He ran to see what had happened and dust was pouring out of the bedroom, so thick he could hardly see the bed. He felt for Bill and pulled him out from a mass of plaster that had fallen from the ceiling. Large chunks had barely missed his head, but he was not even scratched. When we came home, Dad Cole was so excited and overcome, he could hardly tell us about it.

The next few days I looked for us another apartment. I found one in Kansas City, Missouri, nearer the Coca-Cola plant and much nicer. We enjoyed it so much as it was in a residential area. There was a large front porch we had access to and I enjoyed sitting in the porch swing with Billie Jon. I guess Dad Cole didn't like it as well as the downtown location as there was not much to do and no traffic to watch.

The Coca-Cola bottling plant was an interesting thing to visit. You could watch lines of Coke bottles pass by on a belt as they were being inspected for chips or trash. Or they would go to be given a "shot" of syrup, filled with carbonated water and finally capped and cased for shipment.

One of the things that happened at the Coca-Cola plant that summer was an attempted robbery. A deaf employee was shot to death when he tried to ward off the robber. I went with Merrill and Lonnie to the funeral. It was my first time to see signers interpreting the songs and sermon to the congregation.

Our apartment was near Penn State Park with its beautiful statue and fountain. We often spent our Sunday afternoons there. One evening that summer, we left Bill with Dad Cole and went to a theater to see *My Blue Heaven*. "*Just Molly and me, and baby makes three, we're happy in My Blue Heaven*" really hit home to me. Here we were so poor, yet so happy.

At the end of August we returned to Harrison and prepared for the move to Arkadelphia. Billie Jon was a big boy now, almost ready to start walking. We were happy to show him off, and we had plenty wanting to see him.

Dear Ones,

Circumstances force me to stop writing but hopefully I can pick up where I left off and continue my reminiscing with you.

I hope from the things I have told you already that you are beginning to see how God holds our lives in his hands and how *"day by day he pours His steadfast love upon us."* Psalms 42:8

There is a verse in Proverbs 20:24 that says, *"Since the Lord is directing our steps, why try to understand everything that happens along the way?"*

As I continue my story, this will become harder and harder to understand and we will say with Solomon, *"We can make our plans, but the final outcome is in God's hands."* Proverbs 16:1

And now I pray with the Psalmist, (Psalms 71:17-18), *"Oh, God, you have helped me from my earliest childhood— and I have constantly testified to others of the wonderful things you do. And now that I am old and gray, don't forsake me. Give me time to tell this new generation (and their children, too) about all your mighty miracles."* The Living Bible

Merry Christmas and Happy New Year!

Much, much love,
Granny, 1984

Part 2: 1930-1941

Billy Jon was a darling baby as you can see by this picture made by Case Studio in Harrison. James Carl and Una Ruth thought he was a doll. They loved to carry him around and loved to hear him talk. He would say, "Mine" and, of course, it was fun to tease him and hear him shout "Mine!"

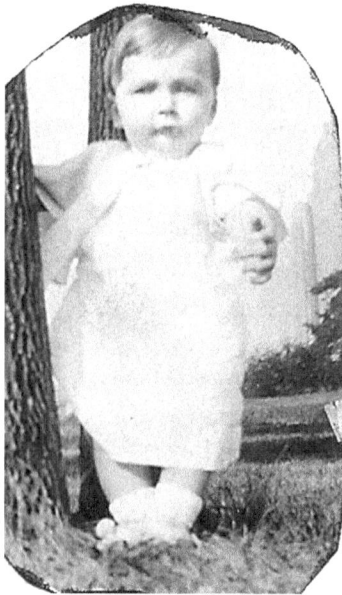

From the news, we knew the United States was suffering from the worst economic problems in the nation's history. The stock market had crashed. Over two thousand banks had closed. Factories had shut down. Railroads were having a rough time with trains running almost empty most of the time. Foreign trade came almost to a stop. Taxes could not be collected. The number of unemployed Americans was rising fast into the millions. We heard about men selling apples on the street corners in cities and how lines were forming in front of soup kitchens set up to feed the hungry. Shacks called "Hoovervilles," named for President Hoover, were the only homes many people had. Farmers got only a nickel a pound for cotton and less than fifty cents a bushel for wheat. Hourly wages dropped sixty percent and salaries fell by forty percent. Hunger and suffering was a daily reality and suicides were many.

Picture of Bill

But all that is not my story. As I said before, most of this seemed far away, but it was getting nearer and nearer to us every day. We were beginning to feel the effects of it. The Great Depression, as we call it now, was upon us and we didn't know what lay ahead.

After much consideration, praying and figuring, we decided this was not the time for me to go to Ouachita with Merrill, perhaps next year. Billie Jon would be larger and we could leave him easier. So, I stayed at home.

It was hard to see Merrill leave after spending the summer with him. But Granny, Mother, Billie Jon and I had a good time together during the day, while Daddy worked and the kids were in school. We worked hard, spent lots of time washing, ironing, cleaning the house and yard and keeping all the chores done, but there was always time to play with Bill, practice my piano, do a little needlework, crack some walnuts or read and study the Bible.

One Saturday, we went into Harrison as usual. Jane went with us this day. We knew this was Flora Hudson's wedding day. Flora was our grocer's daughter and we knew her well. She often visited Era, her cousin and one of my best friends. Jane and I decided we would slip in the back of the church, uninvited, and sit on the back seat and see the wedding. This was the first chance I had ever had to see a "sure enough" wedding. All went well for a while. We were aghast at the gorgeous dresses the bridesmaids wore. We saw the beautiful bride walk in on her father's arm and the minister was performing the solemn ceremony, when Billie Jon became restless. I couldn't let him disturb the wedding, and I must see it all. I remembered how he loved money, so I quickly got a nickel out of my purse for him to hold. That lasted about three minutes and he dropped it. It hit the tile floor with a loud clang and rolled and rolled and rolled down the floor toward the altar. Everyone, it seemed, turned and looked at us. I wanted to crawl under the seat. Here we were uninvited, and I felt everyone knew it.

When the wedding was over, we hurried out the side door and went back to "our territory" on the square. When Jane told her mother about this, Myrtle almost whipped us. She told me that was not the thing to do.

Soon after school started, I had a letter from Merrill that brought good news. The Norphlet Baptist Church near El Dorado, wanted to lend some support to a needy ministerial student, so the business office had picked Merrill to receive the $10 a month. With his tuition scholarship, his campus job, which more than paid for room and board, plus Uncle Willie's $10, he had about $25 a month spending money. This was great! He felt the Lord had blessed him bountifully.

Quilting bees were the social activity of the fall. I remember one day when we went to Mrs. Byron's to quilt all day, I carried along the walker I had bought for Billie Jon. I put him in it and sat down to quilt with other ladies of the community. The quilt was hung in a frame from the ceiling and several persons could quilt at one time. It was a great time for sharing news, gossip, recipes, remedies, experiences, etc.

I had just gotten started good, when I heard a loud crashing noise and a scream from Billie Jon. I ran to him and found his lips bruised and bleeding. He had started through a doorway and the piece of wood, called a sill that was in the doorway, had turned the walker over, throwing him out on his face. I wanted to cry. I picked him up, cleaned his mouth and soothed him as best I could. I said, "Well, that ends the quilting for me. I will just hold Billie Jon and watch and listen, which was exactly what I did until the children came in from school. Some of the larger children wanted to play with the baby. I thought, "This is my chance to quilt some more." So, I found a spot to get in and started. Not many stitches were taken until I heard that awful thud again and more screams. The kids had wanted to see Bill in his walker and he had run over the doorsill as before. I was heartbroken that it happened the second time.

Watching Billie Jon grow was fun. He stood alone a month before he took his first steps. We called him a "fraidy cat" because he wouldn't try to walk alone but would walk everywhere holding to one finger.

Just before Christmas, we were in town one Saturday walking around looking at the toys and things in the stores. Billie Jon saw a little black doll that he loved. I had no money to buy it, even if I had wanted to, so I tore it out of his arms and put it down and hurried out of the store with him screaming to the top of his lungs. The street didn't quieten him at all so down the street we went with everyone staring at us. Who would we meet but Uncle Willie? He said, "What is the matter with my boy?" I told him he wanted a doll he had seen in the dime store. What did he do? He went up to the store and bought the doll and brought it to him.

Christmas came and went and with it Merrill's vacation. He was fun to be with. He was very shy and the majority of people, I expect, thought he was uninteresting, but he talked a lot to those close to him, often saying the unexpected. He had a good sense of humor. His green eyes were kind, gentle and serious most of the time but sometimes there was a roguish look in them. It was always so good to have him home and the two weeks afterwards were so hard. Then it seemed I began to get adjusted and was able to get along until his next homecoming.

Billie Jon was so much company to me. On cold winter nights, we snuggled under the warm covers and I was so thankful for him. Sleep was often a long time coming, as I thought of Merrill and the days not too far away when our little family could be together. During the days, we bundled up with wool coat, cap and mittens and played outside for a short time. The cold wind from the north really made pink cheeks and runny noses.

The winter was a good time for reading. Billie Jon loved stories, even before he was a year old. And, he was a great talker. He would try to say anything but it wasn't always plain. We had a black dog on the farm and he called him "Iger." When he wanted milk, he would ask for "bilk." His first birthday was a time for great celebration. During the winter, Mother and I had made him an appliquéd tulip quilt for a present. (*Don't you know he loved it?*) His cake was an angel food with one candle on it. A telegram came from Daddy, "Greetings for Billie's birthday."

With March came gardening. This year I wanted to really help plant, harvest and can because, hopefully, in the fall I would be going to Arkadelphia with Merrill.

Spring was always so pretty with the peach and apple trees blooming in the orchards and the jonquils and other flowers in the yard and garden. Mother had a Bleeding Heart that was her pride and joy. There were little pink hearts hanging from the long stems of the plant. There was much to do with incubators to be set, baby chickens and turkeys to be cared for, garden to be planted, baby calves to be looked after, etc. Mother and Granny took care of these things and I did most of the housework.

Billy Jon was walking everywhere by late spring. One night I set the table for supper and he walked over and reached up and pulled a plate off. It broke into a million pieces. Mother smacked his hand and said, "Don't do that!." He cried loudly for a minute then stopped, stomped his foot and went back to the table and pulled another plate off before Mother could catch him. This time he got a good spanking he deserved.

Merrill decided to stay at home this summer instead of going back to Kansas City. He preached on Sundays at Gaither and they paid him a little. Since I was pianist at Union, I could not go with him. One Sunday I did go and I remember how friendly the people were. Many of them were his relatives. After church, he took me to White Hall Cemetery in the neighborhood and showed me his mother's grave. During the week he worked for neighbors who needed an extra hand. About once a week, Noah needed his help with butchering beef, so he was able to make a few dollars. He helped us can and get food ready for Dad and Mother's cellar, plus ours to take to Arkadelphia. The garden produced lots of vegetables. There were English peas, green beans, corn, greens, carrots, etc. to can. Potatoes, both Irish and sweet, were dug. Onions and beans were dried, as were apples and peaches.

Mother had an apple peeler that you attached to a table, and it had three prongs to hold the apple and a knife that went round and round the apple, removing the peel. When we turned the crank, we could peel apples fast. One peeled and the other trimmed off any peeling left and cut the apple into eighths, removing the core. Then the apples were either cooked and canned or they were put out to dry.

The method we used for drying was very simple. The apples were put on a clean blanket or heavy sheet and put out the dormer windows on the roof over the front porch. It took several days for them to dry. They had to be brought in at night because of heavy dews and during the day in case a cloud came up. It was worth all the trouble because the fried pies in the winter were so good. We boiled the good peelings and cores of the apples for a short time, then put them in a flour sack or pillow case and pressed the juice from them to make jelly. We also made jelly from wild plums and blackberries the same way.

One day, the telephone rang and it was for Merrill. Our friend, Era Hudson, wanted him to marry her and Vance Hickman. He agreed to do it. This was a new experience for him, but he couldn't refuse Era. They had been such good friends at Union school and in the church, and he was an ordained minister. So, after a while a little black Ford roadster pulled up by the side of the road and parked under the walnut tree. Merrill went out. I watched from inside the house. Era and Vance stood by the side of the car and Merrill said the ceremony. After a few minutes, they got back into their car and drove off, husband and wife. Merrill came back into the house grinning like a Cheshire cat.

That summer we had our annual revival at Union. We took a blanket to make a bed on the bench for Billie Jon to sleep on. One night we got in the car, Mother, Dad, Granny, Ruth, James Carl, Merrill and I and drove halfway home before we missed Bill. No one had picked him up, we had left him on the bench, asleep. We turned around and went back to the dark church. Merrill unlocked the door and found the little fellow asleep right where we had left him. Poor thing!

Merrill's favorite pastime was playing the harmonica. He could play any tune he wanted to. He would lie on the bed and play for hours. One evening, he had been playing his harmonica while I was helping clean the kitchen, after I had put Billie Jon to bed. He became sleepy and crawled under the sheet. As soon as I was finished, I climbed the stairs and found him apparently asleep. I quickly slipped into my gown and crawled in beside him. He didn't move a muscle. I thought, "You are no more asleep than I am." About that time a wasp that was in the bed stung me. I hopped out of bed grunting and holding my leg. He didn't move, just pretended he didn't hear me. Then, suddenly out of the bed he came with a bound. The wasp had found him. I could not keep from laughing, but I did go down to the kitchen and get some baking soda to put on our stings. Granny always said that was the best remedy for a wasp sting.

Fourth of July was always a holiday for us. We dressed up and went into Harrison for the big celebration. Flags and bunting were flying and the town took on a real patriotic atmosphere. There were stands set up in the courtyard. You could buy pink lemonade "*stirred with a spade, good enough for any old maid,*" cotton candy, hamburgers, soda pop, popcorn and lots of things to eat. You could buy balloons, flags, patriotic hats, walking canes, etc. Merrill was reminded of his childhood days in Harrison. He told us how he would shine shoes on the square for weeks before the Fourth, save all his money, then spend it all that day and go home sick as a dog and lose all the "gunk" he had eaten. The bandstand in the courtyard was the place for politicians to speak in the afternoon. Then, in late evening, a "sure 'nuf" band played a concert. We stayed to hear it all then dragged our tired bodies home to bed.

We always went to the revivals or "protracted meetings" in adjoining communities. One night we were at one at New Church when, in the middle of the sermon, we heard horses stampeding toward the church. They came to a stop just outside the front door. Someone burst through the door and started down the aisle toward the pulpit. To my amazement, it was a white- robed Ku Klux Klansman. He marched right up to the preacher, disturbing his sermon and the whole congregation. He handed the preacher an envelope. The minister tore open the envelope and pulled out a note. He read it. Then the Klansman took a match and lighted the note and burned it. We had no idea what the message was. Then the Klansman turned and stomped out the door as strangely as he had appeared. We could hear the horses' hooves as they galloped away into the distance. Cold chills ran up my spine. The sermon continued.

There was an active organization of the KKK in our county, even though there were no blacks within miles of Boone County. Dad and Mother once attended a KKK meeting in a pasture just outside of Harrison, but they could not go along with them. That was their last meeting. They never joined and never told me why.

September came and it was time to go back to Ouachita for Merrill's junior year. Mother and Dad helped us get ready for the move to Arkadelphia. We packed the canned fruits and vegetables, sacked the apples, potatoes and onions, and got our clothes ready. We asked Leo Davis, the school bus driver, if he would go down with us and drive Mother back. He was glad to do this. Merrill located a trailer to haul our things in, and we were off in Dad's car, pulling the trailer behind.

Everything went well until we got to Malvern, a few miles from Arkadelphia. The highway went down the main street of all the little towns in those days. There was lots of traffic on this day. When we were in the middle of town, the cars in front of us slowed to a stop. Merrill applied the brakes, but the weight of the trailer pushed our car into the back of the one in front of us. Bill was asleep on a bed I had made for him by the side of me in the front seat. His head went into the dashboard. He cried more from fright than pain, but it was an exciting time. We saw that no damage was done to either car, and Billie Jon was not hurt.

We found a small apartment near the college. It was upstairs in a large house that had been converted into an apartment complex. The trailer was unloaded and Mother kissed us goodbye, and she and Leo set out on the long trip back to Harrison. She hoped Billie Jon might soon be coming to stay with them, if I entered college as planned and if we could not locate adequate care for him in Arkadelphia. We wanted him to stay with us if we could find a babysitter.

I made arrangements to take the college entrance tests. I was greatly inadequate. I knew I did not do well and it was no surprise when the results came. I had failed. After all, I had been out of school two years, so I should never have tried. At least some of our problems were solved—I would be home to care for Billie Jon.

Since our apartment was on the second floor, I had to go downstairs and around to the back of the house to do our laundry. One day, I got Billie Jon to sleep and put him to bed and I ran down to do some washing. Suddenly, I saw a bundle coming down from the window of our apartment. I realized it was Billie Jon. He landed in a rosebush, screaming to the top of his lungs. The landlady ran out and saw what had happened. She put us in her car and rushed us to the hospital. While the doctors were examining Billie Jon, I called the college and asked them to get word to Merrill. The doctor did not find any broken bones but lots of scratches from the rose bush. It broke the fall.

In a short time Merrill came running in, completely out of breath, as he had run all the way across town. He looked at Bill on the table and saw all the Mercurochrome on him and, thinking it was blood, fainted. So they put him to bed and treated him. Billie Jon and his dad were released at the same time.

That evening we heard a knock on our door and it was Dr. Johnson, president of the college. He had come over to see about us. Billie Jon had a big time playing football with him. We felt real good that he cared that much about his students.

Life in the apartment was not what we had dreamed it would be. We had to share the bathroom with college boys across the hall. They complained to the landlady about the baby. Merrill was not home much. He had classes to attend, library work required and campus duty from midnight to 6 a.m. Bill and I got lonely and felt so cramped. I rolled him down the street some, but with no chores, no piano, no friends and no money, life was a little hard for me.

Before the month was over, we decided that I should return to Mother and Dad's and go to high school and get my diploma. Then, I could enter Ouachita the next year. They agreed and Mother and Leo made the trip once again to Arkadelphia to take Bill and me home.

I started to high school and Mother and Granny took care of Bill for me. I rode the bus with Ruth and James Carl. At last I was in a class with kids my own age. I enjoyed studying more now because it all seemed so important to me.

A trip into Harrison on Saturday was our one outing during the week. Walking around the square was fun. When we got tired window-shopping, we often crossed into the courtyard around the courthouse. There were benches where one could sit, if you could find an empty one, and watch the people. Often you would see an acquaintance and have a visit. This seemed to be the most popular place in Boone County on a Saturday afternoon. When we got tired of this, we would go to the car and sit and watch the people pass on the sidewalk. We had to kill time until Daddy got off work at the post office.

When Dad came to the car, he often had a handful of mail. On the way home he would deliver letters to our neighbors. He felt they should not have to wait until Monday for the RFD delivery. He would pull close by the mailbox and drop the letter in, then honk the horn so they would know it was there. Usually they were watching for him.

Hardly a month had passed after I came home when Era and Vance Hickman came by in their new sports car with a rumble seat and said, "How would you like to drive to Arkadelphia and see Merrill?"

Car with rumble seat

Of course, there was nothing I would have liked better. Mother said it would be fine for me to go and leave Billie Jon, so I quickly got ready and we were off. We found Merrill and he made arrangements to get off work for the night. We drove over to Hot Springs to spend the night. It was so much fun riding in the rumble seat and seeing the sights of Hot Springs. The Hickmans had a camera and were making pictures just like they knew travelers should.

We were really dressed up in the nicest things we had. Era and I had coats with fur collars. Mine was a beautiful shade of blue with a gray collar. Era's was black. Merrill decided he would ride back to Little

Rock with us and catch a train back to Arkadelphia. This gave us a chance to see the State Capitol and to be together a little longer. What a wonderful weekend—I went home feeling so good, but lonesome. It wasn't long before I realized we would have something to remember that weekend by for a long time. I was pregnant.

This ended our dream of my going to college. We decided we would tell no one outside the family that I was "expecting" and I would continue my high school education. I was very careful to dress so I would not reveal my secret. We made it through the Christmas holidays real well. Of course, Merrill came home and we went into town on Christmas Eve and bought a few little gifts at the dime store to put on the Christmas tree at the church. Billie Jon really enjoyed his daddy. They had fun playing together. He talked a "blue streak." Someone said, "He must have been vaccinated with a phonograph needle."

The winter was long and cold. I was very interested in my classes at school, especially my Bible and history classes. I remember in history class we talked about the Great Depression we were in. Mr. Russell said this was the first tarnishing of the American dream and that it was the first thing that had touched all Americans. As awful as the Civil War and WWI were, many had escaped its full impact. Nobody was escaping the effects of the Depression.

Spring came and not too early for me. I was finding it difficult to hide my secret and my body was getting weary. Near the close of school, all the senior activities began to take place. I wanted to take part in everything so no one would suspect anything. I even went on the senior picnic at the top of Boat Mountain. We hiked up the mountain, had a good picnic lunch. Everything went well until I turned my ankle. It was hard getting down the mountain, but J. W. and Elam Atchley helped me along and I made it with flying colors.

Then came the senior play. I had the crazy part of a silly waitress named Daffy Down Dilly. Even fifty years later at our class reunion, one of my classmates, Charlie Fullerton, said when I walked toward him, "Oh, there is Daffy Down Dilly." I had a bone felon on one of my fingers at this time, and it was so painful. I remember holding my hand

and crying with pain when I was off stage but when the time came for Daffy Down Dilly to be on stage, I had to go on with the show.

Graduation day came—field daisies and all. This year the junior class did the decorating. I put on my long formal, participated in the graduation and received my diploma, thinking I had fooled all my classmates and kept my secret well. I heard later that everyone knew it but they were playing the game along with me, wanting me to complete the year.

Now that school was out, I had more time to be with Bill and to get things ready for the new baby.

We always listened to a program on the radio, Station KWTO, Springfield, Missouri, sponsored by the Colonial Baking Co. They advertised Rainbow cakes for thirty-nine cents. They offered a free cake for a winning jingle each day. I decided to send in a jingle and sign Billie Jon's name. It went like this to the tune of "The Crawdad Song":

Picnics now are all the go, honey
As the schools are 'bout to close, baby
In each basket be sure to take
Lots of Colonial Bread and Rainbow cake.
Honey, Baby, Mine!

You can imagine our surprise and joy when we heard my jingle sung and the announcement that Billie Jon Cole was the winner and a cake would be shipped to him by mail. The Rainbow cake did arrive and it was very good!

Bill's favorite story was about a train, "The Little Engine that Could." We read it over and over to him. It thrilled him to death to see a train if one happened through when we were in Harrison. I didn't know whose idea it was, but we decided Bill should have a ride on a train. So, Mother, Dad, Ruth, Jim and us took a train at Harrison and we rode four miles to Bellefonte. The fare, I remember, was a quarter. It was worth every penny of it.

Merrill came home when the term was over. It was good to have him home. He was a great help on the farm. I remember one day he went to the field back of the house to pick mung beans. Billie Jon followed him. When he got ready to come back to the house, Bill refused to follow. Merrill came on, leaving him in the field crying. Mother got so mad at Merrill for leaving Bill in the bean patch. It was the only time I remember seeing her mad at Merrill.

The last three weeks in July was the date set for C.M.T. (compulsory military training) camp at Ft. Leavenworth. All R.O.T.C. members at Ouachita had to attend. It was an interesting experience for him. We were glad the camp was in July because the baby was due in August. Merrill was glad he could be home for this baby's birth and so was I.

On the twelfth of July, a few days after Merrill left, Dr. Blackwood stopped by our house to visit a minute and get a cup of coffee after a long night's vigil with a patient down the road. "Helen Marie," he said, as he left, "I'll see you in about three weeks." Dear old Uncle James, he was such a good family doctor. But he had hardly gotten out of sight when I began having labor pains. "They might be false labor pains," Mother said, "but we will time them and see what happens." After the experience I had with Billie Jon, I was getting more nervous with every contraction. About the middle of the afternoon, I told Mother I was really going to have that baby and she better call Uncle James. She reached him and he said, "Oh, my goodness, not another night!" remembering the long labor I had before. He had not been to bed for

thirty-six hours, but he came right over. To everyone's amazement and happiness, it was soon over. The baby boy was born at 8:45 p.m. and Uncle James and everyone else got to bed at a reasonable time. Merrill had missed it all.

Naming the baby was Merrill's job, so he called on Jane to help him. They decided on Jerry Merrill Cole, Jr. Merrill Jr., as we called him, was a beautiful baby. Everyone

"oohed and aahed" over him. His hair was the biggest sight, so black and thick. Someone remarked, "He looks like a little old person." We didn't think so. When Merrill came home, he said, "He looks more like a doll to me."

I had to stay in bed fourteen days, doctor's orders, so when I got up, I was ready to get out of the house. Dad suggested that we go for a short drive. I quickly got the baby ready for his first outing. Bill was so excited. Daddy said, "We'll drive over and see MC's Camp, a new picnic area near Bellefonte. When we got there Billie Jon looked so frustrated and puzzled. I said, "What's the matter, son, don't you like this place?" He said, "I thought my daddy was at camp." Poor child. After all, wasn't his daddy supposed to be at camp?

After two months passed, we decided that the baby's tongue was tied, so we carried him in to see Dr. Blackwood. Uncle James clipped it. A few more days passed and Mother said, "This baby still doesn't nurse right. I believe his tongue is still tied down too much." Back to Uncle James we went. He cooperated. He clipped his tongue a little more, the he said, "Now, if he can't talk by tomorrow, bring him back."

Something kept happening to Granny's turkeys. She found one or two dead each morning. She decided to set a steel trap. This was a trap for animals on top of the ground. Anyway, she hoped to catch whatever was killing her turkeys. She went out to see about the trap the next morning and we looked out in a few minutes and saw her walking a skunk (she called a polecat) down toward the house. Mother and I began to call to her to stop, to turn around or do something. She laughed and kept coming, holding the trap and walking the skunk that was caught by one foot. She walked it down to the wood pile, picked up the axe and hit at the skunk. She missed him completely and the skunk did what he knew to do for protection. He sprayed with all his might. Granny struck again, this time hitting her mark and the animal lay dying, but he had left his calling card. We left home for the day because the odor was so bad. But, we couldn't run away from it. It stayed on and on for weeks and, every time it rained, it was as strong as the first day. Funny thing was, it didn't bother Granny.

We spent the rest of the summer enjoying our babies. Merrill helped on the farm and did extra jobs that he could pick up.

No summer ever passed without a revival. For two weeks in August, the farmers planned to quit work early enough to go to church. This meant a lot to us, and I will be forever grateful for these experiences.

One thing the Union Church contributed to my life was the memory of scriptures. In Sunday school we had memory verses for every lesson. And on Sunday evening and Wednesday evening and during revival services, there was always a time for quoting your favorite scripture verses. Most people said different verses, but not my dad. He had a favorite verse and he stuck with it. He always stood up and said, "*I beseech you, therefore, brethren, by the mercies of God, that ye present your bodies a living sacrifice, holy, acceptable unto God, which is your reasonable service.*" Romans 12:1

Now I had no conception of what this verse from Romans meant at the time or why it was so meaningful to Dad, but it was imprinted on my mind. When I read this scripture, I always think of Dad. The Living Bible makes it easier to understand than the King James Version, from which he quoted. Notice the difference: "*And so, dear brothers, I plead with you to give your bodies to God. Let them be a living sacrifice, holy—the kind He can accept. When you think of what he has done for you, is this too much to ask?*" No wonder this was a challenge to my dad, and he wanted others to hear it over and over, again and again.

There was a dear old minister at the First Baptist Church in Harrison that we had to hold our revivals often. Before he came to Harrison, he lived in Little Rock, and he was our favorite evangelist. His name was M. L. Voyles (my dear friend Evelyn Burdine's father). Bro. Voyles had feared blindness and, as a result, he memorized much of the Bible. When he would have our scripture quotations each evening, he would always add his quotes to every verse, either quoting the verse or verses preceding the scripture or following it. For instance: If one said, "*I am come that you might have life and that you might have it more abundantly,*" Bro. Voyles might say, "Yes, John 10:10. And, John continued, '*I am the good shepherd, the good shepherd giveth his life for his sheep.*'"

Or, suppose someone said, "*I can do all things through Christ who strengtheneth me.*" Then he would comment something like this, "Oh yes, Paul in Phil. 4:13 was writing encouragement to the church at Philippi. He had just said, '*I know both how to be abased, and I know how to abound; everywhere and in all things, I am instructed both to be full and be hungry, both to abound and to suffer need,*' and he realized where his strength came from in all situations. Thank you."

One time someone, to be funny, said, "*Jesus wept.*" This gave Bro. Voyles the chance to sermonize on the compassion and love Jesus felt for his grief-stricken friends. He said, "John 11:35, the shortest verse in the entire Bible, but, oh how much it says." Then he told the entire story of Lazarus' death and what the person thought was a "cute" verse turned out to be a real thought provoker. Sometimes someone would pick an unfamiliar verse to try to fool him, but none were unfamiliar to him. It was amazing, not only to us but to Ripley. The fact that M. L. Voyles had such knowledge of the Bible was featured in *Ripley's Believe It or Not.* (And I believe he deserves a page and a half in my story.)

September came and Merrill was off again for his senior year at Ouachita. The family wished him well. Mother, Dad, Granny, Ruth and Jim were all so devoted to him and no one could have been nicer than he to each of them. He was very eager to get an education, and they were anxious to help him all they could. Now that money was scarce, they could not contribute financially toward his education, but they wanted to take care of me and the children. We were all happy living off the food from the farm, supplemented by Dad's pay check. At this time, he was earning sixty-five cents per hour. As I thought of this, I figured "that is a penny a minute"—sounds pretty good to me.

We had less food than in pre-Depression days, but it sure was good. I remember lettuce wilted with hot bacon grease and chopped green onions. That, with potatoes, was a good meal. Fried chicken was our best meal. Mother would go out to the chicken house and grab a fat fryer, quickly wring its neck and watch it flap and flop to death on the grass. She would then scald the fryer in boiling water, pluck out the feathers (saving them for pillows), pick out the pin feathers and finally singe it. She could cut up the fryer in the wink of an eye. Then she would salt it, break an egg over it, dip it in flour and fry it in Crisco.

Without the chickens we raised, our table would have been much barer during the Depression.

We raised several chickens each spring. We kept about two-dozen laying hens and a rooster. This kept us in eggs throughout the year. We ate the rest as fryers. Mother often fried and canned chicken for the winter. Since we had chickens and hogs, we had a good food disposal. Not a scrap of food was wasted. Everything, even potato peelings, went in to the slop bucket or the chicken pan. We even saved eggshells and dried them, then crumbled them for the chickens. This was their source of calcium.

Granny baked a pan of cornbread every day at noon, enough for two meals. Half was eaten hot with the noon meal, which we called dinner, and the other half was eaten at supper. Cornbread and milk—sweet milk or buttermilk—was our standard evening meal. Occasionally Granny would make hot mush. I still like to crumble cornbread in a glass of cold milk. To me, it is better than dessert. Fried apples were a great treat for breakfast.

Billie Jon had reached the age where he was so interesting to talk to or read to. We all enjoyed him. Mrs. Bryan told us one day that she felt sorry for Merrill, Jr. because he was such a good baby we neglected him and played with Bill. Of course, that was far from the truth. We always accused Mother of being partial to Jerry, and he was so fond of her. He wanted to trade Granddaddy off "to play with Bill," and let him live with Mother.

Merrill Jr., as we called him then, was so cute. He was the strongest little fellow. Before he was two months old, he was trying to take steps. If he could get his feet against something, like your stomach, he would raise himself up and step off like a gentleman.

Letters came from Merrill every day. We looked forward to them, sometimes only a few lines, but we knew he was thinking of us and we were in his heart and mind.

November brought the general election and a new President was elected, Franklin Delano Roosevelt—a polio-crippled man, but a man with great promise and the thirty-second President of our great nation. We were hopeful that he could bring us out of the Depression.

The Christmas holidays brought Merrill home for a few days. We went to Union, as usual, to the "Christmas Tree" on Christmas Eve. According to Jerry's baby book, Santa Claus brought him a bathrobe, a tinker doll, fork and spoon set and a jumper swing. Billie Jon had written Santa Claus a letter telling him what they wanted him to bring them. We guessed he must have received the letter.

It was not so hard to see Merrill go back to Ouachita in January because we knew he would graduate in May. On March fourth, 1933, the new President, Franklin D. Roosevelt, was sworn in. In his inaugural address, he said, "This nation asks for action and action now." The situation throughout the nation had become critical. Thousands of banks had closed their doors, affecting the checking and savings accounts of many Americans, and there was no deposit insurance. So, you can imagine how fear stalked the streets of every city, town and community. Many could not face it and took their own lives.

Roosevelt acted quicker than anyone thought he could. Congress passed an emergency banking bill and within a week the banks reopened and most people received fifty cents for each dollar they had deposited. At least, this was something. In less than three months, a series of emergency measures went into effect. $500 million dollars were funneled into programs that became known as the New Deal.

The President used letters of the alphabet to identify the various government programs aimed to help the hungry and unemployed. The one we heard the most about was the WPA (Works Progress Administration). Thousands of the unemployed went to work temporarily on WPA. They worked on public buildings, schools, roads, bridges, airports and other projects.

Some folks thought it a stupid act and laughed at those who worked under WPA. Some nicknamed it "We Piddle Around." Others described the men as lazy guys leaning on a shovel, instead of working hard to clear the right-of-way and open up ditches along the roadside. But it gave men the chance to buy food for their families, even though they may have been humiliated and embarrassed to apply for such a job.

One of the things I remember they did was build toilets. This was a "sanitary" outdoor privy, known as the "WPA toilet." I have read that they constructed 150,000 toilets.

Work wasn't steady. After a few days work, a lay off would follow when funds ran out. The highest wage was about $40 a month.

There was another work project around our part of the country called CCC (Civilian Conservation Corps) for young people. They did a lot of worthwhile construction, especially in the state parks. Every time we go to Petit Jean State Park, we walk on walks that they built. For the hungry, there were NRA soup kitchens where long lines formed before time to open. There were also surplus food distribution points and "relief orders" for groceries that could be redeemed at the store.

All this was promising but only a beginning. I can assure you the economic crisis was far from over. We were more or less protected up to this point, as Daddy and Mother provided for our needs. We had the necessities and never suffered like so many did. To add to the misery there were flu epidemics. I can remember waking up with a raging headache. When I tried to get up, the room began to spin. Weakly, I called Mother and sank back into bed. Finding I had fever, she said, "Stay in bed and drink plenty of water. If you still have fever tomorrow, we will call Uncle James," our doctor.

Jerry was just beginning to talk. He would look at me in bed and say, "Hi!" This was music to my ears. He said something that sounded like "Momma" and "Daddy," but the word that we could really understand was "Ruth." He would call "Ruth" so plainly. He liked her because she would carry him around and play with him.

One time we drove over to Parthenon to visit Aunt Letha and her family. On the way home, Dad stopped at a little roadside zoo to let the boys see the animals. The one Jerry liked best was the raccoon. He called it a "paccoon." Ruth and Jim had fun asking him what he saw at the zoo and he would holler, "A paccoon!" He walked early and he looked so small. He was a brave little fellow, not sure of himself, catching many falls and once cutting his nose on the leg of the stove. But he always got up and tried again.

Merrill studied hard and when time came, he graduated *cum laude* with a degree in English. He was selected to lead the ROTC parade at ten o'clock the morning of graduation day. J. W. drove Mother and me down for the graduation exercises. We decided to surprise Merrill and get up early and drive to Arkadelphia in time for the parade.

Merrill's graduation from OBC

We were up early, at 1:30 a.m. to be exact, and reached Arkadelphia in time. We stopped at a tourist court just outside the city limits and changed the children's clothes and cleaned up a bit. We asked the man at the desk where we should park to see the parade. He said, "Parades come down the main street from the college into town. If you will park in front of the post office, you will have an excellent spot to see it." J. W. drove to the post office, parked, and we waited and we waited and we waited! We could hear the band and every minute we expected it to come into sight, but it never did. Finally, we gave up and decided to drive up to the campus to see what was going on. We made it just as the parade broke up. The parade had been on the campus and we had missed it.

I caught sight of Merrill in his uniform—looking like a million dollars. I called to him and he heard me and came running to the car. We were all disappointed but, at least, he knew we tried and that pleased him. When the day was over and the car was loaded and goodbyes said, we left, diploma in hand and a commission as 2nd. Lt. in the U. S. Army. We drove part of the way toward Little Rock before stopping to spend the night in a tourist court.

Merrill had received a scholarship to the Baptist Theological Seminary in Louisville, Kentucky. If he went, this meant more years without him and more years that Mother and Dad would have the extra burden of caring for us. Dad insisted that Merrill plan to go—this was an opportunity that he should accept. So again our summer was spent getting ready for another year of separation.

The month of July was the date for Reserve Officers Training Camp. Now that he was a commissioned officer, he got good pay for the month. This would enable him to buy some clothes and other things he would need for the year at the seminary and have some in the bank for spending money.

On Jerry's first birthday, I took him and Billie Jon up to Ross Tucker's, a neighbor, to get him to cut their hair. He sat them on a nail keg and, with scissors and clippers, soon had the job done with no charge. The Tuckers had a bunch of small children, so I decided to confide in him. I told him I had just learned I was "expecting" again. I expect he suspected my anxiety about having another baby so soon. In his home-style philosophy, he consoled me. He said, "Well, Helen Marie, I'll tell you how it is. Before they come, you wouldn't give a nickel for another one, but after they get here, you wouldn't take a million for them." Nothing could be more true. I left feeling better and invited his children to come over that afternoon to eat birthday cake with Jerry and play with the boys and James Carl. They came and they had a good time.

Often in the summer we would have surprise—or very unexpected—company drop in. Dad's sisters, Aunt Maude and Aunt Angie from Kansas City, or his brother, Uncle Cyrus from Mississippi, or Uncle Riley and Aunt Maude from Memphis. They visited us each summer. When the cousins came, I especially enjoyed it. When this happened, Granny would go into action like a mess sergeant. "James Carl, go carry in some stove wood. Helen Marie, run to the cellar and get a pan of potatoes and a couple of jars of green beans and a jar of peach pickles. Una Ruth, you set the table—wash your hands first," she would tell us. Soon she and Mother would have a good dinner on the table. When we sat down, Dad would ask the blessing then say, "Now you all help yourselves. If you don't see what you want, just ask for it." That really meant, "We are glad you are here; just eat and enjoy yourselves." And that is exactly what they did.

During the summer, Aunt Ethel and Marjorie Fay came from Ft. Worth. What a delightful visit that was. I had never seen them before. Uncle Harvey had died and they wanted to visit his mother, Granny, and his sister, Mother. I remember we had a watermelon feast outside. Marjorie Fay got such a kick out of Bill. He was eating a slice of melon when a chicken decided to have a bite. He looked up at Marjorie Fay and said, "Dat ole wooster eatin' my vatermelon."

When they went home, they took Granny with them for a visit. How much we missed her, but how thrilled she was to go. The first of September Merrill drove Mother, Ruth, Jim, the boys and me to McAllister, Oklahoma to meet Aunt Ethel and Marjorie Fay and bring Granny home.

We visited a cousin of Mother's who was a guard at the Oklahoma penitentiary. He took us on a tour of that facility and that was very interesting. Merrill left for Louisville soon after we returned home.

Granny brought home some hedge plants that she had rooted. Aunt Ethel had a hedge across her front yard and Granny thought that would be so nice at our house. She carefully set them out and they grew nicely for several months. But it happened that James Carl got a little hatchet for Christmas and one day Granny discovered her plants were all chopped down to the ground. There lay the hatchet. Who did it? Wouldn't you know it had to be Billie Jon. We asked him, "Why did you do it?" "Well, they wouldn't bloom," he said.

Bill was always into something. One day I had bathed him and Jerry and sent them out to play. Jerry had coal-black hair and it wasn't long until Bill led him back into the house and announced, "Now Merrill, Jr. is white

Bill and Merrill, Jr

headed." I looked. He had put dust in his clean hair just to change his looks. I was sick. That meant another bath.

Now if you think it was easy to bathe a child in those days, you are mistaken. There was no bathtub with running water at our house. Water had to be drawn from the cistern and heated on the wood stove. This meant starting a fire with either a newspaper, a corn cob that had been dipped in kerosene or a piece of pine kindling. A zinc tub served as a bathtub. It was brought into the kitchen and placed near the stove so the oven door could be opened for a bit of warmth if it was cold. When more than one needed bathing, you started with the one who was the least dirty, using the same water for all.

Jerry was in his terrible twos and I had my hands full. He was into everything. We turned the sewing machine around so he could not open the drawers. Everything had to either be put up or nailed down. He soon learned to climb and he could climb like a squirrel. One day he climbed up on the sewing machine and fell off. He hit his head just back of his ear, and he was knocked out for several hours. Mother said we would take him to the doctor when Daddy got home from work. But before Daddy came, Jerry came to and was lively as ever.

When the days grew cold and snow fell, we had to stay inside. I fed the children their lunch, then Mother would make some snow cream. I would carry them into the fireplace room and let them eat the snow cream in front of the warm fire. I would then snuggle them up in a warm bed and they would go to sleep. This would give me time to write a letter, practice piano or study my theory or my Bible.

One woman gave me a pep talk one day when I was at a Bible Study class. She said, "Just remember that God is preparing you and Merrill for a great task. Now you are making a sacrifice but remember God will make it up to you. You will have long years of wonderful service in His name." I often recalled this that year. When things got rough, I would picture Merrill pastor of a large Baptist church and us living comfortably in the parsonage.

During the winter, I was cooking supper one night when I heard a blood-curdling scream. It was Merrill, Jr. Where was he? I ran frantically trying to locate him. Then I saw him behind the cook stove with his head hung between the stove pipe and the wall. His head was seared in one spot. For months we carried him to the doctor for treatment. The doctor called it "proud flesh," and it was hard to cure. If you look closely you can still see the slick scar it left on Jerry's head.

Spring came and with it baby chicks. The boys were always out in the yard playing. One day, Mother took them to see the chickens while she was feeding them. Jerry thought they were so cute. He reached down and picked one up and pulled its head off. Mother turned to stop him, but he beheaded another one. She got him out of there in a hurry.

I continued my music lessons and studied hard on theory. In early April, I took the examination and received my Arkansas Music Teacher Certificate. I felt now I could earn some money to help feed and clothe my growing family.

My third baby was due on April 30th and Merrill would be out of school April 25th. This meant he would be home in time for the birth of baby number three. But true to form, on April 20th our baby girl was born. We named her Bettelyn Adele. She was a beautiful child and we were happy to have a little girl.

Merrill came home while I was still in bed. He announced that he had decided seminary would have to be postponed for a few years so he could provide for his family. He had arranged a leave of absence and had withdrawn indefinitely. He began searching for a job

Since Merrill majored in English at Ouachita, he wanted to be a high school English teacher. He located a job as principal, basketball coach and English teacher at Omaha High School, a small town eighteen miles north of Harrison near the Missouri line.

During the summer, he went to Reserve Officers Training Camp

Bettelyn

again. He came home with money in his pockets. Now we could buy some furniture. We took $100 and went into town to a secondhand furniture store and bought a complete housekeeping outfit. I remember a wicker sofa and rocker for the living room. Bettelyn always called the rocker her basket chair. She loved to curl up in it and go to sleep. We also bought beds and a mattress for each (we used a straw mattress and a feather bed on one bed). We bought a cook stove, a kitchen cabinet, a table and chairs, and a heater for the living room. How happy we were. At least we were going to have a home of our own.

Dad loaned us his car to drive to Omaha to look for a house. We found a small brown house on the highway in the middle of town that belonged to Mrs. Creedon. She was on the school board and she was glad to rent it to us. Merrill wrote in his diary, "Rent is high, $6 a month."

On September 5, 1934, we moved to Omaha and school started the next week. Merrill's salary was $65 a month. Not much money, but our lives were filled to the brim with happiness.

On basketball nights, when Merrill had to take the team out of town, I was afraid. I can remember getting scared once when I heard horses running fast by our house. I pulled the furniture against the front door. One time, Merrill found me with his .22 in one hand and a butcher knife in the other.

We did not have a telephone; in fact, there was only one telephone in the whole town. Merrill said we could ask to use it in case of a dire emergency. We didn't have a lot of communication with the outside world. Sometimes I felt "sorta" stranded. We had no car, no radio, no TV, of course, and no newspaper. We didn't worry about it. We had each other and it seemed enough.

Dad came out to get us on Thanksgiving Day to take us home for the day. It was good to see the family again and hear about school and the community news. Mother and Granny had a good Thanksgiving dinner.

A winter storm was coming in so Dad said, "We better get started back to Omaha before dark." We said our goodbyes and started but not in time to miss the storm. The snow began to fall and Dad could hardly see how to drive. The roads began to get very slippery and dangerous. In fact, they were almost impassable. Dad decided he better not try to drive back; it would be better to wait until daylight because the blinding snow was coming down worse than ever. He pulled the car off the highway by the side of the house, came in the house, never thinking Mother would be worried. We all huddled around the wood stove to get warm after our frigid ride home. Cars did not have heaters in those days.

Later we all snuggled down in our warm beds and went to sleep. About 2 a.m. there was a loud rap on our front door and Merrill went to see who it was. There, shivering in the icy weather, stood Noah Dearing and Floyd Stinnett, Dad's neighbors. Mother had become so worried when Dad didn't return, she called them for help. The men volunteered to brave the danger and go searching for Dad. When Merrill told them Dad was there and asleep, they were relieved. They said, "Well, let him sleep." They would not come in to warm or get a bite to eat. They wanted to get back and report to Mother. Dad woke up and said, "Wait, I better get up and go back with you." They insisted that he wait until daylight.

When daylight came, Dad was up ready to get on his way. He looked out and his car was gone. He and Merrill quickly got their coats on and went out to see about it. There were tracks where the car had left the pasture, crossed the road, went down the embankment, curving to miss a pine tree, and on into the ravine several yards below the highway. To make things even worse, this was not Dad's car. His car was in the shop and this car was loaned to him by the garage. Now this was the time to go to the neighbors' house and ask to use his telephone. They called a wrecker to come.

Everyone in town gathered to see the men work to retrieve the car. When they saw it set down on the highway without a dent or a scratch, the whole town cheered. Dad paid the men the price they asked, which was $18. When the townspeople heard the price, they said, "Well, next time we need a doctor, we will get the wrecker to bring him out." So, evidently they thought Dad got a bargain. I am sure he whistled all the way home, as that was his custom when he was nervous.

We were very active in the community life of this little town where the people thought teachers and their families were something special. We attended the First Baptist Church, P.T.A., every home ball game, etc.

One day we had been away from the house for something; as we were walking toward the house, we saw a man sitting on our front porch. "Now who could that be?" we wondered. We discovered when we got closer that it was Dad Cole, Merrill's father. He had come down from Kansas City with a handful of clothes, his Prince Albert smoking tobacco and his best friend, his pipe.

He had never seen Jerry and Bettelyn. Bill had grown so much since we were in Kansas City for the summer. He was delighted to see them. We had no idea that he had come to make his home with us, but he continued to stay and stay and stay.

Bettelyn was cute. She was really winning our hearts with her charming personality, especially her daddy's. The boys thought she was wonderful. They would jump around and do their antics to make her laugh. She was content to play with empty spools or clothespins while I sewed or mended.

Soon after Christmas, she began trying to walk, but she was afraid. Holding to your finger, she would stand up and walk, but was afraid to walk alone. One day I took her to Mrs. Creedon's, who lived next door. Mr. and Mrs. Huntley, her parents, lived with her. Mrs. Huntley was a real sweet lady. I thought she was beautiful. She kept saying, "Bettelyn, walk to me," and suddenly she stepped off like she had walked forever. This really thrilled Mrs. Huntley. She picked her up and "loved her real good."

We were hit with a thud the last of February. The school was going to close. The district was out of money and could no longer pay the teachers. What were we going to do? Merrill was among the unemployed we had heard so much about.

When we talked about the situation, I watched the emotions written on Merrill's face, as troubling thoughts whirled through my mind. We had tried so hard. It seemed another door had closed in our face. We not only had three children to feed, there was also Dad Cole. He had not mentioned going back to Kansas City and we never questioned him.

He didn't require much, just his food, bed, laundry and Prince Albert. His uniform was a pair of bib overalls and a long-sleeved cotton shirt. My family had been so good to take care of us; how could we complain when Merrill's father wanted to stay with us?

But back to the problem —we had to do something and do it quickly. There was not much money left, as we had to live from paycheck to paycheck—and I was pregnant again, I guessed, as I had missed my period. We prayed and prayed hard.

I can't remember how it happened, but word came that one of our friends, Norman Phifer, who was teaching at Western Grove High School, had gotten a Civil Service job in Washington D.C. and would soon be leaving Western Grove. Merrill rushed over to apply for the job. He was successful and he was again employed. This, of course, meant another move. Western Grove was twelve miles south of Harrison. We found a weather-beaten house out in the country with a garden spot. So, we believed that once again God had guided us on our way.

Mother and Dad had sold the farm and moved into Harrison. They rented a large two-story house on West Stephenson. Ruth was thrilled to death because now she would be going to Harrison High School. Dad was nearer his work and Mother and Granny were relieved of all the work on the farm. It never felt like home to me, in spite of the familiar furnishings and the people who were the same. I guess the old farmhouse was home too long for me to adjust quickly to a new place. I was not home often either—with no transportation and so many children, it was hard even when Dad came for us. I can remember opening up the suitcases when I got home and seeing all the dirty clothes. I almost wished I had stayed at home.

When time came to put out a garden, Merrill and Grandpa Cole went to work. Merrill caught a ride to Harrison one day. He wanted to get seeds and fertilizer for the garden. He got Dad's car to pick up the stuff. After his shopping was finished, he found James Carl and brought him home with him so he could unload the car and Jim could drive it back. When they drove up, I was surprised. I said, "Are you going back to Harrison? How are you going to get home?" Merrill said, "No, James Carl is going to drive the car back." Now, James Carl was only twelve years old. I could not believe Merrill would do this. Of course, I had driven the family everywhere when I was twelve, but James Carl was still just a baby, it seemed. I guess it was a good thing neither Dad nor Mother knew he was doing this until he pulled in home, safe and sound, feeling "too big for his britches," as Granny probably said.

Someone gave us a German shepherd dog. They guessed it had been lost by a traveler. It was a beautiful thing, and we named him "Grayboy." Merrill and the boys loved him so much and played with him like another kid. One day I went away with the children for something and when I returned, Merrill was sitting on the back door step sobbing his heart out. I said, "What has happened?" Dad Cole said, "Helen Marie, he is just killed. He went walking with Grayboy and a car struck Grayboy and killed him. Seems like Merrill has not stopped crying since it happened." We all cried and hugged each other. Even though we had him only a few weeks, he had become like a member of the family.

We harvested and canned as many vegetables as we could. They dug potatoes and sacked them. Knowing we would return to Omaha for the opening of school in the fall, we wanted to have all the food we could to take back with us. It would help us so much. With another baby coming, we needed every penny we could save.

Merrill located a nice little white house near the Baptist church for us. We moved before time for school to start. Dad let us have a cow to milk, as there was a small barn and pasture on this place. We also had some hens. Things were shaping up pretty well for us.

The baby was due in November. We knew we would need some help for a few weeks. We got in contact with a friend, Opal Daniels, who lived near us at Union. She agreed to come and do the housework and care for the children while I was in bed.

When I began to have labor pains, Merrill went to the telephone and made three calls. He called the doctor, Mother and Opal. Mother came out as soon as she could to help and be on hand when the baby arrived. Finally, Merrill was home for the birthing of a baby.

The baby came just after midnight on November 25th. Another little girl, how wonderful! We tried to think of a name for this beautiful child. We settled on Carolyn. Merrill said, "You can give her a middle name." I considered many names. I thought and thought. Then I thought of the Dionne quintuplets that had been born in Canada a few months before. One of those babies had a very odd, cute name. I remembered it was Yvonne. So I decided that was the name I would choose, Carolyn Yvonne Cole. Sounded wonderful to me.

Opal came to take over the housework and Mother returned home. She was an excellent housekeeper. (By the way, she is in charge of the Housekeeping Dept. at the Holiday Inn in Harrison now). Anyway, my house had never been so clean. I remember one day when we were going out for a walk, she took great care to see that everything was in order. She said, "I never leave my house without being certain it is straight because you never know what might happen and who might come in." This has come into my mind many, many times since then. I often think, "Is my house ready for anyone or everyone to come in?" This has usually been put out of mind without answering it or doing anything about it.

I don't know when I took over the full responsibility of my big family, but soon I am sure. I can remember as the days grew colder what a job I had doing the laundry. Mr. Cole helped by building a fire under the big black wash pot in the back yard. The pot was filled with water, and I separated the clothes, the white ones from the colored ones. I filled the pot with white ones, cut up some White Naphtha soap and punched them around with a big clean stick, and left them to boil. Zinc tubs, two of them, were placed in the kitchen on chairs turned together. One was filled half full with warm water to wash the clothes in, the other filled with cold water to rinse them. A large dish pan was placed by the rinse tub with bluing water in it. Bluing came in round balls about the size of a marble. We tied three balls in a square of cloth and swished it around in the water until it was the color we wanted. This was used to bleach the clothes.

Starch had to be made. I made flour starch. I mixed a cup of flour with cold water to make a paste, stirring it until it was without lumps. Then I poured boiling water from the teakettle into the flour mixture and stirred hard to keep it from lumping. All the cotton shirts, blouses, dresses and aprons had to be starched. When the clothes had boiled a few minutes, they were removed with the stick into another pan and brought inside and dumped into the washtub. Sheets were hard to handle without splashing the boiling water on you.

I usually had two pots full of white clothes, so the pot was refilled for the second boiling. The babies' diapers were usually in the second pot. We had Birds Eye diapers and the night before, they were put in to soak. If I got the kids to bed early and wasn't too tired, I washed them out before I went to bed. If you have never washed out a tub full of dirty diapers, you have missed a dirty job! I needed a clothespin on my nose and dark glasses over my eyes. If the babies had a cold, the diapers were green—I always dreaded trying to get the green stains out.

After the second wash pot was loaded, I was ready to get the washboard and start scrubbing the clothes. I scrubbed, wrung out the clothes, put them in the rinse tub, wrung them out again, put them in the bluing water and wrung them out again—this time separating the clothes that had to be starched from the others. When all were separated, I dipped the ones to be starched into the starch water and wrung them out for the fourth time. Now they were ready for the clothesline. I bundled up and carried them to the line. Quickly I pinned them to the line, while keeping an ear open for the children in the house.

By this time, the second pot would have boiled enough. I would start the procedure over and, if I did well, I got the white clothes on the line by noon. I put the dirty overalls and coveralls in the wash pot to soak, not to boil. The coals were pulled back from under the pot so it wouldn't boil again.

Now was time for lunch. Merrill would be home. Usually our lunch on washday consisted of leftovers. The baby had to be fed. The kids' hands had to be washed so they could eat. Hopefully, they would all go to sleep after lunch and I could get on with the colored clothes. All day long I washed. I can remember days when it was so cold I could not pin the clothes to the line, I could only throw them at the line and they would freeze by the time they hit it. If snow or sleet was falling, they would freeze dry.

Our cistern went dry that winter and Mr. Cole and Merrill had to carry water from a neighbor's house. I can remember them driving our cow a mile or more to a spring for water. It was down in a ravine, so it was quite a job getting up and down the ice-covered slopes.

Jerry was sick so much that winter. He had bad tonsils. We told Mother and Dad about it. They took us to Uncle James (Dr. Blackwood) and he said the tonsils should be removed. The only way he could have the operation was for him to stay with Mother and let her take him for the operation and care for him until he was well enough to come home. It was hard to leave him, but we knew it was best. He got along real well and enjoyed his stay in Harrison with Mother and Dad. In fact, he enjoyed it so much when Mother was ready to bring him home, he rebelled, he wanted to stay. She said, "You need to go home so you can play with Billie Jon." Jerry quickly replied, "Why can't Granddaddy go play with Bill and let me stay with you?"

One thing that was so attractive was a little girl who lived next door. One day they were outside playing and Mother heard her scream. When she went to see about them, Jerry was trying to take her tonsils out—"playing like"—of course. He had a shoe spoon to use as a tongue depressor. When he held her tongue down, she got frightened and decided that wasn't for her.

Merrill decided before the winter was over that we should hunt another house with a good cistern or well. He found one on the outer edge of town. It was a weather-beaten old house with a garden spot. So we moved and made another garden, which was a real blessing to us.

This was a fun place to live. It wasn't much to look at. The chickens ran freely over the yard. We didn't need a lawn mower, we swept the yard with a broom.

Our neighbors up the road on the right of our house were the Ben Andrews. They had two daughters, Sue and Diane, about the age of our girls. Ermal and I became close friends and the children had fun playing together.

A neighbor on the other side, across the road from our house had a cedar post business. Mr. Dickey told Bill he would pay him to peel cedar posts for him. How wonderful! Bill worked and worked and, when he got a post peeled, Mr. Dickey would pay him a good salary, about a nickel a post, as I remember. But it was enough that he wanted to keep on working. Don't laugh! A nickel was a lot of money to a kid in those days, especially at our house. A nickel would buy a candy bar or a package of gum and that was a real treat when your dad and mother couldn't afford to buy one for you.

As Granny used to say: "Money was as scarce as hen's teeth" at our house, especially during the summer. Schoolteachers were paid only for the nine months they taught, so the summers were hard. With our garden, cow, chickens, together with the money Merrill received for his two weeks reserve officers' camp, we could get by. This summer Merrill managed to have access to the only barber chair in town, in a closet-like building on the street in "downtown" Omaha. He had no license, but he did have "talent." He sat down there and hoped someone would need a haircut badly enough to pay him twenty-five cents to cut their hair. But haircuts were few and far between. He always had books to read and studying to do while he was waiting.

Jerry loved to roam the neighborhood. This I would not allow. I wanted to know where this four-year-old was all the time. I struggled and struggled with him. I had too much to do to be running after him all the time. So, I decided to discipline him. I put him to bed, I spanked him, sat him down and made him sit there, but nothing worked. One day I had an idea. I got a short rope and tied him to the garden fence. This did the trick. He was so humiliated, he never ran away again.

Granny was in Ft. Worth at this time living with Aunt Ethel and Marjorie Fay. Ruth went down to spend a month when school was out. Dad and Mother were planning to drive down to visit and bring Ruth home. Daddy asked me if I would like to take the girls and go down with them. Merrill said that would be fine and he would take care of the boys. I didn't know what to do. I wanted to go, yet I didn't want to leave Merrill and the boys that long. I had never been separated from the boys, except for the time when Jerry had his tonsils out and stayed with Mother. "This will be my only chance to ever visit Aunt Ethel and Marjorie Fay. If I can scrape up some money, I believe I'll go," I thought. I talked with Merrill about it and he said he would probably take in some money at the barber shop before time for us to go.

So, the next day I washed all day to get everything clean. It started pouring down rain and I could not get them dry. I decided to hang the things I would need for our trip inside the house. However, the air was so full of moisture, they did not dry. Morning came and they were still wet. I hung a few things around the cook stove while I fixed breakfast. I kept the fire going in the stove and the oven door open so some things would dry. But, with the dozens of diapers, dresses, etc., I could not get them all dry. I ironed some of the lighter weight clothes that were nearly dry, but the heavier things were still too wet to iron.

Dad would be coming out after supper to pick us up, as they were going the next day. Merrill came home from the barbershop with the announcement, "Haven't had a haircut all week." Our money was, in fact, gone. He would be going to summer camp in a few days and would come back with a "fat" paycheck. That would get us through the end of September when he would get his first paycheck from the Omaha High School. This was July 1st, so for a month we would be living on our garden produce and what he could make cutting hair. I looked at my partially packed suitcase. I knew I could not go—not without a penny. But I wanted to go so badly now that I had made up my mind.

Dad came. I said, "Dad, it doesn't look like I can go. It has been so rainy I couldn't get the children's clothes dry." He was sorry. He visited a while then started to leave. He gave each child a dollar bill to spend on the Fourth of July. Well, now this was a different story. The girls had a dollar each—that was two dollars—as much as eight haircuts would have been. I quickly changed my mind. I said, "Wait Dad, I believe I will go. I'll carry these damp clothes separately and hang them up to dry overnight." I hurried to get ready while Daddy patiently waited. I kissed Merrill and the boys goodbye. I could not keep the tears back. It seemed I was going so far away. Merrill said, "Now don't worry, I'll take good care of Bill and Jerry." We left them and Dad Cole standing on the porch. I couldn't stand to look back as we drove away into the night.

When we got home, Mother was beginning to get uneasy because she hadn't expected it to take so long. I started to pull out the damp clothes and hang them up to dry. She quickly got the ironing board and started ironing the dresses, saying that would dry them. After an hour or two, we went to bed saying they would all be dry by morning. The next day, we traveled to Ft. Worth. When we stopped for gasoline inside the Texas border, Mother said, "I'm going to call Ethel and tell her where we are." They were surprised to learn that I was with them.

We arrived at Aunt Ethel's and received a warm welcome. Her house was nice and city living was quite different from the life in Omaha, Arkansas. My mind kept going back to Omaha. I wondered what they were doing, what they were eating, and if either of the boys had gotten hurt or sick.

Marjorie Fay had a little girl named Jo Rae and she and Bettelyn were good playmates. Aunt Ethel thought they were so cute together she had to take us into town to have their pictures made.

One day, Aunt Ethel said, "Helen Marie, I'm going to take care of the girls and the baby and Marjorie Fay is going to take you to see a movie." To go to a movie was a big treat and I was excited. We went to a downtown theater. I had never seen anything like that. The theater was beautiful with plush carpets, padded seats, lovely wall hangings and gorgeous light fixtures. Soon the curtains opened. There were some Vaudeville acts and two guys did some tap dance routines and slapstick comedy. I laughed and laughed. Next came the main feature. The movie was *San Francisco,* a wonderful show. I was enthralled. I could not thank Marjorie Fay and Aunt Ethel enough for that special treat.

Saturday came and all the Atwood family (Aunt Ethel was an Atwood before marrying Uncle Harvey) planned a big overnight fishing trip on the Sam Saba River. There must have been twenty or thirty of us. Aunt Ethel gave me a quilt to use for a pallet for the girls. I remember sitting on the pallet playing with them while others were up and down the river fishing. We had a big picnic supper on the riverbank. Dark came and everybody was still fishing, visiting and having a good time when someone came to tell us that heavy rain had fallen up the river.

They were expecting the river to rise to flood stage in the area where we were. They were warning us to get off the riverbank.

I don't know how the arrangements were made, but we moved to a little Methodist church for shelter. This was a one-room country church and everything was ready for Sunday morning worship service. Each person took a pew and made their bed for the night. I put the girls on one and I took another just in back of them. I didn't sleep much for fear they would roll off the benches. Morning came and the women made sure the church was spic and span, just like we had found it. And the men put several bills in the collection plate on the communion table.

Ft. Worth had a slogan posted everywhere. It was "*Where the West Begins.*" Well, I saw enough interesting things that I hoped someday I could really see the West. I yearned to see what was beyond "where the coyotes howled and wind blew free." It was almost forty-five years before that dream came true.

Our goodbyes were said and we started home. Ruth did the driving. We came back by Oklahoma City to visit Aunt Lola, mother's brother's ex-wife, and the three cousins who had lived with us for about three years after the separation. Uncle Oliver had been left with the children, and there was no way he could care for them. Granny and Mother took them temporarily. It was three years before Aunt Lola decided to take them. I remember there were court trials at Jasper, as she was a native of Newton County. It was a pitiful situation and was dragged out for three years.

Aunt Lola lived in a large house near the state capitol. There were oil wells around, even one in her back yard. Somehow she had gained possession of land in Oklahoma and they had "struck oil." She was a rich lady. The girls had changed, I thought, since they had money. R. O. was still the little cotton-haired boy that was so cute. He was especially glad to see us.

I was glad when morning came and we were on the last leg of our trip. I was nervous about the trip as Ruth drove so fast. We were all nervous but when Dad and Mother suggested, "Ruth, you better slow down," she would answer sharply, "Now, don't talk to me, you are making me nervous and you will cause me to have a wreck." Well, she had had wrecks before when none of the family was along, so we all knew it could happen. I froze in my seat and held the girls close. I wondered if I would ever see the boys and Merrill again.

Now, I expect she must have been going 50 mph, but to a country girl accustomed to driving about 35 mph on a dirt road, that seemed like drag racing to me. I could have been a bit homesick, too, and perhaps had guilt feelings for leaving in the first place. We stopped in Fayetteville for some reason. I remember we were parked on the street in front of a store. I saw they were having a big sale. In the window were hats marked $1 each. I still had the $2 Dad had given the girls. No one allowed me to spend a dime on the trip. I looked at the hats and thought of the $2. Finally, my wishing for a new hat became so intense, I couldn't resist it. I had to buy me a hat! So, I did. After all, it had been so long since I had had a new hat and this one would last me a long, long time. Still, I felt guilty.

I was real glad to reach home. Merrill and the boys were waiting for us. Everyone tried to talk at one time. There was so much each one had to tell. They had made it real well, but I really believe they missed us. When I opened the suitcase and saw all the dirty clothes, I knew my work for the next day was cut out for me.

It was not many days before Merrill left for summer camp and I was left alone with the children and Mr. Cole. He was good to me when Merrill was gone. He milked the cow and took care of the chickens. He drew the water for the wash pot and tubs on washday. He would go to the store or post office or stay with the children if I needed to go somewhere.

I remember going to Mrs. Gilbert's to a Womens' Missionary Union meeting one afternoon. I had lots of friends in the W.M.U. There was Aunt Martha Mathis, an elderly lady I dearly loved. I remember the two Middleton sisters who lived together. They had never married. One was named Addie, but I can't recall the other one's name. But, I remember she got real sick, in fact, seriously ill. The women in the church were taking turns "sitting up" with her at night. It so happened that I was sitting up with her the night she died. I had never watched anyone die before, and I shall never forget how she grew weaker and weaker. I called her sister to get up. Soon, her heart stopped beating and then the most peaceful look came on her face. I knew she was with the Lord by her radiant expression.

Back to this particular meeting of the W.M.U. —I learned that Mrs. Gilbert was moving and her house would be for rent. It was a cute little yellow house. It had linoleum on all the floors. All the houses we had lived in in Omaha had pine floors that had to be scrubbed. And that wasn't easy, not even for Merrill.

When Merrill came home from camp, I told him the house was for rent. With winter coming on, he decided we should see about renting it, because he knew it would take so much wood to heat the one we were in. We had noticed how the wind blew unchallenged through the cracks around the windows and under the front door. We were afraid the rent would be too high but he went to inquire. Luckily, we were able to rent it. In August, we moved for the fourth time in two years.

Merrill said he was going to buy us a radio with some of the money he earned at camp. We were really out of touch with the world, as we didn't take a newspaper. I still remember how good it sounded to again hear, "This is KWTO, Keep Watching the Ozarks, Springfield, Missouri." KWTO was our favorite station and the one we always listened to at Mother and Dad's.

At 5:45 p.m., we always listened to Lowell Thomas when he came on with the evening news. "Hello, everybody!" he would say and then he brought the world to us right in our own kitchen. And when he signed off on Friday night, "So long until Monday," we felt bad because it would be three days before we knew what was happening in the world.

We moved in time to have company before school started. I remember James Carl coming for a few days. One night I had homemade beet pickles for supper. He loved them; in fact, he liked them so much that, when he had eaten all the pickles, he turned up the jar and drank the vinegar. This made him deathly sick before morning. I doubt if he ever ate beet pickles again.

Merrill's brother, Uncle Lonnie, and his wife, Aunt Katherine, came from Des Moines, Iowa, for a visit. Lonnie was superintendent of the Coca-Cola plant in Des Moines. We always loved for them to come. Uncle Lonnie was so much fun, and Aunt Katherine was a real sweet lady. All the children had a ball. He was a great moviemaker and he always had his camera focused on someone. Lonnie brought in Coca-Colas when he came. He thought they were necessary for your health.

Aunt Cassie, Merrill's sister, Uncle Louis and their kids, Martina, Lonnie, Maxine and Bob came from Kansas City and we had a family reunion. Uncle Lonnie and Aunt Katherine stayed at a motel but Aunt Cassie's family stayed with us. We made pallets and had wall-to-wall people. All this added to the enjoyment. This is the only time I remember all of us being together.

Something funny I remember happening at this house was the time I had dinner ready and put Bettelyn in her high chair at the table. She was calling the boys to come on. They didn't want to come and they shouted, "Oh, it's not ready yet." Bette yelled back, "Dinner is ready, ain't the dinner is?" We really thought that was funny. The entire family had a big laugh.

We were fortunate to not have serious sicknesses. One time Jerry had a lot of boils on his head. Mother took him home with her for a few days so Uncle James could lance them and take care of him. We didn't have to consult a doctor often. When a child would complain, I would put my hand on their forehead to see if they had a fever. If I thought they did, I would wet a cloth and put it on their head and keep them quiet for a while. If that didn't help, I gave them a couple of baby aspirins. When they complained of a sore throat, I fixed warm salt water for them to gargle. Soda was good for upset stomach or to put on insect bites. Castor Oil was used for a laxative, or "purgative," as Granny called it.

I always kept a jar of Vick's salve and I rubbed that on their chest if it seemed congested. At night, I would put some on a flannel cloth and pin it inside their gown or underwear. A good test for sickness was to look at their tongues. If the tongue was coated, then they were bilious. Epsom salts was good for that. Occasionally, we would have a case of "seven-year itch" that called for a paste made of lard and sulfur.

Merrill was very allergic to poison oak and we had to fight that, especially in the springtime. Sometimes he would have it so bad, he could not stand his clothes and would have to stay in bed with only a sheet over him.

September came and with it the opening of school. This was a special occasion because Billie Jon was starting to school. He was so happy. We went to the store and bought him a red Big Chief tablet, two pencils, a book satchel and a box of coloring pencils. He had new overalls to wear and did he feel big! His teacher was Miss Moore, a beautiful young woman from Everton near Valley Springs.

The schoolhouse was a marvel to Bill because it was so big. He liked everything about school. One day he came home put out and disappointed. He still talks about that day. It happened that they had a coloring book and, sometimes during the day, Miss Moore directed the children in coloring one page. There was a picture of a cow that Bill could hardly wait to color. He had looked forward for days for them to get to the cow picture. This day he was bothered with a touch of diarrhea and had made three trips to the outdoor toilet. On his third trip, a kid came running in the toilet and, much to Bill's disgust, announced that they had just colored the cow picture. Bill quickly pulled up his pants and hurried back to the schoolroom, hoping he was not too late to color the cow. Well, he was too late and Miss Moore, seeing his excitement, took him by the arm and gave him three spats on the seat, thinking he had just been out there goofing off. To this day, he regrets not getting to color that cow.

Clothes for the family were beginning to be a problem. We bought some new clothes for Bill to wear to school. Jerry got the hand-me-downs. Bettelyn had to have new things, and Merrill needed to replenish his wardrobe. It is amazing how long clothes lasted in those days. They were not bought for one season, but for as many years as the cloth would hold out. Anything new was an absolute necessity. No one minded because the majority of the people we knew were wearing the same things over and over and over. If you wonder what Merrill and I looked like then, here are some school pictures. We had no camera to make pictures ourselves.

Merrill and Helen

We took care of everything we had. When the weather began to get cool, I would pull out the winter clothes to see who could wear what. Hand-me-downs were the rule of thumb at our house. Sometimes Jo Bill's things were handed down to Billie Jon and Jerry always got the clothes Bill could no longer wear. Bettelyn's clothes were passed on to Carolyn. We bought only as few clothes as we had to.

We took care of what we had. Every piece of clothing that wore out was reused as a dishrag, washcloth, dust cloth or something. The good parts could be used for quilt scraps. Old worn out sheets were saved for bandages or torn in strips to tie boxes or tie up pole beans. Feed sacks, sugar sacks and flour sacks were washed, bleached and made into dish towels, or sometimes curtains, underwear or even dresses. It was not unusual to see Gold Bond flour stamps on slips or underwear. Every bit of string was saved and wound into balls for later use. We didn't throw anything away.

When the days began to get cool in the fall, we would put up the black heater. This meant we could keep warm during the long, cold winters. In cold weather, we heated only the rooms we were using during the day. The bedrooms were closed off until late in the afternoon when we would open the doors to knock the chill off.

There was just enough room between the stove and the wall for a pallet. Often the kids would argue over whose time it was to lie on the pallet. Words can't describe the security and warmth of a pallet made out of homemade quilts in the back of the stove. I made them take turns so everyone had their opportunity of catnapping there.

We huddled around the stove on cold evenings and listened to the radio. We all enjoyed *Lum "n" Abner*, two old codgers who lived in Pine Ridge, Arkansas, where they operated the Jot-Em-Down Store. When the party line rang in Pine Ridge, everyone listened. Cedric Wehunt, Grandpappy Spears and Squire Skimp seemed like real people to us. The philosophical conversations of Lum to other characters often drove home a lesson we would remember a long time.

When this was over, I usually began getting the girls ready for bed while the boys, their dad and Grandpa listened to *Fibber McGee and Molly*, *Amos and Andy* or some of the oldies. Often I would carry their pillows and blankets to the stove and warm them good, then it wasn't a big task to tuck them in and kiss them goodnight. The boys would often get too sleepy to stay up any longer and go to bed on their own before we announced, "Bedtime!"

Dad Cole always had to check the weather before he went to bed. "Think I'll step outside and get a breath of fresh air," he would say. If it wasn't too cold, he might stay outside several minutes and smoke his pipe. Other nights, he barely opened the door before a blast of arctic air drove him back. When he came back in on his way to bed he would give his weather report: "It's clearin' off.......startin' to sprinkle...... cloudin' up in the south west....wind's pickin' up....believe we'll have snow by mornin'.....it's lightnin' in the east.....full moon makes it light as day out there," or maybe, "stars are really bright tonight."

Then, Merrill and I would enjoy some time together. The *Hit Parade* was always fun because we were challenged to name the top song of the week. They started with the Number Ten song and continued backwards to the Number One. Another show we liked was *Lux Radio Theater*. This was always a good play, and it was almost like going to a movie. Everything seemed so real with the sound effects and we would laugh or cry as the moment dictated. When our bedtime came, Merrill had to "bed down" the fire. That is, he pulled back any logs that were not burned so they wouldn't blaze up and burn before morning. Ashes were shoveled over the coals so they would be there to start the fire the next morning. After the fire was bedded down, the clock had to be wound. I checked the kids to see that no one had kicked the covers off. Then we were ready for bed.

It was a simple life, but a good one. The Depression may have denied us some of the things we would have liked and really needed, but it didn't keep us from being happy.

We thought we were settled for the year at Omaha High School when word came the Holly Springs School Board, upon the recommendation of Mr. Russell, the Superintendent, had selected Merrill to fill a vacancy at our beloved Valley Springs Training School. We were ready to move again. Nothing could be nicer than to go back and work with Mr. and Mrs. Russell. To think they wanted us was a great compliment and it raised our spirits sky high.

I wish I could remember exactly what happened, but I can't. I know Mr. Russell wanted Merrill to teach Bible and English and coach the basketball team. Mrs. Russell wanted to retire from teaching piano and turn it over to me. To be chosen by them was truly a feather in our cap. Merrill said teaching the Bible and Shakespeare to high school students was next to pastoring a church. "Maybe that is what the Lord is calling me to do."

Merrill turned in his resignation to the school board at Omaha and we began to make plans for the move to Valley Springs.

Mother and Dad learned that a house built by one of the teachers was being offered for sale. This house joined the school property. They came out and told us about it and said if we wanted to buy the house, they would help us with the down payment. They explained that they had sold the farm and, rather than waiting until they died for me to receive a share of their estate, they would rather see us "have it now when you really need it." This was the most generous offer we ever heard of and, of course, we were grateful beyond words.

That weekend, Dad came out and we all went home with him. The next morning, we drove down to Valley Springs to see the house.

Our house in Valley Springs

It was BEAUTIFUL! It was a pink sandstone with black mortar between each stone. We loved it! We were spellbound! There was a living room with a fireplace, a dining room with window boxes beneath the window, a music room, three small bedrooms and a kitchen with a built-in table that pulled down with open cabinets in the wall behind it. There was a porch across the back of the house, a large basement, a large garden plot, a barn, big pasture and a beautiful flower garden.

There was electricity and "running water"—not really, that was a joke. The only running water for this house was water running from a spring at the bottom of the hill. Water had to be carried from a spring a few hundred yards down the hill. The outdoor toilet was something we had grown up with so that was no problem. We all agreed this was the house for us. Arrangements were made for our loan. Since Merrill was getting about a fifteen percent increase in salary, from $65 to $75 a month, we felt like we could make the monthly payments which, as I remember, were $12.50.

The job of packing and moving was upon us, but hopefully this would be the last move for a long, long time. As the old man said, "our chickens had been moved so many times, when they saw a truck in front of the house, they crossed their legs to be tied." You see, that was the way we moved chickens—crossed their legs and tied them and then they couldn't get up and run off.

So in late November, we "rolled up our tents," said goodbye to Omaha and drove off down Highway 65, our fifth move.

You have heard of a "wide place in the road." Well, that describes Valley Springs. As you approach it from the northwest on Highway 65, you see the road widen as it approaches a bridge over a stream.

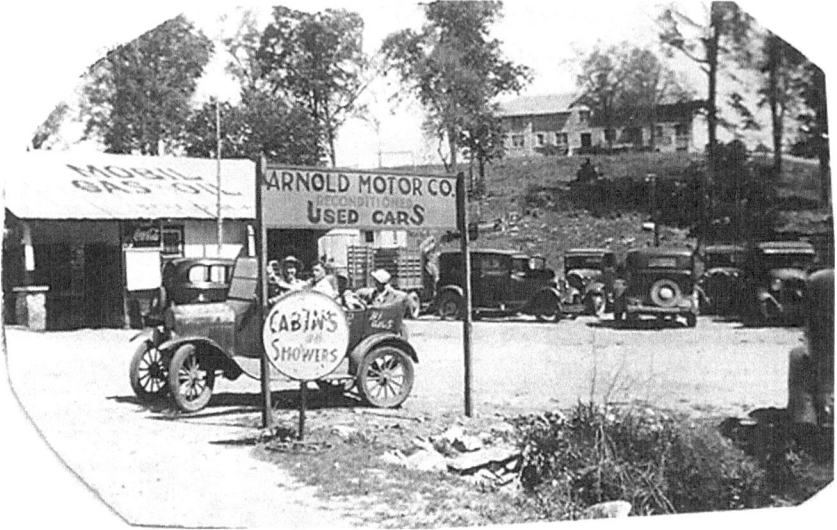

Downtown Valley Springs with Model T in foreground

One road leads to the left and one leads to the right, and that is where the town lies, part on the left and part on the right.

The first business on the left was Frank Fullerton's service station, run by Frank and his tiny wife, Mae. This was the gathering place for the men of the community. You could always see two or three sitting on the long wooden bench just outside the office. Here the talk of the town took place. Nearby was Arnold Motor Co., dealing in used cars. Behind the businesses were two or three cabins for tourists who wanted to spend the night in Valley Springs. Next to this used car lot was Frank Fullerton's home, and then the spring, for which the town was named.

Albright Hall, the school building, was on the hill overlooking the town. On the left, facing the highway, was Beauchamp's. This was the Jot-'em-Down store of Valley Springs, the only merchandise store in town and they sold everything from soup to nuts.

On the street running behind Beauchamps was the post office. Mrs. Zola Askew was the postmistress. She had been for years. A pickup truck delivered the mail from Harrison post office each morning, and Mrs. Zola put it in the boxes for the residents of the town.

Further down the street was the Valley Springs Milling Co., owned and operated by the Atchley family. Mr. and Mrs. Atchley lived across the highway. They had nine children. Four were boys, and they helped Mr. Atchley run the mill.

On the right side of the highway across the stream, was Dalton's Canning Factory. Mr. and Mrs. Dalton lived nearby. They canned several kinds of vegetables here, but mostly tomatoes, corn and green beans.

Nearby on the right was Mr. Sam Crawford's Blacksmith Shop. This, too, was a gathering place to sit and talk a while. There were no benches there, only nail kegs to sit on.

The town barbershop was just outside—in the summer only—the blacksmith shop. Here the chair was a box on top of a nail keg. The barber used other nail kegs for his tools, barber supplies and a white enamelware wash pan.

Further out the highway on the right was Brice Fullerton's store and gas station. Brice was a brother of Frank's. He sold Esso whereas Frank sold Mobil. His home was on the hill back of the store. Also, on the right side of the highway was the two-story school building for primary and elementary grades, the Methodist church, parsonage and the Baptist Church.

We unloaded and set up our furniture. I was painfully aware of the sparseness of our furnishings, but it would be all right. Someday, we would have furniture to fill the house. Just to be in a home we could call our own was wonderful. The children were so excited. Even ol' Jersey mooed and the chickens cackled with joy. We had some Bantams. Merrill named all of them. I can remember the rooster's name was Prince Albert, for Dad Cole's tobacco, I guess. One of the hens was named Queen Elizabeth. They were such fun to watch. We moved them, too.

Everyone had to do some exploring. The boys got so excited when they found an old cistern that had been covered up. It was in the barnyard. We thought it would never cause any problems, but one time a big hog we had got to rooting around at the cover and moved it enough to fall into it. We were fattening it to butcher anyway, so hog killing time just came earlier than planned.

There was a retaining wall that separated the lawn from the barnyard with about three steps down to the barnyard. This was fun for Bettelyn to run up and down the steps. Someone had made a "formal" flower garden by the side of the house. It was laid out with stones outlining the sections with a round bed in the center filled with dusty miller. We had dreams of a birdbath in the center some day. The paths were fun for Bettelyn to run around.

Carolyn was walking, but we could not trust her to walk alone—I should say *run* alone. She was so tiny but so quick. After two or three falls, I learned she had to be watched every minute. When a door was opened, she would run out and continue running right off the porch. On moving day, someone had to be responsible to hold her.

Merrill got buckets and rounded up his dad and the kids and they all went to the spring. A wall of stone blocks had been built to enclose the spring, and a retaining wall had been built out from it. A walk had been made across it where one could stand and stoop to fill their bucket. The spring must have been gushing out hundreds of gallons of water because the "spring branch," as we called it, was wide. The overflow served as a refrigerator for many in the community. Buckets and bowls, tightly covered with a rock on top of the lid to hold it steady, were placed in the runoff. It kept the food remarkably cool. A lot of watercress was growing in the water and looked real pretty.

Springs at Valley Springs

Once more moving day was over. We fed the kids and put them to bed. Then we breathed a sigh of relief. We were dog tired. As we laid our weary bodies down, we wondered how long we would be in that house in Valley Springs. We hoped for a long, long time. At least, we felt we had reached our "promised land." We thanked God for leading us thus far.

During the first three months we were in Valley Springs, there was hardly a cloud on our horizon. Merrill was so happy to be back in Valley springs, this time a member of the faculty rather than a student in dear old Albright Hall. That he was principal in a little town stuck away in the Ozark Mountains of Arkansas did not occur, nor would it have mattered, to him. He wanted to become the best English teacher that Valley Springs Training School ever had.

Mr. Russell was so dear. He was a father-image to all of us. He was one of those rare persons who, even in the Depression, seemed to smile when he carried on an ordinary conversation. He radiated hope and enthusiasm and not only believed the best about tomorrow but helped you believe it too.

We felt so good being in our home when so many people were losing theirs by foreclosure. We were grateful to Mother and Dad for making it possible. Billie Jon started to school. I would get him ready and see him out the door with, "Now button up your coat, it's cold out there." He had to walk or run across town to the two-story white-frame school building where I went to school years before.

I started teaching piano lessons in our home.

Helen teaching piano

I needed to be there with the children. I scheduled a few lessons during their naptime and hoped to have more as the children grew older. I also taught our boys. Jerry learned to play the piano before he learned to read.

Going to church was never a matter of choice at our house. We always went. Since there were no services at the Baptist Church, we attended the Methodist Church. Merrill was asked to teach the Young Peoples' Sunday school class.

Christmas came and Merrill and the boys brought in a cedar tree from the woods and we trimmed it with our old standby decorations.

Merrill popped popcorn and the boys made long strings to wrap around the tree. We didn't have money to buy toys for the kids, but Merrill made slingshots from inner tubes and forked limbs for the boys. He made them stilts so they could walk tall and feel like giants. They each had a hoop to roll. Merrill got a ring of iron about ten inches in diameter and made a wooden roller, using a piece of broom handle and the lid off of one of Granddad Cole's Prince Albert cans nailed in the middle for the pusher. Most of their playthings cost practically nothing. He made a swing for the girls and everyone was happy.

Mother and Dad drove down on Christmas Eve and brought dolls for the girls, toy cars for the boys and Christmas stockings filled with oranges, nuts and candy. It was a great time we had together.

It was wonderful to have electricity and not have to bother with coal oil lamps. We never burned more lights than absolutely necessary. When I cooked supper, Merrill and the kids were in the kitchen or still outside. After supper, when the dishes were finished, everyone went into the living room to do homework, read or listen to the radio. We cut back on everything possible. I find it amazing what we did without. We had no toilet paper (we used the old Sears Roebuck and Montgomery Ward catalogs), no newspaper, magazines, no soft drinks, potato chips or snacks, no restaurant meals, no Kleenex or paper towels. We had no water bill, no telephone bill, no car expenses, no dry cleaning, no income tax, no TV repair, no long-distance calls and no barber or beauty shop expenses. I trimmed the girl's hair and Merrill cut the boys' and Granddad Cole's hair. (Now he *did* have to get himself a haircut occasionally.)

We always counted our blessings when we heard of disasters in other areas, like the heat and drought that resulted in the Dust Bowl out west that John Steinbeck wrote about in *The Grapes of Wrath*. Then there were the tragic floods of the 1930s which struck the Mississippi and Ohio Valleys, claiming many lives. I remember the pleas for clothing for the homeless people and how we shared a few of our meager belongings for those less fortunate. We were glad we lived in the mountains far from the raging rivers. Crooked Creek and Dry Jordan caused havoc enough when the heavy rains flooded Harrison.

But, in February, a flu epidemic hit our part of the state. It seemed no one was escaping. Dad and Mother drove down one afternoon to see about us. Carolyn was real sick with a high fever. Dad said, "We are taking this child to the doctor." So, we bundled her up and drove over to Western Grove for Uncle James to see her. He examined her and said it was the flu. He gave me medicine for her and said, "Keep her as quiet as you can." He and Dad talked about how many people had the flu. Dad said so many of the men working in the post office were sick. Uncle James said, "Well, folks better be careful and not get out too soon or they will be wearing a wooden overcoat." I had never heard that expression before and it haunted me.

Dad and Mother got us back home and, after playing with the other kids and visiting a while, they left for Harrison. I never dreamed that I would never see my dad alive again. I never suspected that the next time I saw my father, he would be wearing a "wooden overcoat."

This must have been about Tuesday when they drove down to Valley Springs. On Saturday, someone came down from Harrison to get me. They said Dad was real sick with pneumonia. I quickly changed my clothes and rode back to Harrison to Dad's house. They had just recently bought this home on the corner of Cherry St. It was across the street from Ralph Hudson, mother's cousin, and near Arvel Barker, Dad's cousin. They were so proud of it.

Upon arriving, I found Dad upstairs with a private duty nurse, Mary Wilgrub, a large German lady Dr. Kirby had brought down from Springfield. I did not go upstairs as he was so sick. Mother told me that he came home with the flu Wednesday night, but since there were so many off at the post office, he went back to work on Friday, very much against her wishes. She told how she heated irons and put them in the car near the brake pedals to try to warm the car a little for him.

When he had to come home early, he said, "I know now I shouldn't have gone back to work today, I feel so bad." He ate a bite of supper and stayed up to listen to his favorite show, *Lum "n" Abner,* before he went to bed. When they signed off, he pulled himself up the stairs for the last time. Granny was also in bed with the flu. Things were really hectic with the doctor coming often and Mother running up and down the stairs. Mother said there was nothing I could do and should let someone take me back home and she would let me know if Dad got worse.

Sunday morning, the following day, came. It was Valentine's Day—always a special day at our house. Before we were all dressed, a car came for me saying Dad's condition had worsened. All day, we waited and prayed, but there was no good report from upstairs. Late in the afternoon, I went back home to see about my family. Merrill and I decided to go to church, and when I got home, a car was waiting to take me back, as they said Dad couldn't live much longer. The doctor said he had three types of pneumonia and they had done all they could. By the time I reached the house, he had died. I was stunned. My dad, who was so much alive and a part of my life, was gone! It couldn't be. Then Mother said, "We have not told Granny. We wanted you to do that."

I braced myself and went in her bedroom, only to find her greatly sobbing. She said, "I know it, you don't have to tell me. I heard him breathe his last breath." Her room was just underneath his and the little thing had been there all that time alone. I expect she might have preferred it that way. She knew God was with her and she could talk it over with Him.

Mary Wilgrub, the nurse, was still there. She seemed hesitant to leave. She had become like one of the family in the three days she had been there. When she left, she promised to keep in touch with the family. This promise was kept. For almost fifty years, Mary—now Mary Stubblefield—has been like one of the family, especially to Ruth. Visits and letters are exchanged regularly.

In those days, the "corpse" was brought back to the home and placed by a window in the living room. Family and friends came by and neighbors "sat up" with the casket throughout the long hours of the night. Members of the family gathered from far and near for the funeral at the First Baptist Church, and he was buried in Maplewood Cemetery.

As the days passed, I recalled over and over the years he had shared my life, my joys and my sorrows. I could remember the rough stubble of his beard against my cheek when he picked me up at the end of the day when I was a child. I recalled how he played "rough house" with his "pig" and his "pup" (Ruth and Jim) when they came along. He was so proud of them.

I remembered him in church leading the singing with his fist closed. I always knew he was my friend who understood my trials. Many times I took him to work at the post office, just the two of us, talking over my and Merrill's situation. He had taught me fine principles and true Christianity. His memory was and is truly an inspiration.

Mother faced a real crisis in her life, but how we admired her courage. The loss seemed to revive her energies and made her more alert and self-sufficient than ever. When school was out, Mother, striving to deal with her deep grief, decided to sell the house and all its furnishings, and move to Flint, Michigan, taking along Ruth and Jim.

This was a sad time for us. I was distressed to have no family to go back to in Harrison. Flint seemed so far away, there was no way that we could ever go home again. The only happy thing about it was Granny came to live with us, bringing her trunk, her low chair, her featherbed, her Bible and her clothes.

Granny

Now our household numbered eight. But it was a privilege to have this great woman living with us, loving and teaching our children. The little stooped body on her crooked feet, working in the kitchen, is a scene I shall never forget. She had a beautiful face with a twinkle in her eye that made one know she enjoyed living. Her long, black hair was twisted into a knot on the top of her head. The children loved to watch her brush her hair as she bent over and it touched the floor.

Some of the grandchildren have been interested in Granny's sayings. Now is a good time to tell you some, so you will understand what a joy it was to have her around.

She always challenged the child who was saying, "I can't" with "I can't never did do nothing." When a child's hair needed combing, she might say, "Go comb your hair, you look like you had crawled through a brush pile backwards." Or, if she were combing and hit a tangle, "Rats have been sleeping in your hair."

To stop someone from doing something, she would say, "Now, hold your horses," or "Hold your tater." To slow them down, she might say, "Take a cold tater and wait," or if they needed to do something better, she often said, "You better lick your calf over." Now, if she thought one couldn't do it, she might say, "Yes, and you will flitter and fall back in it." Or, if one was mistaken, "You are barking up the wrong tree." When we were getting ready to go somewhere, she often called, "Are you ready or Reddy's calf?" You see, we had a cow named Reddy.

When a child was wiggling, she would say, "You are just like a maggot in hot ashes." When a child wanted too much, she thought they were a "greedy gut," or when a child had eaten a lot, she might tell them they were "as full as a tick." If she suspected someone was not being honest, she might say, "I smell a rat." She was often "too busy to spit," or things were "too rich for my blood." When she was "dumbfounded," she might say, "That beats a hen a-peckin' with a wooden pecker." When she had to change her tactics, she sometimes said, "There are lots of ways to choke a dog to death besides on buttermilk." When she had enough of anything, especially foolishness, it was, "Enough's enough and too much is a dog's bait." To her, "A miss is as good as a mile."

She used words like "catty-cornered." When she wanted to locate something like a house across the road, she might say, "It's catty-cornered from here." Or, if something was a "little out of kilter," she was apt to describe it as "whopper-jawed."

In the kitchen, she had her sayings, too. If you burnt the bread, "Your husband is mad at you," or, if you dropped the tea towel, "someone is coming dirtier than you are." She added much spice to our everyday living. And, as I said, she loved having work to do—and there was plenty around our house. It seemed God had given me four hands instead of two.

That spring, the P.T.A. sponsored a special program. One of the things on the program was a doll parade for preschool children. We thought our little doll should enter. I made a little yellow dress for her to wear and a matching one for her doll, and she won first place. We were so proud of Carolyn.

The Depression was hitting us hard. We fought it with spades, hoes, rakes and our little garden plot. Sometimes the hot dry summers almost defeated our efforts. We had to fight cut worms and all kinds of insects that threatened to kill our plants. I remember one time Merrill had to spray our potato patch to try to save it. He mixed up arsenic and water in an old paint bucket and set it at the end of a row to refill his sprayer. Bettelyn was walking around and for some reason she picked up the spoon and took a bite out of it. I saw her, grabbed her up and rushed into the kitchen. Quickly, I mixed up some mustard water and made her drink it. This caused her to vomit and empty her stomach. We watched for indications of reactions, but I must have acted soon enough to prevent something terrible or even fatal.

Merrill kept his eyes out for anything wild that was edible. In the spring, he picked poke salat. He dug sassafras roots and I made hot tea. This was said to be a good spring tonic. There were wild fruits like blackberries, dewberries, cherries, mulberries, grapes and plums. In the fall, we gathered nuts and after the first frost persimmons were good to eat.

In midsummer, around the Fourth of July, blackberry-picking time came. We were up before sunrise. We rubbed kerosene on our legs and arms to keep the chiggers off, and wore long-sleeved shirts and denim pants to protect us from the briars. We took off with as many buckets as we could carry. Merrill and his dad usually had two large buckets each and a small one to use for picking. The boys and I had smaller buckets. It was easier to pick in a small bucket and empty it into a larger one than to carry the big bucket until it was filled, and less danger of spilling the berries, too. Granny took care of the girls at home and fixed lunch for us.

Berries meant jelly, cobblers, or just a bowl of fruit in the winter, and they were free. We picked several gallons. Hard work followed, because water had to be carried from the spring to wash them all and it was hot, canning over a wood stove in July. So I wasn't glad to see berry picking time come nor sorry to see it go. But, I did take delight in the rows of jars of berries and jelly on the shelves in the basement, along with the many jars of vegetables from the garden. You might say we picked, canned and dried everything that could be swallowed.

The hog we raised each year rooted himself up to about 200 pounds by fall. So we had our bacon, sausage, hams, lard, etc. to supplement our vegetables. We always had a Jersey cow and she gave enough milk for her calf and all of us. And, we had chickens—layers for eggs and fryers to eat. You can see, we weren't hungry but many times we were penniless.

After Merrill returned from camp that summer, we arranged to buy a secondhand washing machine, one with an agitator and a wringer. What a help this was.

Used washing machine

Helen hanging clothes on line

This was my first luxury. I could hardly believe it. Now washday wasn't the chore it had been. The water was the big job now, carrying it from the spring. We didn't waste the wash water. It was carried bucket by bucket to water our flowers and vegetables.

When the clothes were dry, they were brought in and prepared for ironing. Ironing day followed washday. A basket of clothes, which had been sprinkled, rolled and left to stand overnight, was ready for the all-day chore. Irons heated on the stove while breakfast was cooked. Dad Cole always washed the dishes for us. I can see him now smoking his pipe and washing dishes. Anyway, I got right to my ironing. The cotton sheets were folded and pressed. The pillowcases were starched and had to be ironed. The tea towels were folded and pressed, handkerchiefs were perfectly folded and quickly pressed. At noon I stopped to feed everyone and get the children down for a nap. This was the time to do Merrill's starched shirts, our dresses and the boy's school clothes.

Clothes that needed mending were hung to one side and the next day the needle and thread took care of the rips and tears before they were ever put away.

Saturday was cleaning day. Just as Saturday is next to Sunday, so "cleanliness is next to godliness," the old saying went. We not only cleaned our house but we cleaned our bodies top to bottom. Water was carried from the spring for both waters. In the summer, we might let it set in the washtubs in the sun to warm, otherwise it was heated on the stove. After an early supper the Saturday-night-bath special got into high gear. Everyone had a bath in the washtub, hair was shampooed and all got a clean nightgown or pair of pajamas. All the shoes were cleaned, polished and buffed. Sunday clothes were laid out before going to bed, as were Sunday school books, Bibles and pennies for the collection. Granny never went with us because of kidney troubles she had, but she read her lesson and studied her Bible at home. Mr. Cole didn't go either. He always sat on the front porch and smoked his pipe.

One day Jerry got deathly sick. He lay around the house all day, still and pale. He was too sick to take to the doctor, and we had no car. So we called Dr. Kirby to come down to see him. He diagnosed it as flux, a rare disease from South America and was carried by flies. Only one other case had been reported in Arkansas, so it was very strange that he had it. He told us how contagious it was and how dangerous, often fatal. He said if Granny or Dad Cole took it, they probably would not last a day.

Jerry grew thinner and thinner by the minute. He could not keep anything inside him. His bowels were so bloody and flowed almost continually, so this caused him to get paler and paler. I called Mother in Flint and told her about the situation. She and Ruth started driving immediately. They stopped in Springfield, Mo., and called the doctor to see if Jerry was still alive.

Dr. Kirby came to see him every day. I remember one day he hesitated before going into the back bedroom where we had Jerry isolated. He looked at me and said, "I can hardly make myself go into that room. I would not take this disease to my children for anything in the world." Nothing was said about hospitalization. The nearest hospital was eight miles away in Harrison and it was just a big white house the doctors had converted into a hospital. We had such a feeling of isolation and helplessness. I think not having a car or telephone added to this feeling.

I sat by Jerry's bed dipping pieces of white sheets in a pan of cold water and bathing his hot forehead. It seemed he was slowly dying before my eyes. His body looked like the pictures of starving children in India that we had seen. Only a covering of sallow skin stretched over his bones.

Mother and Ruth arrived. Mother insisted that she go in and help care for Jerry. He could hardly recognize her and was too weak to raise his body from the bed. She could not believe her eyes when she saw this limp child who had been so very active.

When it appeared like we were beginning to gain ground in whipping this terrible disease, Dr. Kirby said, "Give him a tablespoon of apple juice every two hours. Apple juice will help to coat his stomach." To our joy, he was able to retain the apple juice. This gave us hope. After a day or so, the doctor said we could try a little Jell-O. Well, this was a problem. It was summer and Jell-O would not set on the porch in the summer. The spring was not cold enough to set it. Mother said, "Merrill, do you think you could manage to make the monthly payments on an electric refrigerator if I make the down payment?" Merrill said, "I'll make it somehow." So off to Harrison they went to buy a refrigerator

Helen at refrigerator

How thankful I was to have this wonderful appliance in the dining room (there wasn't room for it in the kitchen).

Now Jerry could have all the Jell-O he could eat. This poor child continued to progress until he was able to be up again. By some miracle, none of the family took the disease. Mother and Ruth returned to Flint when they felt the danger was passed.

The refrigerator was such a blessing. It kept the milk and

butter so cold, and now we could save more leftovers. Also, water could be chilled. The spring water was exceptionally cold. Before we got the refrigerator, when we wanted a cold drink, someone would run to the spring and get a fresh bucket. All of us would drink from the same dipper.

When September came, Billie Jon was eager to go to school. He was anxious to see his friends. Recess and ball were his favorite subjects. Merrill was also eager to get back to the classroom. His scholarly mind yearned for books. He had his lesson plans worked out for fall and he was ready to go. His students were very fond of him. His jaw was the key to his character. It showed strength, courage and tenacity. He looked stern, but when he forgot himself and his dignity faded, his smile was one almost with a schoolboy's mischievousness.

Eight boys came out for basketball. They practiced on a dirt court not far from our house. We often looked out and saw J. W. Fullerton shooting goals. By the time for the season to start, seven boys were suited out in their green and white, ready to go. Frank Edwards (the center) was captain of the team that year.

I started teaching some music students over at the schoolhouse, since Granny and Dad Cole were both there to stay with the children. I traded music lessons for anything we could use, such as sewing, ironing, food, etc. I remember one year I had traded lessons for eighteen gallons of molasses. We had molasses on hot biscuits for breakfast, molasses on hot cornbread for supper and often more molasses on cold cornbread at bedtime. Two or three gallons had been overcooked and the kids could stick a knife into the bucket and twist it around a few times and pull out a sucker. This was fun, and we thought the iron in the molasses was good for them.

Merrill and I tried to plan our work so we would have as much time together as possible. He came by my room after school and we walked home together. There was much work to be done at home, but we were a good team. We worked together and, with his help I was soon finished and we all settled down in the living room. We had fun playing with the children and listening to their tales. We all liked music. Often after the dishes were done, or on Sunday afternoons, I would go to the piano and Merrill would sit beside me and we would go through the old Cokesbury Hymnal singing *Amazing Grace, How Firm a Foundation* and all the old favorites we sang in church. Granny loved this. She would sit in her chair and sing or hum along with us.

Christmas vacation came again. On Christmas Eve, we went into Harrison and bought some presents for Noah, Myrtle, James and Joe Bill and took them out to Union for the Christmas tree that night. As we were driving along the levee near the church, Merrill stopped the car suddenly and jumped out. He had seen a possum out in the field. He chased it down and caught it, even though it took a plug out of his finger. He came carrying it by the tail back to the car. He said, "Now we have us a Christmas dinner." I couldn't believe he was going to cook that possum, but he did, along with some sweet potatoes. It was so greasy that no one could eat it, but it was what you might call an interesting experience, I guess.

Another thing I remember about that Christmas was that Merrill and I agreed that we would not buy each other a Christmas present and use the little money we had for the children's presents. We wanted to get them a little red wagon and a few other things. Christmas Eve came and I pulled out the box I had for Merrill. I couldn't stand to not buy him a white shirt. I felt guilty because I had broken our agreement. Apparently, he had kept our promise, as there was no package for me. But on Christmas morning when I put my feet off the bed, to my surprise, there was a pair of house shoes he had bought for me. They were the funniest little black-felt slippers with a bow on the toe. And I loved them. They said so much.

The kids had lots of fun with their red wagon and some exciting times. One day Bette and Carolyn were riding on the back porch, which was a concrete slab about three feet high with no banisters. They ran off the porch with both of them in the wagon. No real damage was done either to the girls or the wagon. Later Bill was pulling Jerry in the wagon up the mountain road along side our house, and they came running back to the house, shouting, "We ran over a snake." Merrill went to see. There lay a copperhead dead in the road with wheel prints on its body. The boys were really excited.

On New Year's Eve, Billie Jon wanted to stay up and see the New Year in. He could imagine seeing the old year, 1937, bent and gray, carrying his scythe, groping his way out at the stroke of midnight, while the infant, 1938, crawled along behind. We told him he could stay up. All the family told him goodnight and went to bed—but his father. When he wound the clock, he ran it up an hour so Bill would get to bed earlier. Bill waited and waited and watched the clock as it ticked away toward twelve o'clock. When the hands reached the midnight hour, he ran out on the front porch and yelled, "Happy New Year! Happy New Year!" to the top of his voice. Satisfied, he went to bed, his mission accomplished. We could not keep from laughing as we heard it all.

We greeted the New Year, too, but 1938 brought with it the gloom of war. We kept listening to the radio and it was really getting bad in Europe. It seemed like Hitler was a mad man, determined to conquer the whole continent. We worried, even though it seemed far away from us.

Soon after the first of the year, Mother wrote and asked if Ruth could come stay with us and finish her last year of high school. Of course, we were glad we could at last do something for Mother. We talked it over and decided to ask Dad Cole to go to one of his other children's homes for five months so we could have a bed for Ruth. We immediately wrote Ruth to come, assuring her she would be welcome.

Then Merrill told Dad Cole. He was so angry. He picked up his few clothes and walked off, just as he had come nearly five years before. Merrill called to him to wait and talk it over, but he was determined to leave and not look back. He didn't tell the children goodbye or tell us where he was going.

About two months passed and one day Cassie, Merrill's sister, her husband and children drove up. They lived in Kansas City, Kansas. Cassie told us she had received a letter from her dad saying, "Come and get me. I am starving to death." He had gone to Harrison and found a room in a run-down hotel. How he had lived that long was a mystery. I never could figure out why he never worked or why he retired so young. He seemed able bodied. I never saw him take a dose of medicine. He didn't have a dime, but was content to smoke his pipe, wash dishes, carry water, work in the garden some and sit on the porch. He never left the house except to walk to the store for another can of Prince Albert or something I needed. We all loved him and never said one word to him or anyone else about his lifestyle. Cassie and her family spent the night with us and left the next morning to pick up Dad Cole and take him home with them. She understood our situation and she wished her dad had.

About three weeks passed and our children began to get sick—bang! bang! bang! Before the day was over, all four were sick with a high fever. We could not believe it. We had no idea what was the matter. I gave them aspirin tablets and bathed their foreheads, trying to get their fever down. They had rigors and begged for more and more cover. After about thirty-six hours, I began to see a rash. They were breaking out with something. Granny took one look and said, "It's the measles." She was right. They all broke out with the measles. I called the doctor and said, "What do I do?" He said, "There's nothing to do now, the worst is over." He did suggest getting some formaldehyde to spray Merrill and Ruth before they went to school each morning to try to keep from spreading the disease. "There is not another case in Boone County," the doctor said. So we wondered where they got them.

Merrill, Ruth and I divided the nights into three shifts and one of us stayed up and took care of them. The mystery remained until a letter came two or three weeks later from Aunt Cassie. She said, "I hope your kids did not come down with the measles. Before we got home from your house, both of ours were sick and beginning to break out." That was the solution. That was where they got the germ.

When it was about time for school to be out, along the first of May, I began to feel sick every morning. This continued morning after morning. They made no pregnancy tests then, but I knew either I was pregnant or I had terminal morning sickness. Time would tell. I was pregnant all right! Between pregnancies and the Depression, our outlook would have been grim to most folks, but we were so in love with each other we didn't really worry. Merrill just hugged me and said, "We'll make it!" He had an inner core of courage that refused to be defeated. His strength made me want the same kind of stouthearted spunk he had.

As school neared the end, Merrill was always busy. One of the things he did was chaperone the senior class on a trip. This year they went to Lake Taneycomo, near Branson, Missouri, a favorite spot. I went along, as did Mr. and Mrs. Russell. Mr. Russell was retiring at the end of school and they would be moving to their farm near Conway. We had such a good time. Everyone had such a good time. Everyone agreed this was the best Senior trip ever.

That was Saturday. On Sunday afternoon, Frank Fullerton and another man came to our house to talk to Merrill. They told him the sheriff from Taney County had called and said the group from our high school had stolen a lot of things from a gift shop at Rockaway Beach, and if they were not returned within three days, they would be down to make arrests. Poor Merrill, he didn't know what to do. He was so disappointed. To make matters worse, Mr. Russell was leaving Monday morning. Merrill went over and told him what had happened and talked the situation over with him. None of us ever dreamed this had happened and Ruth refused to comment.

Monday came and Merrill called all the senior class together. He said, "A dear old man went down the road this morning with a broken heart. After Mr. Russell has been here all these years, he had to leave knowing his students had committed a crime and the law was after them." Then he told them about the telephone call and said, "I don't intend to ask any questions. I don't want any confession, but what I do want is for everyone who has anything from that gift shop to wrap it up and bring it to school in the morning and put it in my office. I am going to appoint a committee to go with me and Mr. Watkins, who has agreed to take his car, to return the articles and apologize to the owner for taking them. I think the president and vice president of the class will be the ones I will ask to represent all of you."

To our amazement, it worked. The next morning the things began to come in and there were a lot of packages deposited in his office. He boxed them up and, after lunch, the group started on their distasteful mission. They arrived at the shop and carried the boxes in.

The president of the class was the spokesman. He began to talk to the owner. The owner couldn't understand. He knew nothing about it. They had not missed anything. Then, Merrill figured out what had happened. The kids had bragged and talked about their episode around Frank Fullerton's service station and the adults overheard them and decided they should not be allowed to get away with the shoplifting. So they had made up the tale about the telephone call. Merrill appreciated it, as did the shop keeper, but the kids didn't, they were angry. We hoped a lesson was learned.

The big day of graduation came. Instead of wearing formals like we did when I graduated, they wore caps and gowns. They looked very scholarly.

Mother and Jim came to be there for the big day. We were all glad to see them. When they came, we always went with them to visit Dad's brother, Uncle Clyde, and his wife, Gladys. They lived on a farm near Sulphur Mountain. It was always fun to go there. Their oldest son, T. J., was one of Bill's closest friends. They had a son just a few weeks older than Jerry who was injured at birth and was never able to hold his head up or say a word. He grew in length, but his body was just skin stretched over bones. I felt bad when I took Jerry out there, but it did not seem to bother Aunt Gladys, and we always felt welcome.

Aunt Gladys got the name "Our Cooking Aunt" because she was such a good cook. When she called us to the table, we knew it would be laden with food. There would probably be two meats and perhaps six to eight vegetables, topped off by a wide choice of desserts.

Merrill went to camp early in the summer. The camp reflected the anxiety everyone across the country was feeling, because it looked as if war was raging on and on in Europe. Hitler had taken over Czechoslovakia and this ended the hope of permanent peace. France had pledged support of the Czechs and England was determined to resist German attempts at expansion. Merrill came home and said we must pray for peace in Europe.

With his camp earnings this summer, he decided to buy a car. We needed one so badly, especially since I was pregnant and needed to go to the doctor regularly. He decided he could make a down payment and we could meet the monthly payments.

This gave us a chance to get away from home for a picnic or a trip to Buffalo River and a visit at Parthenon with Aunt Letha and the cousins. There was a spring near home called Pigg Springs that provided a fun place to explore—and could be reached in a short time after a busy day.

Buffalo River at Pruitt near Jasper was our favorite place. The bluffs were high over the nice swimming hole. Here we could picnic, walk on the sandy beach, or swim and play in the river. There were cabins nearby for overnight guests. I remember staying there one night.

We tried to take a trip to Aunt Letha's in the summer. It was fun to cross the swinging bridge and fish with cane poles for anything that would bite a worm.

One day, Bette screamed the kind of scream that brought us all running. "What happened?" I asked. She said, "A rock flew up my nose." Billie Jon was hoeing the flower bed nearby. He contended that he didn't do anything. We told him we were not accusing him of doing anything. We could see the rock in her nostril, but it was too far up for us to remove it. Quickly, we put her in the car and headed for Uncle James' office at Western Grove, four miles away. He took one look at it and said, "You better take her to Harrison to Doctors Kirby and McCoy. I think it is a bigger job than I can do."

I held her in my lap and soothed her as best I could as Merrill drove as fast as he dared the twelve miles to Harrison. When we arrived at the doctors' office, Dr. Kirby took a look at it and shook his head. Then he told his nurse to get a sheet. All the time Bette was crying hysterically. I was holding her on the examining table. She refused to lie down. When the nurse brought the sheet, Dr. Kirby wrapped her tightly with her arms by her side. He said, "Get another nurse." Then he laid her down on the table and told one nurse to hold her head "and don't let it move!" The other nurse held her feet and legs. They held her like a vise and the doctor took some long sharp tweezers and very carefully removed the rock. There were only a couple drops of blood. What a relief! The doctor and nurses were real pleased with their accomplishments, too.

Once in the car, Bette cuddled her head against my breast and went to sleep. I breathed a prayer of thanks. But I wondered, "Now, honestly, how did that rock get up her nose?"

I felt so bad all summer, it was a real chore to get our canning done. The children were all required to lie down and rest after lunch. Sometimes nap times were just too quiet for comfort. "Never would they go to sleep so soon," I thought. So, I would slip and open the door and sure enough, they were pillow fighting, rolling and tumbling.

I guess, really, it isn't the kids that benefit from nap time, it's the mother. I wasn't too surprised and I had been able to rest a little. When rain kept the kids in the house all day, they were more quarrelsome than usual, amusing themselves by picking at each other. Between settling arguments and soothing hurt feelings, I managed to get through the day. When night would come, I would fall in bed exhausted. I didn't need a sedative. I slept like a log.

Merrill was always interested in the poor. Knowing there were several children in Valley Springs School District who went hungry, he investigated the possibility of securing a school lunch program that the government was sponsoring. Most of the supplies would be surplus food. It would require some outlay of money, and the proper facilities for the kitchen, dining hall, etc. "The basement of Albright Hall would make an ideal location," he said.

After thinking about it and talking with me about it, he decided to present it to the school board before September. They listened as he described the poverty of the district. Then one board member said, "We are in a serious Depression and many people don't have the clothing and food they need, but sometimes I wonder why people who struggle to survive have to support those who don't have the push to work hard like we do." Merrill answered, "One reason for their lack of enthusiasm is the unemployment situation. There is no work available for many of these people. At least, not full-time work."

"Who's going to do the cooking? Who's going to run this thing, plan meals, buy supplies, etc.?" "If we find the place, the W.P.A. will find the cooks and the manager and hire them," Merrill answered.

"Don't you see the danger of all this? It's the beginning of government control. Whenever central government grabs power—with whatever emergency excuse—no matter how they bait the hook with handouts, every citizen loses part of his liberty. What's more, in the long run, handouts do nothing but weaken a man's character," someone said.

For a moment there was silence. Merrill waited for someone else to speak. Then the question came, "Who would decide who would eat free and who would pay a small charge for lunch? Wouldn't the kids who have to pay look down on those who ate free?" Merrill answered these questions by saying, "A study will be made after applications are received for free meals and all who are selected will receive the same type of tickets as those sold, so the students would never know who eats free."

The board voted to start the school lunch program and many of the patrons in the district volunteered to help set it up. So work began immediately with Merrill heading up the project. It was a big job but one he enjoyed.

Ruth decided to come to Arkansas to go to Central College in Conway that fall. Mother told her she could bring the car down and we were looking for her arrival. One afternoon, we looked out and there she was pulling up in front of the house. We all ran out to meet her. Just as I got beside the car, Mom jumped up from between the seats and shouted, "*Boo!*" I jumped, too. She really surprised us. After a short visit, she returned to Michigan to be with James Carl.

Jerry started to school that fall. Up until this time, we had called him "Merrill, Jr.," but we decided now that he was going to school, we would call him Jerry and soon all the family, even Mom, Ruth and Jim, called him Jerry.

Mrs. Arnold Watkins was Jerry's teacher. He came home every recess to hug me, maybe get a cookie or a drink and just see for sure that home was still there, I guess. I loved that.

Jerry's first-grade class

I taught my music students at home that fall because I was just not up to going to the school. When the morning teaching was over and lunch was finished, Merrill and the boys went back to school, Granny, the girls and I lay down for our naps. I thought of the girls sleeping and, as I felt the delicate movements of the child within me, I was filled with warm emotions. My swollen abdomen was a constant reminder that it wouldn't be long before the little bassinet in the corner would be filled.

When the girls woke up, we settled down in a rocking chair—one sat beside me and the other snuggled down in my lap. For thirty or forty minutes they listened as I read *Little Red Riding Hood, Billy Goat Gruff* or some other favorite book before the idea hit one that it was time to have a tea party. Down they crawled, running for their dolls and the little tea set and their imaginations took them into another world of make believe. About then I would hear a noise on the outside and the front door would swing open, and in would come the boys. School was out. "Wipe your feet," I would holler as they yelled, "Watcha got to eat?"

I got so tired of the questions that were asked me—typical questions asked pregnant women—"Do you want a boy or girl?" "It doesn't really matter," I would answer. Another one was, "When is the baby due?" or "Not again?" As many times as I heard this question, I never could think of a good answer. It looked like, under the circumstances, they could have answered that one for themselves. When asked, "What are you going to name it?" I always said, "We haven't decided."

We found a lady who promised to come and stay with us when the baby came. We drove over to her house one afternoon after school to finalize our plans and before we got home I started having labor pains. Merrill ran to the telephone downtown to call the doctor and hurried back to help me get things ready. He put water on the stove to heat. When the doctor and his nurse came, Merrill held my hand and waited for instructions from them. For the first time, Mother was not there and he felt more of the responsibility of helping deliver the baby. He was glad he could be there to receive daughter number three into the family and the wide, wide world. She was tiny and dainty, a perfect baby.

We wondered what to name her. Merrill thought she should have my name, so we decided to name her Helen Annette and call her Annette. It so happened that she was born on December 15, which was Granny's birthday, so Granny thought she had a real birthday present. This brought about a close relationship between the two. A couple of days later on December 17, Ruth, her roommate, Jean Dixon, and two boys from Arkansas State Teachers College stopped by to pick up our boys to go to Michigan for Christmas. Mother wanted them to come, thinking this would help with my recovery.

Of course, we were lost without Bill and Jerry. We kept the Christmas tree up for them and their presents on the window seat. When they returned, they were excited to get home. They had had a grand time. They saw a lot of snow and ice, three of the Great Lakes and Mother even took them into Canada. They had much to tell. The riders from Teachers College proved to be a big help on the trip. They entertained the boys and that was fun. But the boys "broke their necks" to get to the window box and their presents.

During the winter months, we had our hands full at night. I would have to nurse Annette and change her diaper. Often I would crawl back in bed and hear the cry, "I need the slop jar," or worse yet, "My bed's wet, and I didn't do it." I would change the bed, get back to sleep and someone would need a drink of water. Well, you know what that meant. Then might come the call, "Mamma, Bill's pulling the cover off of me." One of us would get up and make the round to see that everyone was covered. If one of the girls couldn't sleep, Merrill would walk the floor with their blonde head on his shoulder until they went to sleep. Of course, sometimes there were cases of the croup or the colic. By the time we got ready to sleep again, we would hear the roosters begin to crow, telling us the night was over. Well, it might have been over for them, but not for me. There was at least thirty minutes before I had to hit the floor running.

Now there is nothing as sweet as a cute, tiny baby snuggled up on your shoulder, maybe feeling of your face. What a bonus for the nights you walk the floor when they have the colic or their nose is so stopped up they can't breathe. We said those cute little girls on the floor reminded us of the lines from *My Blue Heaven,* "Babies on the floor, who could ask for more." And questions spouting from the boy's chocolate-covered mouths. "What's this? Can I do this? Can I do that?" *"Why? Why? Why?"* was a real challenge. All this made one agree with Erma Bombeck. "Each baby is a prize package, a reward, a wonderful blessing."

We had an iron baby bed enameled white.

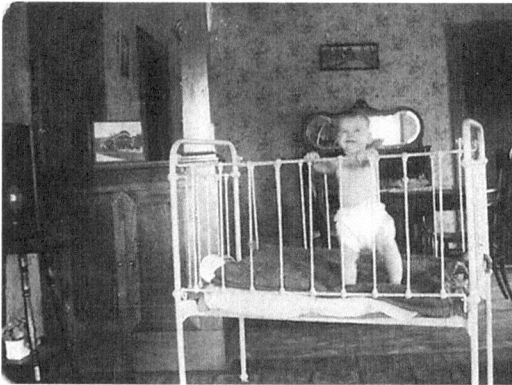

Baby bed

It has been enameled over and over, because Ruth and Jim had used it as well as all of our kids. There were bumps and bumps where the enamel had broken and been painted over. But broken it should be. When the child was big enough to pull up to the sides, they would stand and sway back and forth, shaking the bed as hard as they could. They would bang their toys against the sides and walk around and around the bed smiling at everyone they saw. Not always smiling, maybe, when they got tired, wet or hungry, they screamed "bloody murder" until someone came and rescued them.

Sometimes I would be brave and put Annette down on the floor to crawl. But, everything had to be "baby proofed." That meant no needles, pins, buttons or marbles on the floor, not anything she could put in her mouth. When she was able to pull up, nothing could be on the low tables or window seat, because it would be torn up or perhaps broken. That poor child crawled all over the floor, then sucked her thumb, chewed on toys all the household had kicked around. But despite all the germs, she was a healthy baby.

Granny loved to sit with a pan of apples and scrape a mouthful for Annette and each child gathered around her. Sometimes I thought Bette and Carolyn took advantage of the situation because both were old enough to chew an apple. But Granny loved doing it for them and they accepted her generosity.

It was such a joy to get the baby to sleep and watch Carolyn standing on tip toe peeking into the crib. Bette would sometimes slip her favorite doll in the bed with her while she slept. They were always anxious for her to wake up so they could get down on their hands and knees and crawl with her. The boys were always eager to give her a quick but loving hug. These are the things that thrill a mother and makes memories of a large family wonderful to recall.

It's funny how we waited for the baby to say her first word. She cooed and gooed, but finally one day one of the kids yelled, "Did you hear that. The baby said 'Da da.'" Now why "Da da" instead of "Mam ma"—I'll never know. But she had fun hollering "Da da, Da da" over and over. And, of course, this pleased "guess who?"

As soon as I was strong enough, I started teaching three music lessons each morning. I had fifteen students taking a lesson a week. I also taught Bill, Jerry and Bette. This was a great joy to me. I loved my students, and it was a change from housework and caring for children. Too, it supplemented our meager income.

Summer came and with it more outdoor activities. The kids could play outside. There was the gardening to do, baby chickens to care for and grass to mow. The girls loved to play house and, of course, Bill was happy he had a horse to ride.

Merrill in uniform

Merrill went to Ft. Crook, Neb., this summer. I drove him to the railroad station. I returned home wondering if I could make it alone. How I missed him and his help with all the vegetables to can and the children to care for.

After two weeks Merrill came home talking about the intense training they had had using gas masks and other war-related activities. He said he felt like war was accelerating in Europe. And in the fall it was indeed true. The Nazis swept through Denmark and Norway, the low countries and into France. They began massing their forces for the defeat of England. Everyone in the United States was getting more and more concerned.

Mother decided to move from Flint, Michigan. She took a Civil Service examination and was given a job as an auditor in the War Department. Her ability and love of math had paid off. So Ruth, Jim and Mother moved to Washington, D.C. She put Jim in a high school in Washington and Ruth entered the Washington School for Secretaries. We were glad to see them getting settled permanently. Mother loved her job. She worked in the Pentagon until she retired. She moved to Arlington, Virginia, after the first year and that was her much loved home.

Bettelyn started to school in the fall of 1939. Mrs. Watkins was her first teacher, just as she was Jerry's. The district also had bought new school buses. They put some gasoline tanks between our house and the school, so this was a common sight from our front door. They would line up and refill their tanks before the afternoon run. Since three of the kids were in school, I went back to the school to teach piano. I also organized a small orchestra.

Merrill had a good basketball team. J. W. Fullerton and Louis Brown Tilley were outstanding.

Merrill's basketball team at Valley Springs

This is a picture of the starting five. The old yell the kids had was certainly suitable for this team.

Green and white!

Green and white!

Valley Springs,

Watch 'em fight!

When basketball season started, the school board ruled that only basketball players and cheerleaders could ride the school bus to the games. Some of the girls were determined to go to the basketball games, so they fell on the idea of organizing a girls' basketball team so they could ride the bus with the boy's team. They asked me to coach them.

This was certainly out of my field, but Merrill said he would help me. We had fun even if we didn't win many games.

Helen's basketball team at Valley Springs

In the spring Merrill suggested to the school board that they have a garden for the school lunch program. He told them the WPA would hire a gardener and they could raise vegetables to supplement the surplus food. We offered to buy a mule for the gardener to use. The school board approved the project and agreed to use some of the school property near our house for the garden. So we became the owner of a mule. The old mule had to do double duty. He had to pull the plow and also let our kids ride him. That was fun for them.

The garden was a big success. It produced lots of vegetables. There was a canning project in the summer with the WPA furnishing the labor. A lot of food was provided for the lunch program, making the meals more tasty and desirable.

We were busy with our own gardening and canning. We made sort of a game out of it each summer, seeing how many cans we could fill in a day. We usually had more than 800 quarts by winter. We spent many happy hours together over the sink and cook stove. Don't think we never fussed—we did—but we "made up" in a short time.

Merrill took great pride in his flower beds. Most of the flowers were the old-fashioned hollyhocks and irises.

Annette grew up fast with all the attention she got from Granny and the other children. As I said, she was very special because she was born on her birthday.

When graduation time came, the senior class chose to go to the University of Arkansas. We went in the back of a truck. It rained "cats and dogs" so we had to use a tarpaulin for protection. We had to eat our picnic lunch inside the truck. The students had a great time exploring the buildings on campus. One of their favorites was the museum. Merrill was anxious for them to get a good feeling about campus life. He hoped several of them would make an effort to go on to college. Not many graduates continued their education and he felt it was so important.

This year Merrill went to Ft. Leavenworth, Kansas. When he returned he was very concerned. He said most everyone feared the United States would be drawn into the war before long. As he had done in the years before, he decided on something special to use some of the money for. This year he wanted to enclose our back porch. We needed more room and this would make a nice addition and actually finish the house as it was initially planned. He made arrangements for a carpenter to do the work before winter.

Granny and Annette were almost inseparable. When Granny hobbled down to the henhouse to see about the eggs, Annette was behind her. Or, when Annette wanted to climb up and down the steps separating the yard and the barnyard, Granny was beside her.

Mother and Jim came for a visit each summer. We were so glad to have them come. Mother played with the children just like she was their size. Ruth was not with Mother and Jim at this time.

By fall of 1940, bombing was going on in England. We heard that cathedrals were being destroyed and cities were bombed daily. Palaces were being camouflaged to try to save them from being targets of the German planes that made raids every night. The people spent much time in air raid shelters. It was frightening.

The presidential election of 1940 was very important. We were anxious that F.D.R. be reelected because we believed he would keep us out of war. Peace was the theme of Roosevelt's campaign speeches.

We heard him say, *"I have said this before, but I shall say it again and again and again: Your boys will not be sent into any foreign war."* Roosevelt's policy was to give England all the aid possible, while rearming this country to make it impregnable against attack in case England fell, as we were next on Hitler's list. Meanwhile, we should not fight unless attacked.

Roosevelt defeated Wendell Willkie and was reelected. Despite his efforts to prevent U. S. intervention in the war and policies that could lead to it, the imminence of war was in the air. We all had the feeling that it could not be long before we would be involved. We listened intently to the news broadcast every night. I think all of this drew us closer as a family. We had anxieties but we lived each day to the fullest.

The diaper age was past, but there was always something. Perhaps a loose tooth that had to be pulled. This required a sewing thread and much patience to tie the thread around a tiny slick tooth. It would keep slipping off, or the kid would start hollering, "Wait, wait—oh, it's bleeding now. Stop! Stop!" But, determination would finally get the tooth. Then they were so proud of it, and the hole left by the missing tooth. That was a sign of growing up. And besides, there was a tooth fairy—a very poor one, however.

On occasion there was bubble gum in the hair. What a mess! One could pull and struggle, hair by hair, and usually end up cutting it out, leaving an awful gap on that side of what was a beautiful head of hair. A common ailment was blisters on the heel, especially if the child was wearing a pair of "hand-me-downs" that were a little too large. Problem after problem—but all of them temporary. The good times our family had far outweighed the bad times.

Our back porch was finished before winter, as promised and it really was a good addition to our house. We had more protection, more room and it was more attractive.

As school day approached, the clothes had to be categorized. They fell into three categories: school clothes, play clothes and Sunday clothes. School clothes consisted of new overalls and cotton shirts for the boys and new print dresses for Bette. Play clothes were last year's school clothes (with overall legs cut off for summer). Sunday clothes were a pair of wool or corduroy pants, nice shirt, a long-sleeved slipover sweater for the boys and a nice dress for the girls.

The first thing the kids did after school was change into play clothes. This served two purposes—it cut down on the laundry and made the school clothes last longer.

I tried to mend every tear, replace every button and patch every worn out spot as soon as I saw the need. I had a button box and every time a piece of clothing was discarded to the rag bag, the buttons were cut off and put in the button box to be used again. On our meager income, we had to take care of what we had. And still, carefully laid economic plans made the first of every month seem to always come up short. I often saw Merrill pick up a couple or three hens and take them to the store to sell in order to pay a bill.

School started as usual in 1940–41.

School pictures of Helen and Merrill

The children were glad to get back on the playground with their friends. Billie Jon was out early to meet the school buses because his best friends (and cousins), Joe Bill and T. J., would be on them. They were a little older than Bill but he liked nothing better than playing ball or tagging around with them. He never hurried home when school was out like Jerry and Bette did.

I had more music students than ever that fall, a total of thirty-two. I was glad because I felt it important for many children to have some musical training. There was also another small orchestra, and I continued coaching the girls' basketball team. So you can see, I was a busy person.

Merrill was given a new assignment that fall. He was adviser to the annual staff. He was very creative and he came up with a different format. This year's basketball team was perhaps the best one Merrill ever coached. Some of them received basketball scholarships and played on college teams.

Fall came and with it cool weather. This called for an adjustment of clothes. Coats, sweaters, jackets, pants, dresses, etc. were all tried on to see who could wear what. New warm clothes had to be bought for Bill and Bette because they had grown so much. That left Jerry, Carolyn and Annette wearing hand-me-downs.

Early in the fall, as happened so often, Mother came to their relief. For Carolyn's birthday on November 25th and Annette's on December 15th, she sent two beautiful suits for their presents. Both were a shade of rose, Carolyn's was trimmed in mauve velvet and Annette's in white lace and embroidery. They were the best-dressed kids in town. All went well until Carolyn decided to go to school to visit and when the kids saw her pointed cap, they called her a witch. She never liked the cap any more. Jerry and Bette wanted snow suits that were very warm. Bill chose a plaid wool jacket and a leather cap with goggles.

Ruth was working in the State Department in Washington and she had to dress like a career woman so, as a result, I fell heir to some good suits as she discarded them. Merrill bought a leather jacket for himself, so we were all fixed up for the winter.

Merrill and Helen on school steps

I was glad we didn't live far from school. When it was bleak and cold and the wind howled around the corners, sometimes blowing snow into high drifts, I was glad to get my family home and all warm and safe inside.

Christmas and the winter of 1941 was the last one our family would ever have together. We did not know that, but there was a strange feeling inside me. Haven't you had a feeling that something strange and unknown was happening? Well, I did.

A stormy spring came on. The school board began to take second thoughts about the school lunch program, and Merrill got into trouble with some of the board members. They did not believe social service should be a part of the public schools. Merrill thought the lunch program was a gift of love to the district. We didn't have much money ourselves, but we did have a job, a good place to live (thanks to Mother and Dad) and ample food. Many in the district were not so fortunate. Merrill wanted to help them. Some objected strongly.

One day in early spring, I started having terrible pain in my side. It was almost unbearable. Merrill called Dr. Kirby and he came down to see about me. The doctor took one look at me and said, "That's appendicitis. Go call an ambulance. We have to get to the hospital before this thing ruptures." The ambulance came and the attendants lifted me onto the stretcher. Since it was a cool day, they put a sheet over my face to carry me outside to the ambulance. Now for an ambulance to come to Valley Springs to pick up someone sick was unheard of. A neighbor man coming down the mountain road, saw me being carried out and thought, "Oh, Mrs. Hudson (Granny) has died." He hurried to help carry the corpse to the hearse. When they rolled me into the ambulance and I took my hands and removed the sheet from over my head, the poor man jumped as if he had seen a ghost. I remember as I passed the school, all the windows were filled with kids to see me go by. Granny would say, "It was a sight for sore eyes."

I had a rough time at the hospital. For fourteen days, I was kept in bed. Merrill drove up to see me each day after school. When he came to take me home, Dr. Kirby picked me up and carried me to the car. I don't know when I was allowed to walk. Certainly times have changed in this field.

Six weeks passed and on Sunday afternoon Merrill had the same type of pain. I drove him to Harrison to the doctor's office. Dr. Kirby was out of town for the day so Dr. McCoy, his partner, examined him. Yes, it was appendicitis. "Nothing to do but operate," he said. During the six weeks since my operation, their hospital, a large frame house, had burned. He prepared to operate in his office. He called in his nurses and left word for Dr. Kirby to come as soon as he got back home. When Dr. Kirby arrived just after dark, everything was ready to proceed.

The doctor looked at me and said, "Now if you want to, you can come in and sit in the corner rather than stay out here by yourself." I went in. Since I had just recovered from my operation, I thought I was an old hand at surgery. Well, I wished I had refused the offer and stayed outside. All the strange noises Merrill was making made me think he was strangling to death. When they got to the appendix, one doctor said, "Look at that red hot appendix." I jumped up to look. They swatted me back down—they were not talking to me! I was glad when that operation was over.

A nurse stayed with Merrill for several nights. I stayed after the doctor thought he could release the nurse. One night, he got very sick. He was wild. He got his feet against the wall and shoved the bed across the room. He said he was in very bad pain. I called the nurse and she said she would come help me if I would come for her. I made the trip across town and picked her up. When she saw how he was suffering, she gave him a shot. This quieted him and we made it through the night. The next morning, when the doctor came and found the nurse there, he said, "What's the matter?" The nurse told him what had happened. He said to the nurse, "I told you not to give him another shot. His body is playing tricks on him to get morphine. Now he will have another spell." When I took Merrill home, the doctor told me to expect another cry for morphine, then he added, "Don't call me to come, because I won't come."

Two or three days passed with no trouble. Then one night, about two o'clock, he got deathly sick. It was altogether different from the spell he had had in the office. I thought he was about to die, so I got in the car and drove four miles to the switchboard at Bellefonte to call the doctor only to hear, "I told you not to call me."

"But this is different, Doctor, he is going to die," I said.

"I guarantee you he won't die and I will be down tomorrow," he told me. We struggled through the night. He didn't die and the doctor came as promised and left saying, "It may happen again, but maybe it's over."

It was over, thank goodness! This experience made me know how quickly the body can become addicted to drugs and how helpless the person is who has the addiction.

As the March winds blew and spring approached, war clouds began to gather. It looked as if we might be drawn into the struggle with Germany or Japan. Then news came that all reserve officers were to be called up for one-year's active duty to train a large army.

Merrill was a reserve officer. This meant he would be getting orders soon. Tears stung my eyes. I had thought I had Merrill "for keeps," but it was no longer true. Now I was beginning to understand that premonition I had been feeling.

We continued our work as usual. Teaching, gardening, washing and ironing. There were at least twenty-one starched dresses hanging on the clothesline every week. There was a cow to be milked, chickens to be fed and children to love. All this kept us going but our minds were disturbed.

Merrill knew that he had a choice, he could go or he could withdraw his commission. No man would be required to go if he were an ordained minister or if he were the head of a large family. Merrill was both. Yet, his loyalty would not allow him to think of backing out now that his country needed him. He said, "I have depended on active-duty income to exist when no danger was faced; now that there is danger, I will not pull out. I could not live with myself."

We began to make our plans to accept the orders whenever they came. Merrill said, "I must have some pictures of you and the children to carry with me. So we all dressed up and went into Harrison to have Mr. Case make some pictures.

Merrill, Helen and five kids

Bette wore a navy blue dress that I had made for her out of an old crepe dress of mine. I embroidered it with white, and she liked it. I made a top out of new material for Carolyn and used some old material to make a skirt that buttoned to the blouse. Annette wore a pink dress Mom had sent her, so she was really dressed up. I wore a black chiffon velvet someone had given me.

Orders soon came for Merrill to report to Camp Robinson near Little Rock, Arkansas, on June 13, 1941. We talked it over and decided, rather than living in Little Rock, we would rather live in Conway. I could not think of moving into a city. Conway was about thirty miles from Camp Robinson. With its 8,000 people, it seemed large to me compared to Omaha and Valley Springs. Merrill went to Conway and found a house near the schools at 1129 Davis. So we began to pack to move.

To protect the reserve officers who were being called into duty, a law was passed that said if a man was taken off his job for service, his employer would have to give him a job equal or superior to the one he left at the end of his military duty. The president of the school board wanted to get out from under this requirement. He called a board meeting just before we left and got enough votes to not renew Merrill's contract at the end of the school term, which was prior to June 13. When Merrill was notified of this action, it broke his heart. There was no time for appeal or even to talk with them, so he left feeling defeated.

Dear Ones,

As I promised, I have written down more memories for you.

I thought this Mother's Day would be a good time to pass these pages on to you with a promise of more to come.

I am so thankful that God trusted me with five wonderful children and, in turn, trusted them with children and on and on. I feel so blessed to have had the opportunity to mother, grandmother and great grandmother a fine bunch of kids. I am so proud of each one of you. And, you make Mother's Day a day of real celebration for me!

There may be things I write that you remember in a little different way, but just understand my memory is not perfect. I have been known to make mistakes, but the things I am telling you will help you know how we lived. That is the main purpose of the book—it is not history or a legal document.

I will, someday, take you back to Valley Springs and our experiences there—in the meantime know

I love you,
Granny, 1985

Part 3: 1941-1944

$\mathcal{E}$arly on the morning of Friday the 13th, we pulled away from the little pink sandstone home on our way to Conway, Arkansas, our home for the year of active duty. Bill was eleven years old, Jerry was nine, Bettelyn was seven, Carolyn five and Annette was one and one half. Of course, Granny was with us, too. The truck, loaded with all our belongings, followed us. After about three hours, we arrived at the white frame house. The eight of us piled out of the car and hurried into the house to explore from room to room. The rooms were large. It was a rambling house. It seemed the kitchen was a long way from the living room. Open gas stoves provided the heat. There was running water, a hot water tank and a bathroom. This was a good place for us. There was a little pasture and a shed at the back for Ol' Jersey, our cow. The school was up the street a couple of blocks and a small corner grocery was just a block away.

The men unloaded the furniture and placed it in the proper rooms. We stored our wood stoves on the back porch, along with other things we would not be using during this year. As soon as possible, Merrill paid the movers, kissed us goodbye and left for Camp Robinson to report in, promising to return as soon as possible.

I left Granny with the children and walked up town to make deposits for the utilities so we could get them turned on. When I got back in sight of the house, I saw Bill and Jerry in the top of a big sycamore tree in the front yard. When I got close, I said, "What are you boys doing up there?" They said they had heard a train and they wanted to see it. "Poor kids," I thought, "Country come to town." But, it had been a long time since they had seen a train so I expect it would have been a sight.

Dark came and I got the children all inside the house. Here was a bathtub with plenty of water. What a change! I bathed Carolyn and Annette together in the shining white tub half filled with warm water. I dried their hair and they put on a clean gown and were soon tucked into bed. I went back to the bathroom and called Bette. "It's your turn now," I said. I looked at the grimy waster and quickly pulled the plug. Tonight we would each have our own bath water. The zinc tub in the kitchen was only a memory.

We got ourselves settled down for the night. I felt so alone. In fact, I felt frightened. This was a town of mixed races. All my fears and prejudices of the black race took over. I just knew a black man was looking in every window. I didn't dare say a word to Granny or the children. Granny would have said, "Shut your mouth!" She wasn't afraid of anything or anybody. She would have been ashamed of me. The kids found other children in the neighborhood and soon made new friends.

Merrill came back for the weekend bringing postcard pictures of Camp Robinson, so he could show us where he was stationed.

Post Exchange

He seemed to be pleased with the camp. He was anxious to get back and get into the routine of training the enlisted men that had been assigned the company of which he was commander. We asked him lots of questions about where he slept, where he ate, what there was to do there, etc. After all, that was why he brought the postcards, so we could see. He explained that this was his living quarters and the building at the back was the Mess Hall where he ate.

When it came close to the end of the month after we moved, we were anxious for payday to come. The cabinets held little food, my purse held no money, and worst of all, our bank account was empty. With moving expenses, utility deposits and a month's living costs coming out of our meager bank account, it was really deflated.

Merrill came home that Saturday morning with a depressed look on his face. He announced, "I got no money today. I failed to sign the payroll and it will be Monday before I can get paid." He told me he was going to the bank and borrow enough money to get us over the weekend. He needed a haircut

Lt. Merrill Cole

and we had to have some groceries. Soon he returned. "The bank turned me down," he said and continued, "They said I had no credit rating and they refused to let me use the car or the cow for collateral." There was a long silence. I stood there, frozen, not wanting to say any more yet unable to walk away. Merrill said, "I'm sorry I got us all into this," His voice was almost a sob. He went on, "It was a stupid mistake to not sign the payroll, but I didn't understand so much red tape."

I said, "We will find some way to get something to eat. I'll go down to the little store and ask Mr. Nixon to let us have some bread and a few things on the credit." I, too, was refused. He said he couldn't let me have any groceries. He explained that we were "army people," new in town and they only extended credit to Conway residents. In other words, he couldn't trust us.

The only thing we knew to do was call Mother and ask her to wire us some money. We called and we called, but no answer. In desperation,

I called a cousin, Austin Barker, who lived near her, to see if he knew where she was. He didn't. I asked him to keep trying to get Mother and tell her we needed some money. (We couldn't afford but one telephone call.) He promised, and Merrill waited for her wire until Western Union closed at six p.m. Still no money.

Then Merrill remembered Mr. Russell, our dear old teacher, who moved to a farmhouse a few miles out of Conway. He said he would drive out there and see if he could borrow $5 from him. When he returned, he had the $5 and he told me how Mr. Russell had written a check for $5 and told him to get Horton's Service Station to cash it and hold the check until he picked it up. Mr. Russell had no money either. This was the way Merrill managed to have his hair cut and buy us a few things to eat.

Western Union opened for an hour at 8 a.m. on Sunday morning. Merrill was there waiting, and so was the money from Mother. He got the cash and started out to Mr. Russell's to give him his $5. He met them coming in to Sunday School, so the loan was repaid in the middle of the road and all was sunny again.

Merrill came home often during the summer. We hardly knew anyone, as we lived very selfishly to ourselves. The few hours he had at home were too precious to be spent anywhere else and, besides, we were "army people," very strange, I reckon.

We got the kids dressed and sent them to Sunday school and church, but never went ourselves. When he was on duty over the weekend, I usually drove down to see him on Sunday afternoon. The four oldest kids would go to the movie and Granny and Annette would take a nap and then play or read.

I had to go back in time to milk. I would sit on a tomato crate and stick my head against the cow's flank to keep my balance and also to get my face out of the way of her tail, when she switched flies. One evening, I was milking and telling Annette what a good old cow Jersey was to give us all that good milk. She was so thankful and to show Jersey how much she loved her, she leaned over and kissed her on the hind leg. I didn't intend for her to be that thankful.

Billie Jon wanted to make some money, so we let him sell papers on the street corner downtown. There's where he got the nickname, "Slo Jon." The paperboys were very good friends. One day he brought a little black friend, "Lightening," home with him to get a sandwich and a glass of milk. Bill has told me how fast I fixed that peanut butter sandwich and got them out of the house. I guess that is why they say parents don't actually teach their children to be prejudiced, it is contagious.

We bore the stigma of "Army people" for several months. One day a woman from the Red Cross stopped at the door. She had some yarn in her hand and said, "Here is the yarn you wanted." I told her I had not asked for any yarn. She said, "Well, some woman did whose husband was in the Army, and a man down the street told me some army people lived here, so I guessed it was you."

One Sunday, I remember, soon after the children started to Sunday school, a car stopped in front of the house and a well-dressed lady came to the door. She came in and was friendly, until she found out we were not the Coles she was looking for. She said, "Oh, they said Merle Cole's children had enrolled in Sunday school and they gave me this address." I tried to explain that my husband was at Camp Robinson, but she wasn't interested. She wouldn't give me time to say we were Baptists, newcomers needing a church or anything. I thought, "I don't want to go to your church. We are not strange people. My husband was a school teacher six weeks ago and now he is just a reserve officer on duty for a year."

Fall came and I had not made one friend in Conway. I guess it was partly my fault, but I thought it was the coldest town I had ever seen. None of the neighbors came to call. I was so lonely. In addition to being Army people, I felt I was too uneducated to associate with the college people. After all, there were three colleges in Conway and I probably was the only one in town with just a high school education, I thought.

Another thing—we had five kids. Maybe this was frowned on in a cultural town like Conway. Oh, my imagination was working overtime. But one Sunday afternoon, Merrill was home and we went to the service station to get some gas. Four of the kids wanted to ride with us, so they piled into the back seat. The man filled our car, took our money and, when he brought back the change, he looked in the back seat and said, "Looks like you picked up the whole neighborhood." I wanted to say, "What are you talking about? We have another one at home." But, we laughed and went on thinking, "If that man only knew."

In spite of my inferiority complex, I decided to go to the church with the kids one Sunday evening. When I got near the church, several people were standing outside talking. A sweet lady in a print dress approached me and said, "I'm Olive Ferguson," then turned toward a man and said, "This is my husband, Clarence." I told them my name and they took me "under their wing." I sat with them during church and felt so welcomed. She invited me to a Sunday School class meeting at Clara Mae Speaker's. I was happy to go with her. When we pulled up in front of Clara Mae's house, Olive said, "I have to hurry home and fix supper for my husband; he has a meeting tonight." I asked, "What does your husband do?" Expecting her to say he works in a factory or at a service station, she said, "He is Dean at Teacher's College."

Here were two people I was dodging. They didn't appear educated to me. They seemed like good old common folks. And, best of all, we were already friends. This sobered me up and I joined the Sunday School class and attended when Merrill wasn't home.

The County Fair catalog came out in September and there was an award of $1 offered to the first person that could repeat by memory the advertisers in order of their appearance in the catalog. This was too good an offer for Bill to miss. He took the catalog and began to memorize the businesses, one after the other. This was difficult, since he was new in town and not familiar with such old companies as Farenthal & Schwarz, Hambuchen Lumber Co., Erbacher's Meat Market and hundreds of other strange names. (Perhaps I should have said dozens.) But, Bill was determined to win that dollar. On the first day of the contest, he was there when the office opened and rattled off the names, much to the surprise of those responsible. He came home with his dollar clutched in his hand and a proud look on his face. "Quite an accomplishment," I thought, as I hugged him tight.

Merrill was asked to coach a basketball team for his outfit and so he was busier than usual. His visits home were cut down some. He had games scheduled with various college teams for the fall and winter. We planned to see those in Conway.

On Sunday, December 7th, Merrill was home, lying on the sofa with the radio on. Suddenly, they interrupted the program with the announcement, "Pearl Harbor has been bombed by the Japanese." They continued to tell as much as was known. They kept repeating, "All servicemen are ordered to remain at their bases or return immediately if you are away." Merrill jumped up and ran to the bathroom to shave and get ready to go back to camp. I wanted him to stay around and listen for more news, but he knew where his duty lay, and he left almost immediately.

What a feeling! Hardly six months had passed since he came in for a year and now war was really on us.

He brought his basketball team up to State Teachers and I got to see him for a few minutes. He told me the rumor was that they would soon be shipping out of Camp Robinson. He expected this to be the last basketball game, as they were busy with more important things. We hardly saw him at home again. He wanted me to have a picture made for him to take with him. He had not liked my picture made in Harrison because I looked so grim. He said, "I want you to look as pretty as you can. Have your hair done and smile just for me." Mr. Sam Fausett made the picture. Merrill was pleased. On the surface I may look calm, but my stomach was tied in knots.

His picture was in color. The dress was brown with a pale pink collar. Four years later his picture was returned to me with his personal belongings from Germany. But, I'm getting ahead with my story.

Helen Marie

A week passed and Merrill said, "It is any day now." So for three days, I got up early, milked, left Granny with the children and drove to the gates of Camp Robinson and waited for them to open. I did not know if Merrill's outfit would still be there or not. But each morning I found him. They were all packed and ready, just waiting for the orders to come to move out—where to? No one knew. We held hands and hardly said a word. My throat was all choked up and butterflies were in my stomach. I stayed until time for the gates to close at night, and then we would hold each other close and kiss goodbye, not knowing whether there would be a tomorrow or not.

On the third day, just after noon, the orders came. So, we said goodbye and I left as they lined up to march to their troop train. "*Why? Why? Why?*" I kept asking myself. There was no answer I could hear. I kept hearing President Roosevelt saying, "The only thing to fear is fear itself." I couldn't understand this. I was afraid, very much afraid. I gritted my teeth and drove back to Conway.

This was our baby's second birthday—Granny's, too. It was not a happy birthday—the 15th of December, 1941.

The days passed slowly. One day a card came in the mail. It had been dropped from the troop train and someone had found it and had been kind enough to pick it up and mail it. It read something like this: "Here I am sitting on the track just outside of Conway, wishing I weren't going so far away from my family. I will write as soon as I can, in the meantime, know that I love you. Merrill"

And so it was, the entire 35th Division was moved from Camp Robinson to the West Coast. They were housed at Ft. Lewis, near Tacoma, Washington. Merrill wrote every day, so letters came often. But he seemed to be so far away. They did not know how long they would be there, but they knew it would not be long.

Soon after Christmas, Merrill wrote that he felt I should move the children to Harrison because he might be gone for a long time. He did not want me to move back to Valley Springs with water to carry and so much gardening to do. He thought I would be happier in Harrison near our relatives.

Early in January, I took the boys with me and went to Harrison to find a house to rent. We picked up Myrtle and she went with us to house hunt. After a hard day in the rain, we found a house on North Vine

Street near the First Baptist Church and not far from Uncle Willie's. I gave the lady a check for the first month's rent and returned home.

The fog was so dense around Marshall and Clinton that we could hardly see the road. Bill rolled the windows down and stuck his head out to see that I did not leave the highway. I struggled and strained to see the white lane, sometimes stopping to blink my eyes and get them in focus again. We got home very late, dead tired. My neck and shoulders were killing me.

The next morning I got up early and went to town to get packing boxes and make arrangements with a mover. When I got home, the mail had come and in it my check with a note from the lady saying, "I have decided I should not rent you my house because you have too many children, so I am returning your check. Sorry." Well, that was it! I was too tired to go back up there to look for another house, and the weather was too bad, I decided to wait until spring.

As I look back, I wonder if that was not God who shut that door. Many times I have thought about how different our lives would have been had we moved back to Harrison.

By this time, I had become acquainted with a couple across the street, the Andersons. He offered to help me with anything around the house that he could. I did call on him when a plumber or an electrician was needed, and he could usually fix it. We learned to love the Andersons and all their family. We called them Daddy Ed and Mamma Jewel.

We almost had a tragedy during the cold days of January. Jerry had the flu and was lying on the sofa in the living room. You may say, "That was too bad." Well, this time it was good. On this cold morning the children and I were up early hovering around the open gas heater in the living room. I picked up a book to read them some stories before I fixed breakfast. All the children gathered around and Annette sat in my lap. She said she was cold, so I picked up a small blanket and pinned it around her shoulders. After a while, someone said, "I'm hungry." So, I sat Annette down and forced myself off toward the kitchen to fix breakfast. I had hardly reached the kitchen when I heard blood-curdling screams from several of the children. I ran and found Bill with Annette down in the floor. He was wrapping her up with a quilt to smother out flames of fire. She had switched around and got the blanket I had pinned around her shoulders in the gas stove. She started screaming and running toward the kitchen. Bill knocked her down and Jerry quickly pitched him the quilt that was covering him, and Annette was not even burned. The quilt with the burned hole is still around to remind me of the thoughtfulness of my boys and the goodness of God.

I went to Sunday school and church regularly. The minister was Dr. Blake Smith who originally came from Harrison. That made me like him from the start. He was a real good preacher. He had not been in Conway long and he had followed a man who had been there thirty-four years. The dear old pastor had married, baptized and buried members of the families in the church, their children and their grandchildren. The people loved him dearly and, as a result, were slow in accepting this new minister with a completely different personality. I could sense a lack of trust and communication from the ones I came in contact with, so my heart ached for him. He meant so much to me and I loved him very much.

The Sunday school class I attended was taught by a dear lady, Mrs. Bohner. How kind she was to me, and I always knew she was remembering me in her prayers. In the class I found Evelyn Burdine, my piano teacher at Newton County Academy. Her name was Evelyn Voyles then. Walter Burdine was superintendent of the academy. Walter's wife had died and he and Evelyn had married. It is funny how a difference in ages becomes so unimportant, hardly noticeable, after people reach adulthood. Evelyn and I became very close friends immediately. She was much taller than I was and one day when she was standing at the door to leave, Annette looked up and said, "Mommie, why didn't you grow up like Mrs. Burdine?"

After Merrill had been on the West Coast a couple of months, I received a telephone call from him at 2 a.m. He said, "I am in Bellingham, Washington, guarding an airport. We could be together if you could make arrangements to come out here. Try hard to come just as quickly as you can. I've got to see you again, and we will only have a few days." I promised to try.

There was, of course, no more sleep for me that night. I called to see what time the train left and was told 4:30 p.m. If I were to catch it, so much would have to be done. I hastily got together the clothes I should take. I thought of whom I would call to come to stay with Granny and the children, but I had to wait until morning to call. I had never traveled in my life, so I needed to borrow a suitcase from Evelyn. I checked the children's clothes and tried to think what I needed to do for them. I couldn't go back to bed. I was so excited. My list of errands grew longer and longer.

Morning came and I told Granny and the children about the call and what I wanted to do. I called Evelyn and talked things over with her. Then, shaking like a leaf, I called my friend, Amy Martin, in Harrison and asked, "Would you come and take care of my family while I go to see Merrill before he goes overseas?" She agreed to get a bus to Conway that afternoon, so all was shaping up for me.

The day passed fast. I had shopping to do, groceries to buy and a million things to do. Evelyn came over with a suitcase for me, and we packed it. I left the house for my last errand, which was to the bank to get money for my ticket and Travelers Checks to carry with me. With money in hand, I went to the depot to buy my ticket. It seemed like it took so long to get anything done. The agent had never heard of Bellingham, Washington. He looked and looked through all his timetables. I was getting more and more nervous. I had left Evelyn with Granny and Annette and told them I would be back and Evelyn could drive me to the train and then pick up Amy at the bus station.

Finally, he decided on the route and started writing out the long, long ticket. I had to change trains about four times. When he totaled it all, it was more money than I had. I said, "Wait, I've got to go across the street and get a Travelers Check cashed." He looked disgusted, but what else could he do? I hurried and I looked at my watch and saw I didn't have time to return home, so I called Evelyn and asked her to bring my suitcase to me, as I couldn't get back in time to pick it up. I took the cash and raced back to the railroad station. I heard the train whistle in the distance. It was nearing Conway. I wished Evelyn would hurry. I paid for my ticket and walked out on the platform, watching for Evelyn.

The elation I felt over getting the chance to see Merrill again struggled with other emotions. *Would the children be all right? Did I think of everything? Would Merrill still be there when I got there? Did I have enough money to get me there and back? Should I have depleted our bank account?* The train pulled into the station and the engine stopped across the street that Evelyn would be on. I hoped she could find her way to another street and make it in time.

The billows of smoke pouring out of the smoke stack made me know it wouldn't be long before the train would be moving out. The whistle blew shrilly. Where was Evelyn with my suitcase? I couldn't go without it. The conductor waved his arms and shouted, *"All aboard!"* The train sputtered and wheezed with the familiar *"chuff-chuff."* It jerked forward and was moving. The ticket agent saw me standing there. He motioned for the train to stop. I told him I didn't have my bag. He said, "Go on, it will catch you." The train came to a stop about fifty yards down the track. The conductor stepped off and motioned for me to hurry. I said, "Sir, I don't have my bag. Will it catch me?" He said, "It may and it may not." I said, "In that case, I'm not going." He angrily mounted the steps and slammed the guard rail shut. The train moved on.

As soon as the last railroad car was across the street, I saw Evelyn coming with my bag. Mary and J. S. Rogers had seen the train stop and me refuse to get on. Mary had come down to pick J. S. up at the drug store for supper. He said, "Who is that?" Mary said, "Oh, that looks like the little woman who has been to the church a few times. Her husband is in the army." J. S. said, "Well, let's see what the trouble is," as he wheeled his car into the parking area.

Evelyn and I told them what had happened and J. S. said, "Get in here, we'll beat the train to Morrilton." Away we went, and we did beat that train to Morrilton, eighteen miles away. We were standing on the platform when the train pulled into the station. The conductor came to the door, saw me, suitcase in hand, and he stepped back, seemingly to catch his breath." "Now, Helen," J. S. said, "don't you take a thing off of that fellow."

I got on the train and sank down in the scratchy red plush seat, with my suitcase on the floor beside me. I looked out the window and waved to my newly found friends. The conductor moved down the aisle checking tickets. He asked me, "How did you get to Morrilton?" I told him. Then I learned the train had stopped at a water tank and that had delayed them. "God works in mysterious ways," I thought, as the telephone poles were sliding past. He punched my ticket and handed it back. "So you are going to Bellingham, Washington. That's a long way."

The train wheels clicked and clacked over the rails. It was February and it was a drab winter. The trees were stark naked and the grass was brown. Settling back into the plush seats, I rolled with the motion of the train, as I watched the fields and towns pass outside my hazy window. I chuckled to myself as I remembered how the conductor looked when he saw me at the railroad station at Morrilton. I wondered what the kids were doing. I wondered if Amy got there. I felt bad that I didn't go to tell the kids and Granny goodbye. Maybe it was easier that way.

It was a long four nights to Bellingham, Washington. The weather grew colder and colder. In fact, we went through a blizzard. The mountains were so interesting to me, especially the mountains in Glacier Park, where every color imaginable was reflected back from that ice covered world. I promised myself a return trip to Glacier Park someday, which was fulfilled about thirty years later.

We reached Spokane, Washington, in the night. I raised my window shade a mite so I could see the town. Later, as we were crossing the Cascades, the conductor noticed the window shade was up, and he shouted, "Lady, lower that shade! Don't you know this train is supposed to be blacked out? Do you want to get us blown off the map?" I was so embarrassed. I lowered the shade and felt like crying.

Homesickness was beginning to take over. I thought of the children and Granny. Every turn of the wheels was taking me farther and farther away from them. I couldn't stand to look at a child. My arms felt so empty. Finally, the train began to slow down and the engineer blew a long warning whistle. The conductor announced that we were coming into Bellingham, Washington. The wheels ground to a stop. I hesitated to get out, "What if Merrill had shipped out and was not there to meet me?" I thought. Then I saw, reflected in the glass, a figure so slender and erect. It was Merrill. My trip was not in vain.

It was a gray, foggy morning. We were near the hotel that was to be our home for a few days, hopefully. Who knew how long it would be until they would call them back to Ft. Lewis. The fact that war was upon us was made more real everywhere one looked. At the hotel, men were working feverishly boarding up the windows. The idea was to black out the whole coastal town. I was thankful my family was far back from the coast in Arkansas.

There was only a small detachment in Bellingham. When Merrill wasn't on duty, he had plenty of freedom. So we were able to take walks, go to the movies, watch the boats at the harbor, and enjoy the extra hours together that we felt were a gift from the Lord. One weekend, we went on a special bus trip to Mt. Baker. The snow was banked alongside the road higher than the bus itself. When we reached the lodge at the top of the mountain, Merrill went in and rented ski shoes for me so I could get out and walk to the lodge—my high-heeled pumps were hardly the thing for that kind of weather.

One Sunday when Merrill was on duty, I went to church. I had heard that Northern Baptists were very inhospitable. But that was wrong. Many, many people greeted me after the service! One man said, "Oh, there's a young lady here who went to Randolph Macon and her roommate was from Arkansas. She will want to meet you." Then he motioned to a girl across the church to come over. She told me the same thing and I said, "Sure 'nough?" She grabbed me and hugged me and said, "That's the first time I have heard 'sure 'nough' since I was in school." For the first time, I realized that "sure 'nough" was not common language everywhere. Later in the afternoon one of the young ladies I met came to the hotel and asked me to have coffee with her in the coffee shop.

One of the officer's wives I met told me about her husband leaving Camp Robinson at the same time Merrill did. She said she was in the hospital in Little Rock having a baby. Her husband was with her. The baby came and he got to hold it before a runner came to tell him they were loading and he must leave. The nurses told her how he took her unconscious form into his arms and held her close, kissed her and left with tears streaming down his face. I was glad our departure was a little less traumatic.

Another person I met greatly affected our childrens' lives. This was a young girl who operated the elevator at the hotel where we stayed. She told us about being a baton twirler in the local high school band. Merrill thought she was so cute, and he got the idea that our girls could learn to twirl a baton, so he bought one for me to take back to them. They did learn to twirl and how! I wished he could have seen them fulfilling his dream, because all three of them learned to twirl and were majorettes in the band. Bette was the drum major of the Conway High School Band for two years.

Every day there was the anxiety of not knowing when the last day of our visit was coming, so every minute was precious. Things seemed to be going well at home, according to Evelyn, so I stayed until orders came for them to return to Ft. Lewis.

When we got to Tacoma, Merrill suggested that I go to the railroad station and try to get a shorter route home. He believed four nights on the train were too much. I took his advice and went to the station. I waited in line to talk with the ticket agent. When my time came to talk to the man, I said, "Sir, I have a ticket to Conway, Arkansas," he interrupted me and began to call, "Lady, lady, come back." The lady who had been in front of me turned around and he motioned to her to come back. She came back with a questioning look on her face. Then he said, "Here is someone else going to Conway, Arkansas." Then we introduced ourselves. She was Connie Lee Springer and I learned she was Carolyn's Sunday school teacher. She did not know when she would be going back, neither did I.

After a couple of days passed, I went down to get my train and there Connie Lee sat crying her heart out. She didn't see me, and I didn't speak to her. I wanted the last minute with Merrill alone, and I told Merrill, "I'll find her on the train." I did and we rode back together and became good friends. When Merrill and I separated, we made a prayer pact to pray together at 3 p.m. central time. That is, I would pray at 3 p.m. every day and he would figure out the time difference wherever he was and join me in prayer the same hour. This prayer time meant so much to me during the next three years.

I learned before I left that he was going to the Aleutian Islands, off the coast of Alaska. He said he would write every day and he wanted me to write him every night and tell him all about the kids and their activities.

When I returned home, I found everything okay. The children seemed so happy to have me home again, and I am sure Granny was. They had lots to tell. Granny told about letting Bette and Carolyn go to a movie one Saturday afternoon. Dark came and they had not returned. She was worried and sent Bill to find them. He went to the theater and there they sat watching the movie, and they said that was the third time they had seen it. They had not realized that the day was over.

On Sunday, we dressed up and went to church and Sunday school. Granny never went, but we had to give her a report when we returned. I had not joined the church yet, so when I told her we had the Lord's Supper, she said, "You didn't take it, did you?" I said, "Yes." Then she gave me her thoughts on closed communion.

Jerry and Bill; Bette, Carolyn and Annette

Merrill wanted me to buy bicycles for the four older kids and a tricycle for Annette when I got my next paycheck. They were thrilled to death. The girls rode up and down the street in front of our house and sometimes on the sidewalk. One day, a big boy in the neighborhood decided to have some fun with a very mean trick. He tied a string across the sidewalk to see what the girls would do. Bette was in front and, when she hit the string, it threw her off her bicycle and bruised her up quite a bit. That young man got a tongue lashing from me.

Bette was victim of another accident that summer. One day, Jerry was pretending he was playing golf (a forecast of years to come). Bette got in the line with his golf club and he hit her on the jaw. We thought her jaw was broken. Jerry kept repeating, "I didn't mean to, Bette, I didn't mean to." We hurried to the doctor. He looked at her and felt the outside of her jaw then said, "Bite my finger." She bit down hard. That was what he wanted her to do. The bite proved the jaw was not broken.

"That was it." I asked. "How much do I owe you?"

He said, "$2." It sounded like doctors were over-charging to me. That was a lot of money then, and I reluctantly pulled out the $2 and gave it to him. I went out thinking to myself, "$2 just to have her bite his finger."

Another accident on North Davis happened when Annette was going to the corner grocery store with Jerry to get some milk. She was skipping along, carrying an empty glass bottle. Before she reached the store, she fell, breaking the bottle. It severed a large vein in her wrist. A neighbor man happened to be in his yard and he saw her and ran to help her. He knew how to apply pressure to stop the bleeding until we could get her to the doctor. This probably saved her life.

Merrill reached the Aleutian Islands and sent pictures of their landing. They were transported almost to shore by small barges and then had to wade on to the beach. This was not beach weather. It was still very cold there.

He also spoke about how they were served their meals and how hard it was to eat with cold hands. He said that the hardest thing he had to do was to give orders as an officer, then stand back and watch the noncommissioned men do the work. He wanted to pitch in and help, but that was taboo with the military.

Merrill wrote every day, but the letters came in bunches. I would miss several days then get a stack. I know his mail from us was the same way. One could not expect daily mail delivery in this remote spot. Merrill said it was heartbreaking to see the disappointment on the men's faces when their names were not heard at mail call. That never happened to him.

Bette had a birthday in April and we invited all the children on the block for a birthday party.

Uncle Lonnie and Aunt Katherine came to see us every summer. This was always a treat. Uncle Lonnie came loaded with cameras and film. He liked to make movies as well as still pictures. We did not make many pictures because of the cost of the film and the developing. I tried to take a few to send to Merrill so he could see how the kids were growing and what they were doing.

Another visitor we had was Uncle Jim. He was in the Navy and was stationed at Memphis. What fun it was for him to come.

One time he came and while he was there he milked Ol' Jersey for me. One night he came in the kitchen saying, "Sister, I had to pick up that cow and carry her back into the barn a half dozen times." I laughed and thought no more about it until one night a month or so later, an insurance man came by to talk to me about some insurance. We were sitting in the living room and suddenly Annette spoke up, "You see that man there?" and pointed to Jim's picture, "He can pick up a cow." I had some explaining to do.

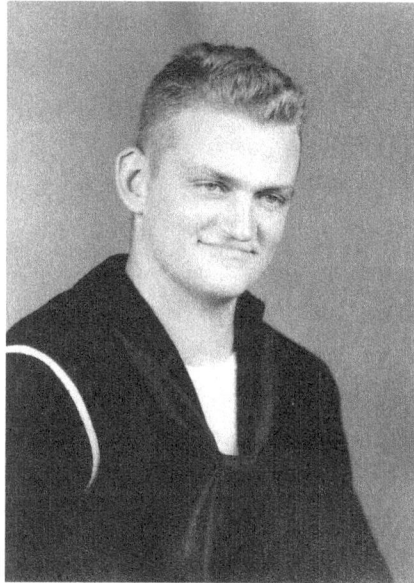

Uncle Jim

That summer I let the four older children go to Vacation Bible School at the Nazarene Church. I thought that would be fine. I was embarrassed when they came home and told me that everyone but them knelt when they prayed. They said they told the teacher that they were Baptists and Baptists didn't kneel to pray.

Merrill loved Granny and he was so glad she was with us. He often wrote something to her in his letters. One time he said, "Buy Granny anything she wants." Annette looked at her immediately and said, "Granny, do you want an ice cream cone?"

By this time, I was beginning to enjoy living in Conway. I loved my Sunday school class. Evelyn, Mary Rogers and Olive Ferguson were such good friends. I continued to write Merrill about our friendships and how much the kids were enjoying Conway. One day, a letter came suggesting that I sell the house in Valley Springs, because he had no plans for returning there, and buy one in Conway. I thought that was a good idea, so I began to look for a house. I found one at 625 Donaghey. The house had not been lived in for several years. A teacher owned the house and had kept it, thinking he might want to move back someday. It was known as the "Parson's House." It happened that Mr. Parsons had decided not to return to Conway, and he had put the house up for sale. There were three lots facing the street and they were lined with chinaberry trees, making it an unusual place.

The house had an upper story. They called it an "airplane sleeping porch"—it had windows on three sides. There was a perfect garden spot. I quickly envisioned rows of vegetables to feed our family. There was a shed or small barn at the back with a place for Ol' Jersey and also room for the chickens. I thought if we could have our own chickens and eggs, what a help that would be. There were three pecan trees in the yard, perfect for the kids to climb, plus nuts. The house was reasonably priced. I hurried to sell our house and then applied for a loan with First Federal Savings and Loan of Little Rock. Mr. Charles D. Johnson was president of the firm. I found him so gracious. He was glad for me to have a loan, not only for the price of the house but also enough to redecorate it, too. So, we purchased the house at 625 Donaghey.

There was a lot of work that had to be done to the house before we moved. Jerry and Bill helped me paint and paper. All was going well until the whooping cough struck. All five kids had it at the same time. What a time! I remember them holding to the posts on the front porch and coughing and whooping until they were thoroughly exhausted.

Friends were good to bring in special things to eat. But they lost every meal. One day, Elizabeth Adams brought them chocolate ice cream. But as soon as they ate it, up it came. Mrs. Bohner had brought strawberry ice cream the day before, so as soon as Carolyn could get her breath, she said, "I wish she had brought the same kind Mrs. Bohner did, it tasted better coming up." I continued to work on the house as much as I could for the six weeks they were sick, but it wasn't easy. I hired a lady to help me at the house during this time. She washed and ironed and cleaned the house for me. It was the first time I had ever had a maid.

One day, I remember getting letters from Merrill telling about their work trying to quickly establish bases on all the Aleutian Islands before the Japanese took possession of them. He feared an attack daily. He sent pictures of the cold ice-covered land and the cemetery that they had set up. All this made me very depressed. I cried and cried. The dear black lady saw me crying. She was ironing. She stopped momentarily and said, "Mrs. Cole, remember George Washington was in the Revolutionary War and didn't get a scratch. Now he got his coattail shot full of holes one time, but the bullets didn't hit him. Maybe it will be the same with Mr. Cole." Bless her heart, she was so serious. I knew she was trying to support me and I appreciated it.

I, too, wanted to be optimistic. I knew the Bible told me that God watched over every sparrow that fell and every lily that bloomed and, even more important, over us. But I was afraid—this was war. I really worried without ceasing instead of praying without ceasing, and I had no peace. I can remember going to church and, as we left the church, Dr. Smith always stood at the door to greet the people. Somehow he knew I could not say a word or I would cry, so he would just squeeze my hand and smile and perhaps later in the day give me a telephone call. He really helped me through some hard times.

I was distressed when my bosom friend, Evelyn, and her husband moved to Fayetteville. They had been such a help to me and were so dear. Our relationship did not end, however. They kept in touch and visited us when they were in our area. There is a card I have kept through the years that have passed, because I thought it was so clever. It was mailed January 3rd and for one-cent postage.

"Dear Marie: This is from the Burdines in the University City, N. W. Arkansas. We are passing thru to L. R. Friday night—five of us and the hound. Now see it is the pause that refreshes. We want to get in there about eight p.m., already 'suppered' up. Then visit till about eleven thirty, then sleep awhile and go on to L. R. Saturday a.m. How about it? Will bring some coffee, eggs and bacon, if definitely necessary, but rather "not." If not satisfactory, get right back to us. Walter."

My answer to this was, "Come on here for supper. I will be standing on the porch with supper on the table." We always enjoyed seeing them.

Another move that affected our lives was a move to Conway. Two of my cousins, Berlin and Ardatha Henderson (married but not related) moved to a house on Western Avenue. Berlin was the grandson of Granny's sister and Ardatha was a granddaughter of Grandpa Hudson's sister. I had gone to school with both of them at Newton County Academy. Berlin was very affectionate and the girls loved that.

Before school started, we were able to move to our new house. The boys were thrilled to have the room upstairs. I told them it was theirs to live in and to keep. The girls had a room, also. It was a great day for us to be in our own home.

The furniture we had fit into the house real well. There was a fireplace in the living room that made the decorating fun. There were built-in shelves on either side of the fireplace. I used an idea I had seen to supplement our furniture. I made some tables out of a whiskey barrel and a nail keg. The other half of the barrel was used for a coffee table. I had glass cut to fit the top of it. The barrels and keg were painted black with the metal bands painted gold. To give them a real "oriental look," I painted a couple of Chinese letters on the nail keg.

Merrill wrote that he wanted the kids to take piano lessons. "Education is not complete without music. Books and music go together," he said. There was a lady in town, Mrs. Bolls, who taught piano. I asked her about teaching the four oldest children. She was happy to have them. I often said she was such a marvelous person that it was worth the price of the lessons to have the children sit for awhile under her care.

The County Fair each fall was a big happening for the older kids. I would give them each a quarter and let them go. I would explain, "Now, you can ride one ride for a dime, have a nickel for soda pop and ten cents for a hamburger. Or, you can have two rides and a soda pop and eat supper at home. I'll be back for you at six o'clock." I guess they took a long time deciding how to spend that quarter. They probably looked over the rides— the Ferris wheel, the merry-go-round, the caterpillar, the dodge-um cars and probably some little airplanes. Or, they could try to win a prize by spending a nickel for three balls to throw at the rag dolls. If you hit three dolls, you won a quarter. That must have been tempting, because then they would have more money to spend. There were balloons for sale, to say nothing about the cotton candy, pop corn, *Cracker Jacks*, hot dogs, hamburgers, ice cream and soda pop. I am sure it was a hard decision to make.

These kinds of things probably caused the boys to decide to get themselves a paper route so they could make some money for themselves. Both delivered the *Log Cabin Democrat*, an afternoon paper, and Bill delivered the *Arkansas Gazette* for a time. This meant he had to get up early, early to make his route.

When Christmas neared, I thought I would take Bette and Carolyn to Little Rock to see the Christmas decorations. They had never seen anything compared to that. We were in Blass Department Store and I wanted to go to an upper floor, so I found the elevator and stepped on when the door opened. As I did, I thought, "Oh, these girls have never ridden on an elevator. They may get frightened." I leaned over and whispered, "Now, this is going to go up." They looked at me with eyes as big as saucers and asked loudly, "Gonna go up?" Everyone in the elevator looked at us so funny. Our secret was out—we were from the country.

Christmas Eve came and we were so lonely. Jim had promised to come and spend Christmas with us but the highways were all closed because of ice and snow. There was absolutely no traffic between Little Rock and Conway, the radio said. We went to bed hoping that conditions would change. When the children woke up, they were still expecting Uncle Jim. We decided that they should open one gift each and then wait for Uncle Jim. I thought it was useless to wait, but it pleased the kids. After a while, my eyes happened to move to the small glass panes in the top of the front door. There I saw a grinning face. It was Uncle Jim! The kids quickly ushered him in. No one had ever been more welcome. He was half frozen. He had managed to get on the last bus to Little Rock, only to find no bus leaving for Conway. He decided to hitchhike and walked to the outskirts of town. He continued walking down the highway, hoping for a ride. He could not see the pot holes and often hit one and went through the ice into water, so his feet were iced over. Finally, a grocery truck from Conway came along and picked him up. He was glad to find us waiting for him.

Ice was not only in Arkansas. Merrill sent a picture from the Aleutians made outside his quarters. He said when he was not on duty, he stayed inside his tent and played his harmonica to try to forget the wind blowing against the flapping tent.

A big change had come over Conway. The Arkansas National Guard had been called up and sent to Alaska. That included the unit from Conway. Many families were touched. If there wasn't a family member included, there certainly were friends and acquaintances. Now the whole town was "Army people." We were no longer a minority. The women organized an Army Mothers' Club, a support group for mothers and wives, that I attended.

I remember a sermon Dr. Smith preached one Sunday entitled, "Staying with the Stuff." He used the Scripture found in 1 Samuel 30:24, *"Whoever stays behind with the supplies gets the same share as the one who goes into battle."* The gist of his sermon was that we who stayed with "the stuff" had as much responsibility to protect the four freedoms our men were fighting for as they did on the battlefield. The four freedoms being: Freedom from fear, Freedom from want, Freedom of speech and Freedom of religion. He told a story to illustrate his point. He said there was once a ship at sea. They had been in search of a valuable pearl. The precious jewel was on board and they were returning home when they saw a pirate ship approaching. They knew if they were to protect the pearl, they must go out and fight.

So one man was selected to stay on board the ship with the pearl and the others went out to fight. The man left kept thinking of the pearl. He got it out of its safety box to look at it only to drop it overboard into the sea. When the men returned to the ship, bleeding and weary, they found the very thing they were fighting for had been lost.

How this sermon spoke to me. Merrill had left me with our five precious children to care for. If I failed—I could not—I would not, I vowed. Believe me, it took me and five guardian angels to keep our five in good shape. There was the time Bette fell off of the monkey ladder at school and hurt her back, Jerry sat down on his thumb at Boy Scouts and broke it, to say nothing of the two concussions Jerry had in bicycle wrecks. Bill had to have an operation for a hernia. There was always something happening, but usually not too serious.

An Easter card came from Merrill that he must have carried with him from the West coast. It was so beautiful I have kept it through the years—to share with you.

Because of you, I've known a lot
Of Happiness and Cheer,
Because of you, my daily life
Has deeper meaning,
Dear;
Because of you, there's gladness
To be looking forward to,
And so I wish you
all the Joy
I know BECAUSE OF YOU!

It doesn't seem so many
years ago when we were
planning & looking forward
to a life together. Just
to live with you, alone,
and be loved by you
is what I'm looking forward
to. I love you,
and I am so
glad you are
my wife —
I love you
Merle

Easter card

Then there was this handwritten note on the opposite page that meant so much to me.

Notes like this kept me going through the years that I waited. During those days there were many pre-breakfast battles. "Those are my socks—if you don't take them off right now, I'll go tell Mother." "Somebody used my tooth brush." "Are you going to stay in that bathroom forever?" "I dare you to hit me! I dare you! I double-dog dare you!" "Mother, he hit me!" Then there were cries like, "Give me time." "I need a quarter for a notebook." "I can't find my pencil. Who got my pencil?" Or, "I need a note for the teacher because I was sick yesterday." I would pray for patience and try to hold my tongue. Often,

Helen Cole Littleton

I am sure, I was irritable and tried to dominate instead of communicate. It was easy to feel sorry for myself.

Probably what saved my sanity were my friends. We had a sewing club and, when we met, the chatter and giggling raised my spirits immensely. This picture of the group was made a few years later.

The Sewing Club

Evelyn and Lila are missing from the picture but you will see from left to right: Maggie Adams, Mary Rogers, Elizabeth Adams, Ardatha Henderson, Olive Ferguson and Katherine Robbins. How often a word of sympathy or encouragement from them helped me get back on my feet.

Time came when the Lord called Blake Smith to the University Baptist Church in Austin, Texas for a much greater service. I remember one Sunday night, he told the congregation that he had received a call from this church and he had been praying for God's guidance. He had asked the Lord for some sign, to ring a bell or something. Then he said, "The bell has not tolled." We thought this meant he would not be going, but a few weeks later, he announced his acceptance. I was sorry he was leaving.

A few weeks later a dear couple, Harold and Retha Tillman, came to our church. Retha immediately came into our little sewing club. She was a real good addition. One day, I remember, we were meeting at her house and Sue, her high-school daughter, came in from school.

She stopped, looked and listened a minute then said as she climbed the stairs, "Well, I thought *we* were crazy."

Each year as school ended and summer began, I dreaded the disorderly house every day, the many arguments I would have to settle, the thousand times I would have to scream, "Close the door, you're letting the flies in" and the million times I would hear, "I don't have anything to do, what can I do?" or, "Can I go?" I took the family to Harrison and Parthenon each summer. This gave Granny a chance to visit Aunt Letha and her kids. There was nothing quite as much fun as getting all our kids together. My cousins had children the age of mine and they had a ball playing together.

Mother came to see us every year during her vacation. She traveled by train, and we met her in Little Rock. She always had a skin irritation because she would get soap poisoning on the train—but that didn't dampen her spirits. The children had so much fun with her. Each one thought that she was just their age. One summer, Jerry spent part of the summer with Mom.

Aunt Ruth was at Mom's house now as her husband, Bill Howard, was in the Army stationed in England. She also came for a visit each year. I appreciated her and Mother coming at different times because that gave us company more often. The children liked everything about her visit except the liver she tried to make them eat. She was worried about their nutrition, and she thought liver would take care of some of the lack of iron in their diet.

When September came and it was time for school to start, we would always try to buy secondhand books from someone. Money was not as scarce as in Valley Springs, but we needed so many things and Merrill wanted me to save as much as I could—but not at the neglect of the children.

After seeing Bette's third-grade picture where she stood on the front row too shy to lift her head and look up, Merrill wrote, "I want you to give Bette "Expression" lessons. I can remember how shy I was, and I think Bette has inherited my shyness. We must do all we can to help her." So, I enrolled her with Mrs. Scales for "Expression" that fall. It must have helped, because she was not bothered with shyness in high school.

Bette when named queen

This is a picture of her when she was named Queen of the Conway High School *Wampus Cats*, the yearbook for the school. Her daddy would have been happy to see her smiling face, as she faced the audience. These were the times I missed him most, times that he would have been so proud of his children.

Jerry had one prize possession, a cat named Dempsey, a beautiful black Persian cat given to him by our neighbors, Mr. and Mrs. Dempsey. That fall, when the County Fair parade featured a pet parade, Jerry thought he had a sure winner. He got a tomato crate and decorated it with orange crepe paper. He was going to put the crate in the red wagon and pull it in the parade. When the day of the parade came, he loaded the crate and the wagon in the car and, holding his cat, we were off for Main Street. I let him out by Erbacher's Meat Market where the parade was forming. Old Dempsey was not anxious to get in the crate. I went into the meat market and bought a small piece of liver, hoping to calm him down. I left Jerry and drove farther up the street where I could see the parade go by. When Jerry passed my corner, the cat looked like a wild cat. I never saw such an ugly animal.

After Jerry and the cat passed, I left the parade and started to a store to do some shopping. I met a friend who said, "Is that your son with the black cat in the parade?" I said, "Yes." Then she told me I better go quickly and help him, as the cat was having a convulsion and they had called the police. She said, "I'm afraid they will shoot it." I ran to my car and hurried down the street. I saw Jerry and the cat. They had left the parade and the cat was on the ground having a fit. I jumped out of the car and raked the cat into the crate and said, "Hurry, Jerry. Get the wagon in the car. We are going home." I could see the police rounding the corner behind us—but I didn't let Jerry know they were coming for the cat. Poor Ol' Dempsey and poor Jerry! A couple of days later I found him dead in the shrub by the front porch. The cat had been literally scared to death. Jerry was crushed.

As the children grew older, it seemed there were more and more problems. All kinds of questions had to be settled and thousands of times I wished for my husband's sound judgment and keen mind. The days and the nights were so long. Often letters were six weeks apart. The war was increasing in intensity. Japanese war ships were anchored just off the coast of the Aleutians. It seemed as if it would never end.

I managed to fix breakfast and usher four kids out the door to school. I looked at the mountain of dirty clothes. "Hadn't I just washed three loads day before yesterday?" I thought, as sudden tears of frustration stung my eyes. I quickly brushed them away, a bit ashamed of myself, and put the first load in the washer. Then I continued to straighten up the house, wiping off sticky finger prints here and there, picking up glasses and crumbs left from snacks the night before, collecting odd shoes and socks, school papers and books. Soon I found myself in the bathroom, scrubbing the tub. Again, the tears started coming against my will. I had little resistance. I can see myself now, sitting in the bathroom floor, rag in one hand, cleanser in the other with tears streaming down my face—fussing and crying. Even though it was still morning, I was tired. I was tired of the same mess every day, mopping the same floors over and over, washing dishes only to get them out in a short time to get dirty again. I was sick of spending time cooking a meal that was devoured in a minute.

After thinking all this, I felt so guilty. I loved my children so much. I was just feeling sorry for myself. I was glad Granny and Annette were outside. Granny was such a strong person, I wished for her faith.

News came often of men being killed in service. It always upset me. In fact, I could hardly stand to think about it. Merrill had talked to me before he left and said he might not return. His words kept coming back to me. He was not being a sad sack, but was trying to advise me about what to do should this happen. I remember he said, "I would hope you would remarry because you are too young to be a widow all your life and the children will need a father. I would never ask you not to remarry, as much as I love you; rather, because I love you, I want you to be happy and cared for. Just be careful who you marry. Don't just marry anybody. Think of me once in awhile, but love him like you have loved me." This seemed to almost haunt me. I felt he had a premonition that he would not return.

Christmas came and went, then New Years Eve, 1944 came. This was our 15th wedding anniversary. Mother, bless her heart, still held out a ray of hope to me. She sent us a set of crystal goblets for our anniversary. The 15th anniversary is the crystal anniversary, according to the anniversary calendar found in jewelry and department stores. They were gorgeous but a bit out of place with our chipped and cracked dishes Perhaps there would be a china anniversary ahead—we could hope.

The weeks passed—six, twelve, eighteen, twenty, then one night the telephone rang. It was a collect call from Lt. Merrill Cole. He was back in the states and would be home within a few days. The world was wonderful once more! It was amazing how much easier everyday living became. I could face the cold winds, as I hung out the wash and watched the clothes freeze stiff on the line, The frozen long underwear of the boys looked like ghosts floating down from the sky. I cleaned the house. It had to be spic and span because he had never seen it. I was busy every minute.

He had promised to call again as soon as he knew when they would give him leave and he had his travel plans made. Of course, I expected his call every day. I was afraid to leave the telephone for fear I would miss his call. I waited, I waited, and I waited. Could it have been just a dream? But, I remembered so well. Granny remembered, too, that the telephone rang and she heard me talking. So, I knew I would hear, but I could hardly wait.

Finally, the telephone rang again and it was the call I had been waiting for. He would be leaving Tacoma by plane on February twenty-first and be in Little Rock that afternoon. I counted the hours until I would be meeting him. But on the 21st another call came. Because of the weather, the plane had been grounded in San Francisco. The passengers had been taken to a hotel. He didn't know, of course, how long they would have to wait. He said he would call again when he knew something more. Before midnight, the second call came. They had made it to Big Springs, Texas, but the plane was grounded for good there. All flights out were canceled. He would have to take a train to Little Rock. This meant several more hours of waiting.

The next day, I thought I should get the house straightened and all the washing done in spite of the weather. I changed the sheets and washed everything and hung them on the line. It had stopped raining but the ground was wet and the sun was still behind clouds. About the middle of the afternoon, I looked out and the clothesline had broken and all the sheets and other clothes lay in the mud, with the wind swishing them around.

I burst into tears. This was the straw that broke the camel's back. I stomped out of the house with my clothes basket to gather the clothes up to wash all over again. I was crying and gathering up clothes when I heard the telephone. I ran inside. It was Merrill. His train would be in Little Rock at 11:30 p.m.

Goody! Goody! Goody! Now I must hurry and get the clothes washed, the cow milked, the kids fed and get on my way before dark. I didn't want to be on the highway after dark. As you might guess, the train was three hours late. It was 2:30 a.m. when it arrived. You cannot imagine the surge of excitement I felt when I heard the whistle blow and I knew the large locomotive was coming around the last curve. When I saw its bright headlight, I knew, at last, he was coming home.

When he stepped off the train, my heart seemed to stop beating. I watched him as the line of travelers climbed the stairs to the ramp where families were waiting. He walked with his shoulders back and head held high. He looked so good. I guess I had expected him to look "battle worn."

How nice it was to be a complete family again, if only for two weeks. The children were so glad to have him home and everyone tried to claim his attention at once. We had two nights alone when we drove to Harrison to visit relatives. We came back to Marshall and spent the night in a little motel there called The Cedar Motel.

Mother and Ruth came for a short visit during the last week. My friends sent in food each day, so I would not have to cook. As the days passed, Merrill became more nervous. He talked about bitterness he felt—bitterness toward the Army. He had seen so much waste and this bothered him. He had expected to be promoted to captain and, for some reason, he felt papers had been shuffled and he had been passed over. He still felt much resentment toward the president of the school board at Valley Springs. He was disappointed that I had not saved more money. Times and prices had changed more than he realized.

I remember when it all came out. We were shopping for groceries and, when I picked up a pound of bacon, he said, "What are you doing buying sliced bacon? Are you too good now to slice bacon?" I just put it back and picked up a slab of bacon. When we got home I tried to explain how I thought the pre-sliced bacon went further than the bacon I had to slice, because I could not slice it as thin and it did not make

Helen Marie on Hwy. 65 on the way back home.

as many pieces. But, sliced bacon was too luxurious for him. He felt I had changed, and I had I'm sure. Living in Conway was quite different from life in the remote villages of the Ozark Mountains. I felt the change was good.

He was most disappointed in himself. Just as Satan tempted Jesus in the wilderness, so he had been tempted in his loneliness. He had, at times, done things he was not proud of, and he wept as he told me about it. He said he was afraid. Had it not been for his harmonica, he might have ended up a suicide as many of his cohorts did. The old songs he played were the way he worshiped during those long months. He had no idea what lay ahead, where he would be next or when he could come home again. So, the last couple of days were real hectic for both of us.

He went back to the West Coast to await orders. I looked for ways to keep busy, looking forward to another homecoming. Soon, word came that he, along with other officers in his division, was being sent to Ft. Benning for three months training and from there they would go to Ft. Crook, Nebraska. And, best of all, the family could go with him. We were excited.

Granny wanted to go and stay with Aunt Letha for the three months we were to be gone to Ft. Benning, then she would go to Ft. Crook with us. I wrote Aunt Letha about her wishes and she answered, saying someone would come for Granny when we were ready to move. Merrill called and said that he would be going by train to Ft. Benning and he wanted me to meet him in Memphis and go down with him to look for a house. He was due in Memphis on Monday morning.

On Friday, April 21st, a telegram came saying, "Sunday in Chicago. Meet me if possible. Wire care of Empire Builder. Signed, Merrill Cole." I made arrangements for the children and boarded the train for Chicago. This extra day with Merrill meant millions to me. My train was due to arrive in Chicago two hours before his, but much to my disgust, we sat on the track in St. Louis two hours before moving out; then we were delayed all along the route until we were three hours late. The Shore Patrol on the train assured me that I had no cause to worry as the Empire Builder always ran three or four hours late.

When I stepped off the train, I asked the redcap who carried my bag if the Empire Builder was in. "Yes," he replied, "Long ago. Came in on time today for the first time in months." I told him I was to meet my husband and asked if he would page him for me. I waited breathlessly. I could hear his voice as he went into all sections of the giant station, "Lt. Merrill Cole.....Lt. Merrill Cole.....Lt. Merrill Cole...." The call sounded fainter and fainter, then clearer and clearer as he made the circle and came back to me. "I'm sorry, lady, he doesn't answer," he said.

He must have read the despair I felt, as he seemed to feel terrible. I told him Merrill was on his way to Ft. Benning. Then he said, "I think you better rush over to the Union Central Station, as he must have gone there to take the train out to Ft. Benning." He motioned a cab and hurried me off, instructing the driver to drive me to the Union Central Station as quickly as possible. The cab door shut, the driver jumped in his seat, the motor roared, and away we sped. In and out among the traffic, he wove like a quarterback carrying the ball. My heart was in my mouth. But, he couldn't go too fast for me.

Then just ahead, at last, was the large station. The clock said nine o'clock. It would only be a minute now. The brakes brought the cab to a screeching stop. I hailed one of the busy redcaps. Stopping briskly by his side, I told him who I was looking for. Up the stairs he went to the loud speaker system. He called, "Lt. Merrill Cole, please come to the information desk. Lt. Merrill Cole, please come to the information desk," and a third time, "Lt. Merrill Cole, please come to the information desk." Surely he could hear this. My eyes searched the swirling crowd for a khaki clad figure moving toward us. My heart beat faster...one minute.... two minutes...three minutes. Surely he would come...but, No! My knees grew weak: I felt sick inside.......I was lost!

I picked up my bags and carried them to a locker room; then, set out on my long search. "What to do" was my problem. Could this be the wrong station? Perhaps trains for Ft. Benning left from another station, too. I saw a Travel Information booth. I asked them, and they said this was the right station and the train would leave at 9:30 p.m. I went to the main information desk and told my story. It was no use, but "there's another information desk downstairs," they told me. Perhaps they could help me. "I'm sorry. I have no name like that, but I shall put your name down and, if he comes here to inquire for you, I will tell him you are in this station," she told me.

That was a small ray of hope. Slowly, I walked away. I wished I were back at the other station to search for him. Then I saw a telephone booth. Why not call over there and have him paged? The woman was very nice; her voice gave me courage. I waited and there was no answer. Sadly, I turned away.

Soldiers, soldiers everywhere, but none was my G.I. I walked to the baggage room. "Perhaps I could see his valve pack," I thought. The baggage man saw me looking and asked, "May I help you, Madam?" Again I told my story and very effectively, I judged, as he went about among the bags, looking at every valve pack. "I'm sorry lady, I don't find it," he said.

My spirits sank lower and lower with every passing minute and how slowly they passed! There was a sign—Traveler's Aid. Now aid was what I needed and I was a traveler, so I turned in the door. Blinking the tears back and swallowing the lump in my throat, I told my story again. I soon learned that I was not the first to be lost. The kind lady called all the officer's clubs in the city and they checked their registers. No, he wasn't there. Undaunted, she rose with a smile and said, "Now, I am going to check the Pullman reservations." I waited until she returned, smiling from ear to ear. She said, "He has been here and made reservations. He has Lower berth No. 4, Car 36."

Now I knew I could find him at 9:30. The clock said 10:35—ten hours and fifty-five minutes to wait. What an age of time! Resigned to my fate, I decided to walk up the street, as the lady suggested. There was the famous Stevens Hotel, the fashionable shop windows, the picturesque crowd of people walking, some slowly, some hurriedly, some east, some west, but no familiar faces. The city that I had longed to see was very uninteresting to me. I could stand it no longer. I turned back toward the station.

Seating myself on the hard benches, I decided to relax and rest. My mind was like an unruly child; it would not relax. I watched the milling crowd. I saw weary travelers arrive, others depart. Babies cried and tugged at their mothers; everyone seemed to be going somewhere. The clock now said 3:30—six more hours to wait. I couldn't take it sitting down.

I got up and started walking when, suddenly—there he was right before me! "Sweetheart, where have you been?" he said, holding me close. "Sit down and I will tell you," I said. My knees were too weak to stand.

Then I learned how he had failed to receive my telegram and, after going to a hotel, he placed a call for me and heard our son, Bill, say, "Mother isn't here; she is in Chicago." Returning to the other station, he had searched frantically for me, meeting every train from St. Louis. Someone told him that a train came in at Union Central Station at 4:30 and he had come to meet it. That's when I found him. He said he would never have boarded the train to go to Ft. Benning without me, so I would not have found him in Car 36 at 9:30. But, together we continued on our journey to Ft. Benning.

We contacted several real estate companies before we found a place to live. Finally we found a furnished house about three miles out in the country, called Shingle Hill.

I returned home and made arrangements to move. I rented our house unfurnished. We moved our furniture upstairs. I wrote Aunt Letha that we were ready to move and one of her boys came after Granny.

Merrill told me to spread a sheet in the trunk and pack all our clothes in there. We could get more in that way than if they were packed in boxes. So I packed and I packed until it was full. We got in the car to leave and I could not find my car keys. I searched and I searched for them. After a while, Jerry said, "I think I saw some keys in the trunk." So, I began to unpack the trunk and there they were near the bottom.

We drove to Jasper, Alabama, the first day and reached Columbus, Georgia, where Ft. Benning was located early the next afternoon. I wanted the children to look as nice as they could when they got there so I said, "You may travel barefoot and in old shorts until we get near Columbus, then you must put on clean clothes and your socks and shoes to look nice for your daddy. As we neared Columbus, they began to get ready. When the girls bent over to put on their socks and shoes, they all got car sick. All their excitement was gone. When we arrived, they were nauseated and white around the gills.

Merrill drove us out to Shingle Hill and we moved into our new home. The kids were excited living out in the country. They soon made friends with a black family who lived across the road. Bill got a job at a grocery store in Columbus. The girls made up plays and programs to present to family at night. We had some good times together.

Occasionally, we went to a park or to a movie on the base. One movie we saw was *Going My Way*. The reason I remember it so well was because when the priest's (Bing Crosby) mother came on the scene, Annette began to cry. It made her think of Granny and she missed her so much. I promised her that we would soon be picking Granny up to go to Nebraska with us.

We listened to the radio much of the time. Those were terrible days in Europe. We listened to D-Day and all its anxiety. I was so thankful Merrill was home and not in the European theater. So often we talked about what we would do when the war was over and his life would be his own again. We had heard many people say they believed the end was in sight. It had been over three years now since he was called into active duty.

A few days before his school was over, he received orders for overseas duty again, this time to the European countries. He was ordered to report to Ft. Meade, Maryland, to await shipment to a Replacement Pool in England.

The air was heavy with unspoken agony. I dared not say how I felt. It really seemed unfair to me that he would be called on again so soon for overseas duty. I tried to go on and not let it spoil the days we had left together, but I found myself often staring into the future, wide eyed and wondering.

We called the people living in our house, told them we would have to return and asked them to find another house as soon as possible When Merrill got out of school, he drove us back to Conway. The Rogers were going away on a two-weeks vacation and they insisted that we live in their house instead of renting a motel, as we had planned to do. That is what we did.

Merrill had to leave soon for Ft. Meade. His bags were packed and sitting by the door ready to be loaded into the car. The children laughed and played while they waited for their daddy to come out of the bedroom. When he appeared, trench coat slung over one arm, the kids ran to him. He took each one in his strong arms, held them tightly, then kissed them goodbye. He had said, "Please don't take the kids to the train—it's just too hard—I'd rather tell them goodbye at home." (*See Appendix 1 for poignant letter he left for his son the night before he left*)

I couldn't bear to look into his eyes because I knew they would be glistening with tears. The kids backed away and watched as we drove away to the depot. Not a word was spoken the few blocks to the station. There he took me in his arms, kissing me warmly and firmly, knowing it might be another long separation. When he boarded the train, at the last second he stood waving as the train pulled away. My eyes were filled with tears; my heart was full of fear; my mind was full of memories; but, I shook myself and gasped a prayer of thanks for the weeks we had had together—surely he would return.

As I look back, I can see how the Lord helped work out our situation. I have often said, the older I get the more see God's timing many times in my life. At this particular time, our renters found a house and moved the day before Mary and J. S. returned, so we were able to get into our home.

I wrote Granny that we were home again. She came right away to stay with us. I have wondered what I would have done without her. She not only helped me physically, she helped me emotionally and spiritually. It seemed every nerve in my body was tense with anxiety, and I felt as if burdens resting on my shoulders were enough to crush the vitality of a giant.

Merrill got to go for a weekend with Mother and Ruth while he was at Ft. Meade. They took him to New York City. They told me how he wished I could see everything they saw. He kept repeating, "Helen Marie would enjoy this. I want to bring her here sometime." So later, when we were visiting them, Mother kept the children and Ruth took me to see the sights of New York, "just for Merrill," she said.

Annette started to school that fall and that left Granny and me alone much of the time, but we enjoyed every minute of it. I enjoyed going to the games. Mary Rogers took her car and a load of girls who were cheerleaders (her daughter, Jeannie, was a cheerleader). She invited me to go along. Being with Mary and Bill's friends meant so much to me. That was such a fine bunch of boys. Jerry was usually along, too. He played in the band and rode the band bus. We were really a Wampus Cat family.

Letters came from Merrill more regularly than when he was in the Aleutians. He wrote that, since he had no duties, he could get away from the base (replacement post) more often. He rented a bicycle and toured much of the English countryside. Being an English major, he found that so interesting. He wrote each day about the cathedrals he saw or the places he visited. He wrote, "Keep these letters until I get back so I can tell you all about these places."

In mid December, a postcard came saying, "I am now in France. I have been assigned to the 19th Division, which is a part of General George Patton's Third Army." I cannot tell you what a disappointment this was. We had heard much about Gen. Patton's army. It was on the move. It had pushed across the Saar River into Germany, the first infiltration into Germany. But after three days had pushed back into France. The casualties were heavy. I was aware of the danger the lower ranking officers were in. I found it very hard to hold my head up and go on.

I remember going to Margurite Westmoreland's house to a Sunday school class party that afternoon. I was there but my mind was in Europe. My friends listened to my fears. They were so kind and understanding.

I had heard a visiting minister tell about how his son had gone through a battle in Italy. He said he prayed and the Lord turned the bullets. I thought, "Now, if I pray constantly, read my Bible and study it daily, the Lord will turn the bullets away from Merrill." So, I prayed and I prayed and I prayed.

Christmas was approaching. I decorated the house as usual. I prayed we could get through Christmas without bad news. Merrill's letters were real hopeful. He thought the war would soon end and he could hardly wait. Once he wrote that after seeing the havoc war had caused in Europe, he would fight for a lifetime to keep war from coming to our shores. More than anything, he wanted to protect his family from the horrors of war.

My prayers were answered. Christmas came and went and all was well except for the loneliness. On the morning of the December 27, 1944, I was up early putting Epsom Salt packs on Jerry's head because of a slight concussion he had from a bicycle wreck the day before. I heard a knock on the front door. When I opened the door, a taxi driver was there with a telegram. He handed it to me, but seemed reluctant to leave. I said, "I am afraid to open this." By then, it was open and I read it:

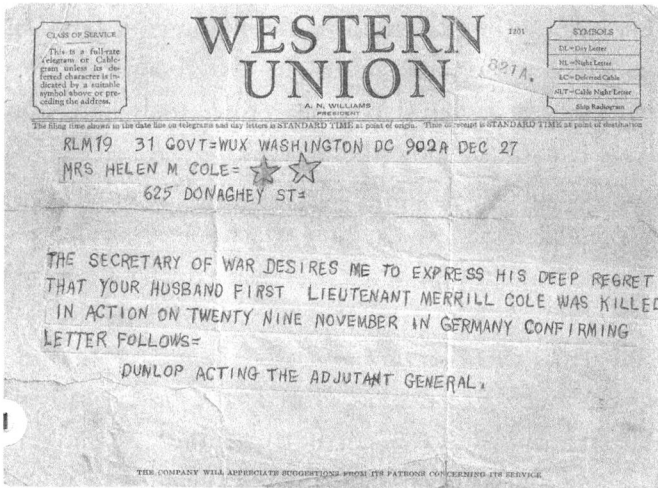

Telegram

The telegram confirmed what I had been fearing. In fact, Merrill had already been killed★ when the postcard arrived saying he had been assigned to General Patton's army. He fought only two weeks. *★The story of Lt. Cole's death is told in "The Fighting Tigers" by William D. Downs, Jr. Phoenix International, Inc. 2004, pp 22-26.*

I stood there with my mind half paralyzed. I tried to speak but stumbled over the words. The taxi driver said, "Is there someone I can tell?"

"Yes," I said. "Go tell my friend Mary Rogers, she lives on Ash Street."

"Yes, I know," he said, and he was gone.

I turned back into the house. I went to the stairs and frantically called to Bill, "Get up, son, your daddy's been killed." He leaped from his bed and hurried down the stairs. I went back to Jerry and told him, then went in the girls' room. They were awake, and I talked to them a minute. Granny had heard it all and she was there beside me. We were all stunned. There were no tears. That came later. The front door opened. It was my friend and neighbor, Delma Turner. The taxi driver had stopped and told her because he could not stand to leave me alone. I vaguely remember phone calls and friends coming and going. I groped in what seemed to be a dense oppressive fog. Later, in the mail came the official letter from the War Department.

```
                    HEADQUARTERS, 357TH INFANTRY
                     APO 90, c/o Postmaster
                       New York City                    /fak

                                          10 December 1944

    Mrs. Helen Marie Cole,
    625 Donaghey Street,
    Conway, Arkansas.

    Dear Mrs. Cole:

        The Regimental Commander has directed that I express to you his
    deepest sympathy in your hour of bitter grief over the loss of your
    husband, First Lieutenant Merrill Cole, ASN O-305994, who was killed
    in action against the enemy in the Saar Region of Germany on 29 November
    1944.

        Your husband made the supreme sacrifice bravely, unflinchingly in
    the service of his country.  It is given, perhaps, only to those who have
    stood on a battlefield to know of this high courage with which he and
    his comrades have so successfully carried the fight to the enemy.  There
    is pride in his contribution to the cause of freedom.

        His devotion to duty, his loyalty and his acceptance of responsibility
    will forever be a credit to him and the nation he represented so well.
    His memory is honored by his comrades in arms.

        He was laid to rest in a plot set aside as a United States military
    cemetery in eastern France.  A Protestant chaplain officiated at his burial.

                                    Sincerely yours,

                                    Roy G. Mosher

                                    ROY G. MOSHER,
                                    1st Lt., 357th Infantry,
                                    Personnel Officer.
```

War Department letter

The *Log Cabin Democrat* came out in the afternoon with the news of his death on the front page. It had to be true. There was no waking up from a bad dream. I was crushed because I felt God had failed me. I had thought if I stayed in contact with God through prayer, everything would go well. I thought I had found an insurance policy. Did not the preacher say, "God can turn the bullets?"

What a shock and disappointment! I wanted to cry out, "What a waste!" Here was a man who not only was a good husband and father, but also a minister of the gospel. "Why him?" So I agonized, "Oh, I didn't pray enough or, I didn't have enough faith or it would not have happened." Was it a punishment? I wept over everything—a song, a picture, a coat, a book—anything and everything. I wandered through memories that kept coming into my mind. The harsh reality was beginning to be felt. I would never be the wife of a Baptist minister of some church. I was a young widow with five children to raise alone.

Family came from far and near. Uncle Lonnie, Merrill's brother, drove on solid ice from Des Moines, Iowa to Springfield, Mo.

On Sunday, we went to the church for a short memorial service for Merrill, following the worship service. In the bulletin, we found this message:

The deepest sympathy of the entire church goes out to Mrs. Helen Cole and her family. The husband and father was killed in action on the Western Front on Nov. 29th. This family is assured of every possible consideration by our church and by other friends in Conway.

The choir sang "Near to the Heart of God"

> *There is a place of quiet rest,*
> *Near to the heart of God.*
> *A place where all is joy and peace,*
> *Near to the heart of God.*

That was what I was looking for, praying for—but there was no joy. I felt no peace and could not rest. In time it did come, but those were dark days—the darkest I have ever seen.

As you read this portion of my book of remembrances, keep in mind that it was during the darker, more difficult moments, when I was at the end of my own strength, that the Lord chose to teach me the most valuable lessons. I hope to relate some of these in my closing pages.

Season's Greetings

Dear Offspring,

I am sorry to end this section of my memories on such a sad note, but this is the end of a period of my life.

You know the story does not end here. I had many hard days, months and years, but I needed to learn that God does not always answer our prayers the way we intend Him to, and I needed to learn that one should not blame God for everything, because sins of men bring on things, such as war, and we are victims of circumstances.

God ministered to me through family and friends. As the passage in Isaiah says, *"Those who wait on the Lord for help will find their strength renewed. They will soar on wings like eagles; they will run and not be weary; they will walk and not faint."*

God did enable me to walk and not faint. Later I was able to run at times, and since then, I have often soared. My life has been filled with so many good things—each one a gift from God. Daddy Lit was one of these great gifts. Not only to me, but to each one of you!

Well, I'm getting into my next and last section. Now, I am not going to put seventy-two years of living down on paper. From here on, I will leave most of the telling to you. That will be your story. But, I do hope to conclude this someday.

I hope this will be a good Christmas and New Year for you. I hope you will be able to "soar" through it; but, if by chance, you are having to "walk," know that with God's help you can walk and not "faint."

Love,
Granny

Last letter from Merrill in form of a card

Lt. Cole's grave in St. Avold military cemetery – *Photo by Bill Downs*

Part 4: 1944-1952

I named this book of remembrances *Bumpings and Blessings*. You may wonder why. Life for me became full of them. War bumped me into widowhood, but blessings were ahead. God did not forget me, rather He used family and friends to minister to me, and I want to tell you how.

For days after the telegram came, it seemed my mind would not work. I vaguely remember friends and relatives coming and going. I would break through to do some necessary things and then retreat into a fog again. I have wondered, had we had a body in a casket to see, if it might have been easier. As it was, just shifting from a life of great expectancy to one of "What do I do now?" was very frustrating.

For a few days, numbness insulated me from the harsh reality. Uncle Lonnie and Mother called to my attention that perhaps I needed to find a job now to supplement my income. I told them Merrill had told me if he should be killed, the Government would provide for me and the children. They thought it would not be enough. Mother said we could come to Arlington and live with her, but I did not want to do that. The children were happy where we were, and I could not consider a move at this time. I did appreciate her offer.

I remember the day she left. I took her to the train. As the train pulled away, tears welled up in my eyes. I knew it might be a long time before she could come back. I turned to go home, and I dreaded the loneliness. When I opened the door, I saw a huge bouquet of flowers sitting in the living room. I looked at the card and they were from the Westmorelands. It seemed like a message from God. How did they happen to arrive at this time when I needed them most? I asked

Margurite this question and she said, "I knew when your mother was leaving, and I knew you would need a lift."

The fact that I had five children to feed, clothe and educate kept coming into my mind. I knew it was up to me to find a way to do it. Conway seemed like a good place for us to live because of the colleges located there. My friends had been super, so I wanted to stay. I was not prepared to do anything except teach piano. Conway had no need for piano teachers. After thinking and talking with friends, I decided perhaps I could open a kindergarten in our home, since there was only one in Conway. This seemed to be my best opportunity, and I could prepare for this in a shorter time than other work I could think of. Another problem that I faced was I needed help to care for my family and my house, if I were to have time to go to college.

Somehow the Lord led me to a dear black woman named Ulma Wilson. She agreed to help me five days a week. Granny was not too pleased when she came to work for us. She had never had a maid and, when Ulma put the dish drainer on the left side of the sink and Granny had always had it on the right side, I saw then that the two of them would find it hard working together.

As the days passed, I grew more and more despondent. I could not make myself do anything. By the end of the second week, I did not feel like staying up. My knees buckled under my grief and misery. I could not understand how my family and my friends went on with their daily living when I was so filled with self-pity. I cried all the time. I remember one day Annette looked up into my face and said, "Mother, when are you going to stop crying?" This shook me momentarily, but not for long. I refused to eat, to talk or to get out of the house.

One afternoon, it was time for the children and Granny to eat supper. I can see her in my mind, setting the food on the table, then calling them in and saying, "All right, pin back your ears and dive in!"

She came to my bedroom and said, "Can't you get up and eat a bite of supper?" I turned my face to the wall and said, "I'm not hungry." The dear old soul turned away to hobble back to the kitchen when she fell. I jumped out of bed and saw she was in great pain. I called the doctor. When he came, he called an ambulance, and we were soon on our way to a hospital in Little Rock. I felt so guilty. X-rays showed her hip was broken and she was rushed immediately into surgery. When she was moved from surgery to her room and I saw her lying there with her leg hoisted into the air, I could have cried, "It was all my fault," I felt.

Mother came back to help us again. She stayed a few days, then she had to return to her job in the Pentagon Building, and Ruth came to help us. We went every day to see Granny. She seemed to be doing real well and was in good spirits. But, one morning the phone rang—Granny had gotten worse. We hurried to the hospital. We found her in a coma. The doctor explained to us that her kidneys had failed and he thought she might not come out of the coma.

It was hard to see her fading slowly away. Each hour she grew weaker and, just after midnight, she died without recognizing us. The only consolation I had was, I knew she was ready and eager to meet her Lord. "She will be with Grandpa and Merrill," I thought. This comforted me. Mother was already on her way—her third trip in three weeks. Ruth and I went to the Red Cross and quickly found our brother who was in the Navy and stationed in Minnesota. We waited for him to arrive at the airport before returning to Conway.

Again, our friends in Conway responded to our needs with food, love and flowers. Family members and close friends went with us to Bellefonte to bury Granny by her husband.

Four generations: Granny, Bette, Mother and Helen Marie

This picture of the four generations was the last one she had made probably three years before she died.

The semester began at Teachers College the day Granny was buried. So I missed the first day. But, the next morning, I got out of bed, pulled myself together and I want to class. I felt like I was too old to go to college. I dreaded it, but it was a necessity.

My first class met, and when the bell rang ending the period, everyone started scrambling, heading for their next class. I took two or three steps on the waxed corridor outside the door and slipped and fell. All the young kids came running to help the "old lady" up. I was so embarrassed that I did not even feel thankful that I was not hurt.

The teachers I came in contact with were all very fine. I felt I had made the right decision and was determined to study and do the best I could.

Every morning, when my feet touched the floor, I said to myself, "This is a day I must use to prepare myself to provide for my children's needs." But I found it easy to fall into the chasm of self-pity and despair.

"Why did this have to happen?" was the question that I couldn't keep out of my mind.

The person who helped me the most was my former pastor, Dr. Blake Smith. A letter came from him in Austin, Texas, pointing out to me that people are often victims of circumstances. God does not send such tragedies but sometimes permits them to happen to us and it is then that He comes to us. He said the miracle I had prayed for did not happen; but, a miracle would come if I would allow God to deal with me in this situation.

I kept thinking about this and began to look for God's help. In time my bitterness began to lessen. The more I thought about it, the more I knew that God had been ministering to me. There were friends who came, bringing hot homemade soup or a cake that delighted the children. Granny had been with us throughout the years Merrill was away, always loving, and I am sure was constantly praying for me. There was Peggy, who spent many nights with me, trying to give me support. Mary and J. S. Rogers were closer than family—always there to help. Dr. Ferguson came and, holding my hand, told me how much God loved me and how He had cared for him and his family during the loss of his wife.

And Berlin Henderson, my cousin, who lost his dear wife at a very young age, and whom I had heard threw himself across her freshly filled grave and beat his fists against the clay, crying, "Lord, why? Why?" Now he comes telling me how a road turns, comparing it with the loss of a spouse. It is sometimes a short turn and it may be a long curve, but someday we would find ourselves traveling along a new road, a different road, but still a beautiful, interesting and wonderful road.

I thought this was a good simile. In fact, when I had to write a term paper for my English class, I wrote a paper on my experience and entitled it *A Road Turns*. I came to the conclusion that, even though God had not chosen to grant me the miracle I had prayed for, he had heard my prayers and had answered them. I prayed he would help me continue seeing His loving hand at work in life's daily miracles, large and small.

Money was beginning to be my big problem. I had been living on our savings because no checks were coming from the government now. In February, we got down to rock bottom. I asked Dr. Ferguson if he thought there was any way I could get an advance from the government or would they help me. He didn't think so, but he had a suggestion. He said the Red Cross would loan me money without interest until my paychecks were issued again.

This was the solution. I asked the Red Cross for a loan, and they were very helpful. In late February, a check in the amount of $1,100 gratuity pay came. I remember taking it to the bank and a young man, whom I had never seen, was at the teller window. He looked at the check and he whistled at the amount. That just burned me up, and I said, "Sir, it's not funny! That's blood money." Poor guy, he was so embarrassed.

I did not think this check was right, according to my understanding, so I wrote for an explanation and received this reply: (*see Appendix 2*)

When we were in Valley Springs, Merrill had been forced to drop his life insurance policy. There was no money to pay the premiums. "We do not have to have life insurance. That can come later," was his thinking. After he found himself in the war, it was too late. Only the $10,000 policy the government offered was all that was available.

It seemed the paper work and red tape would never end. Insurance forms came to be filled out. I had the option to receive $53.60 per month for twenty years, or $37.80 monthly for a lifetime. After thinking about it, I would need money more in my old age than when I was able to work, so I chose the $37.80 monthly. Merrill had died thinking the government would provide for me and the children. But it soon was apparent that this was not true.

In April the following letter came. I knew for certain it was not true. How I hated the word, "pension." But, I was to receive one, like it or not. This meant my monthly income was going to be $137.80. (*see Appendix 2*)

All of us were in school, so we were a very busy household. The boys had paper routes. Bill got up early to deliver the [*Arkansas*] *Gazette* and Jerry had an afternoon route for the *Log Cabin Democrat*, the local paper. The girls were in the band and were sometimes busy after school practicing baton twirling.

Ulma was brave enough to come to our house every day of the week to pick up clothes, make beds, clean the kitchen, wash and iron and prepare lunch for five kids, plus caring for Annette when she got out of school. She could hardly be called a cleaning lady or a maid. She was somewhere between an angel and a saint. We all loved her, especially Annette. She had a little girl of her own, Marcell, and she was special to my kids, too. Years later, when Annette was in college, we asked Ulma and her husband to spend Christmas Day with us.

The spring semester ended and I received [my] grade sheet from the dean of the college. I didn't have a four-point, but it was satisfactory to me.

We contacted Brooks Hayes, our Representative in Congress, about a summer job for Bill. He arranged for him to have a job as an elevator operator in the House Office Building. So, as soon as school was out, he left for Mother's.

Ruth was living with Mother. She had had a tragic thing happen to her. As I remember it, her husband, who was stationed in England, fell in love with a girl over there. He put an ad, or a notice, in a paper in Utah, stating that he was suing for a divorce. According to the law in that state, after it ran for a stated period of time, if there was no objection raised, the divorce was final. She had no way of knowing it was in the Utah paper, so she was divorced before she knew it. My heart bled for her.

I enrolled for the first summer term, as there was another course or two I needed before opening my kindergarten in the fall. By the time the summer term was over, I had most everything lined up for my kindergarten. I bought some tables, chairs and bookshelves from a kindergarten in Russellville that was closing. I managed to buy a record player, some children's records and books. I was just about ready to set it up.

Mother had invited us to come to her house and spend the remainder of the summer. Bill was there and we were lonely without him. It was funny when one child was gone, there was such a void I could hardly stand it. Now going to Arlington, Va., seems like a foolish thing to have done because our car was old, gasoline was rationed, and tires could not be replaced.

But, "Granny the Operator" asked Noah for tractor ration stamps to buy gasoline. I found a friend in the church who would ride with us to Knoxville, Tenn. and Aunt Ruth met us at Knoxville and helped me drive to Arlington. Not one time did a service station refuse to take tractor stamps for gasoline and we made the trip without any trouble.

Our stay in Washington was great. Mother loved showing us the sights. We all felt a surge of pride that we had given something for our country, as we looked at the Washington, Lincoln and Jefferson monuments and, as we looked at the Tomb of the Unknown Soldier, we felt that we should erect a monument to our daddy, if only in our minds.

The kids love to tell about Mom taking them to the zoo and throwing the paper sack in the hippo's mouth, when the peanuts were all gone. She kept them laughing much of the time with her antics. For example, sliding down the banister, rather than using the stairs at home. Ruth and I made our famous trip to New York. We spent all the money I had and, most of all, her paycheck. We went by train and arrived the day the plane hit the Empire State Building—we had to miss visiting that landmark as it was closed to the public. But we saw lots of other sights. We rode a double-decker bus as far as it went—beyond the George Washington bridge and back—ten cents each way, as I remember. We rode the Staten Island Ferry for a nickel. It passed the Statue of Liberty in the New York Harbor. We rode the elevated train, and took interesting tours. We walked so much my arches broke down. Buying arch supports and new shoes big enough for them depleted my purse the second day.

We spent so much seeing shows, taking tours, eating at nice restaurants that we ended up eating at the Automat that last day. This was an interesting experience then, but we do it all the time now in the canteens of our hospitals and other public buildings. Put in your quarter and pull out a sandwich. That was like magic then (it would be today, if a quarter would do it).

Speaking of magic, on the Radio City Music Hall tour, we saw television for the first time. It was just being developed. They asked two from our group to go behind doors and suddenly they appeared on a television screen in our room. How unbelievable!

When our visit was over and it was time for us to return to Conway, Mother insisted that she ride to Bristol with us. She couldn't help me drive, but she was a lot of company and gave me a feeling of security. Before she caught her train for the overnight trip back to Washington and work the next day, she saw that our car was filled, the oil changed, etc.

The next morning we were up early and on our way, hoping to be home by late evening. We had not gone many miles until the car began to get hot. I stopped at a garage and they found that the cap on the oil filter had not been properly put on and all the oil had leaked out. We had to get a new oil filter and more oil before we could go on.

Soon it was time to stop for lunch. The kids began to complain, *"I'm hungry,"* *"When do we stop to eat?"* *"I need to go to the bathroom,"* *"I'm thirsty."* So we stopped and took care of all those needs. We were getting into the Cumberland Mountains. I had checked to be sure the tank was full of gas and everything was in shape for the drive over the mountains. The roads were two lanes in those days, and traffic was often so backed up for miles that it was hard to find a place to pass a slow car or truck. We kept climbing higher and higher. There was no evidence of anyone living in those mountains. It reminded me of pictures and movies we had seen of the pioneers going west in their covered wagons. I was thankful we were in our faithful old Ford and not in a covered wagon. We were not expecting an Indian raid, either—but these were not the friendly mountains of the Ozarks that I loved so much. In fact, there was something almost terrifying about them, and I was anxious to get across them.

We came up on a big truck that seemed to be having a hard time getting its heavy load up the steep slopes and around the curves. I wished he could pick up speed a little bit but, if anything, he was getting slower and slower. "Mother, I think we are nearly to the top," one of the children said. That was encouraging because the engine was getting hot. Suddenly, it chugged to a stop and smoke was pouring out of the hood. I yelled, "Jump out, the car's on fire." Everyone scrambled out and Jerry ran to the front of the car and threw up the hood. The smoke poured upward. The girls began to cry. I looked over to my left and saw how high we were in the clouds. This had to be the most godforsaken looking place I had ever seen. My heart almost stopped beating. "What now?" I thought.

A noise of screeching brakes caused me to look around. There was a lumber truck stopping behind us. This good man jumped out of the cab and said, "Are you having trouble?" This was a real live lumberjack. I had heard of these fellows. He quickly looked the situation over and said, "I will push you over the top of the mountain and follow you down the mountain, until I have to turn off the road. I think you will be able to make it to a garage where you need to stop and have your gas line checked." "Thank you, sir," I said, and we all crawled back into the car. It was not far to the top of the mountain, and then we began to coast down the mountain. Soon the motor choked and sputtered and started running. Around and around the curves we went. The girls watched out the back window and, after several miles, the kind man honked his horn and the kids waved as he turned his log truck off the road to go on about his work.

"Wasn't he nice?" they said together. I agreed.

Years later when we were studying about Joseph being in the pit and the caravan came along just in time to save his life, one of my friends, Lou Calhoun, said, "Now you know, I wonder how long before this event God started that caravan so that it reached the pit at the exact time to rescue Joseph." So, looking back, I wonder now how long this log truck traveled to be there at exactly the right time to help us? Some may scoff at the idea, but the longer I live, the more I see God's timing in so many of my life's situations.

Well, we continued down the mountain, but when we got to the bottom, the car had trouble on the least upgrade. I keep looking for a garage, but there was none. Finally we came to a little country store. I stopped and inquired about the nearest garage. The man said it was twenty miles down the road in a little town called Crossville. We hoped we could make it. When we had to go up a hill, the girls would chant, "*I think I can, I think I can, I think I can,*" as the car struggled to the top. Then, as we picked up speed, it was, "*I thought I could, I thought I could, I thought I could.*" When we reached the garage, we all sighed with relief.

"Your gas line will have to be replaced," the man said. We all got out and waited an hour or more until he could finish the job. Thankfully, we started on. Our peace of mind did not last long. When we got into the beautiful green mountain section of Tennessee, the road was more crooked. I noticed a strange noise every time we went around a curve.

"What's that screeching noise?" the kids asked. "Mercy, I don't know. Guess I should stop and put some gas in the car and ask the service station attendant what it is." That is what I did and he said, "Lady, your wheels have got to be realigned or you are going to wear your tires out. They will never make it to Arkansas unless you do." He told me he did not do that type of work. He suggested that I drive on toward Nashville and stop just outside town for the night, then drive in to the Ford place in Nashville early the next morning. We followed his advice and stopped at a small motel eleven miles from Nashville.

The next morning, we were up early, and I told the kids we would eat our breakfast while they fixed our car. So we arrived at the Ford place before time for it to open.

When I pulled inside the service department, the foreman came up to the car window, but instead of saying, "Lady, may I help you?" he said, "Lady, we are not taking any work this morning because the war is about over and we are going to celebrate with a three-day holiday."

I could hear the radio blaring and I saw dozens of men huddled around it, listening to the news. The man walked away, unconcerned about my needs. He didn't even care what I needed, as I sat there wondering what to do. He turned and came back. I told him my problem and he said, "Lady, you better go out and find you a motel and wait until we open up again, and then we will be glad to serve you." I said, "Well, I need to get the work done today so I can go on home.

Is there any place that you think I could get it done?" "No, lady, there isn't. Everyone is closing up just as soon as the announcement comes."

With that, he walked away again. I still didn't start my motor, and he whirled around and came back and said, sharply, "Lady, did you know there's been a war going on? We are going to celebrate!" I said, "Yes sir, I know there has been a war going on, but I don't feel like celebrating like you do. You see, sir, my husband was killed last November in Germany. The children and I have been to Washington visiting my mother and we are trying to get home to get ready for school. Of course, I'll be glad for the war to be over, but it is a feeling different from yours."

He turned and walked away without saying a word. I saw him walk over to a man and he said something to him. The man shook his head and I said to the kids, "I bet he is asking that man to fix our car." The two men walked toward our car and the foreman introduced the man and said, "He says he will fix your car and, if the war is over before he gets it done, he will finish it for you." I thanked the men and asked where we might find breakfast.

The car was finished, the radio was still blaring and the dozens of men were still milling around when we drove out to find our highway again. Every time the gasoline gauge showed the tank was a fourth empty, I stopped and filled it up because I knew the stations would close when the war was over. When I crossed the Mississippi River at Memphis and stopped and filled up, I breathed a sigh of relief. I knew then I had enough gasoline to drive to Conway.

When we got to Brinkley, we were in the main part of town and I heard a siren. Thinking it was a fire truck, I pulled over to the side of the street and stopped. Then I saw people throwing their hats in the air and jumping up and down, so I knew at last the war was over.

I wished for a radio but there was none in the car. When we reached DeValls Bluff, we saw everyone celebrating. I remember a group of small children marching, stepping high, carrying flags. When we reached North Little Rock, I pulled the car off the street at the end of the Broadway Bridge, and we watched the excitement. Cars were driving down the street with their horns blaring and people were riding with their bodies halfway out the windows, shouting and waving hysterically. We caught some of the enthusiasm and started on to Conway and home, feeling good.

In 1985 I found [an] article that tells the story of all the excitement better than I can. I wanted you to read it and know something of what went on that August day in 1945. (*see Appendix 3*).

The kids were glad to get home and see all their friends. They could hardly wait for Sunday to come when they could see those outside the neighborhood. We moved the furniture out of two of the bedrooms and set up the kindergarten. The girls and I shared one bedroom, but they did not seem to mind. We had four bunk beds that I bought when the Women's Army Corps moved out from Teachers College where they were stationed for a few months.

The telephone rang often, as did the doorbell, with people wanting to enroll their child for kindergarten. I was so happy to show them my set up. By the time opening day came, I had a full enrollment. I was so pleased. In early September everyone started to school. Ulma had all the house to herself, except for the kindergarten rooms. At snack time she prepared the snacks, usually cookies or crackers with milk or juice. Christmas came and I was really busy with preparations in my school, plus for my family.

Our Christmas program went off without a problem. Little Edward Robbins, who was almost blind, read the Christmas story by memory. I can still see his little face turned

A day at school with a pet rabbit. Edward Turner, the blonde headed boy standing beside me, lived next door to us.

upward in thought and hear his angelic voice as he repeated the familiar scripture.

When the New Year came and the excitement of Christmas was over, I hit a low ebb. I became so depressed I had to go to the doctor. Dr. Archer looked at me and said, "Helen, you haven't really faced your loss yet. You have been putting it back into your subconscious mind and now it is surfacing again." He pointed out how I had pushed it back when Granny fell and had later died. Then I started to school and continued to not let it surface. After school, the trip to Washington, opening the kindergarten and the anxiety of getting through our first Christmas without Merrill kept it smothered. Now that things were settling down and I was not so excited about other things, I was meeting my grief again. He said, "You have got to work through it." He told me to go back to bed as soon as the children left in the afternoon and just be quiet and stay there until morning.

"I can't." I said, "I've got to take care of my kids."

"You can't afford not to," he said, but insisted that they could fix their supper. Ulma could have something ready for them to make sandwiches or snack on, and they were large enough to do that.

For a few weeks we did this, and I felt some better. Finances kept hitting me in the face. The kindergarten children paid by the month. As the war came to a close and the fathers returned, several of the children moved away, so that cut into my income. As time went on, I knew I could not continue in this manner. Too, I was facing a summer with no employment, which meant no supplementary income. As much as I enjoyed the kindergarten, I knew I would have to give up the idea.

A new bank was opening in Conway. It would open soon after school closed, so I decided to make application for a job at the bank. I was accepted and, when the First State Bank opened, I was there. I felt more secure now that I knew exactly what my income would be and could better care for my family. The girls were happy to have their rooms again. Bette had the front bedroom and Carolyn and Annette had the middle one. Congress passed a bill allowing time spent in the service to be covered by Social Security, so now we were eligible. The girls were able to draw a check each month, but the boys were past the age. The girls used their first checks to buy furniture for their bedrooms.

Bill left for Washington as soon as school was out. In the House Office Building, he got to see so many VIP's. It was a real thrill to carry generals, senators, etc. on his elevators. He loved to listen to their conversations.

We had many good times and many hard times. I remember one time I had been to Mother's for a short visit and was returning home by train, when a lady sitting beside me, said "Well, I can see you have never had any trouble or had to work hard." I smiled and didn't say a word. I thought, "Lady, if you only knew!" I thought of the hard work I had done in Omaha, Valley Springs and in Conway. How that work had been interrupted umpteen times, how I had settled scores of arguments all the time (most of the time), trying to be sweet and patient, even though I felt anything but! Now, I was not the ideal mother for a growing family—once I was told I was like a warden. I am sure sometimes I neglected them—I was always so emotional. I can recall cleaning up after supper and, all of a sudden, everything would get to me. The burned rice in the pan, the kids fussing when they should have been studying, the telephone ringing, the teenagers talking, the radio blaring—*everything*—I wanted to throw down my dish rag and say, "*Quiet!*" But, I learned, if I dwelled in self-pity, I could not keep going. I worked hard to not worry.

We were always in debt to the grocery store, the dry cleaners and the dentist. Once, Dr. Fleming, our dentist, sent me a bill marked, "Charity," canceling out my debt to him. It made me so mad. You know what I did? I just changed dentists and went to Dr. Weatherly— and owed him. I had to figure out who I could pay each month. It was so frustrating and embarrassing. I will ever be grateful to George and Fritz Simons. They owned the Simons Grocery. I have never seen two more compassionate men. When I could pay only a small portion of my grocery bill, they always seemed to understand. A few years ago, I went in the store and thanked George for his generosity.

And how many times J. S. Rogers came to our relief! One of the kids might just have to have a new notebook or fifty cents for something at school and I didn't have a nickel. So, they could go down to Rogers Drug Store and J. S. would let them have the notebook or the cash. As far as I know, we always repaid J. S. as soon as more money came in.

We had another loss I must tell you about. One quarter of Ol' Jersey's bag went bad, and we had to sell her. How I hated to see that cow go. She had given us so much good milk. We loved her like one of the family. A friend said we could have a cow out of his herd to milk. So, Bill and Jerry went out to his farm and drove the cow in. That afternoon, I went out to milk her. Being accustomed to milking our gentle Ol' Jersey, I picked up my tomato crate and sat down to milk this cow. It wasn't two seconds until she whaled away and kicked the bucket almost out of my hands. I got up and backed away a little bit and tried it again. One thing I learned was, this sister didn't want to be milked. She kicked the bucket harder and all the milk went splashing out on the ground. "This could be dangerous," I thought. "What if she kicked me?" So, to protect myself, I put the tomato crate between me and the cow. This was a big mistake because her foot hit the crate, knocking it into me, bruising my legs, and I thought my hand was broken.

I gave up! Holding my hand, I went back to the house and went inside. A man was there hanging paper. He said, "I'll milk that heifer for you." I told him he was taking his life in his hands, but he insisted. So, the cow was milked. Early the next morning, the boys drove her back to the pasture, and I guess she lived happily ever after. From then on, we bought milk at the grocery store.

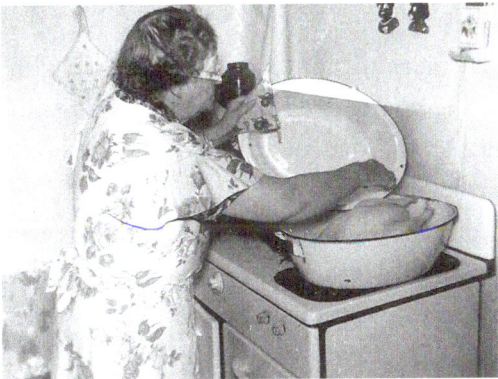

Mother cooking turkey

When Mother (or Mom) came to see us, there was always something special, like this turkey she is cooking for Thanksgiving.

She helped us in so many ways. She and Ruth came regularly to visit us. Ruth sewed for the girls. Especially I remember formals and clothes for special occasions. She continued to pass her clothes to me, and Mother often brought things for the kids. I am grateful!

I don't know how I managed to have time off to take the kids back to North Arkansas. But it seems that every summer we went back to visit family and friends. We always went to Noah and Myrtle's where the kids played in the hayloft. If it was an election year, the girls would find out who Noah was supporting and they would take the opposite side just to razz him. They had lots of fun.

Uncle Willie loved the children like a grandfather. However, they had to be more sober there and act like well-behaved kids. I guess their favorite place to go was Aunt Letha's at Parthenon. She had a bunch of grandkids and we always went fishing in Buffalo River and cooked on the riverbank. They fried potatoes and onions together, fried fish and, best of all, there was a gooseberry pie, or cobbler, they called it. At the house, the kids played *Red Rover, Ante-Over, Hide-and-Seek* and all the old games they never got to play at home. Sometimes, on Sunday, there was church or all day singings with "dinner on the ground." How they could think of so many things to do amazed us.

When the grandkids were old enough to drive, we let them drive into Jasper to the picture show. One time, I remember, we took a picnic lunch to Diamond Cove. There was a skating rink there and the kids got to skate. Annette fell and bruised her leg, but we didn't think much about it. We went from there to Omaha to visit the Andrews. On Saturday, they took us to Rockaway Beach, near Branson, Missouri, to swim.

Annette woke up on Sunday morning with a high fever. We couldn't see a thing wrong with her. She complained of her leg hurting, and there was a huge kernel in her groin. She could hardly walk. I got so worried because polio was rampant at that time. I just knew she had polio. She continued to worsen, and the fever rose. We were twenty miles from a doctor. About the middle of the afternoon, I couldn't stand it any longer. I packed up and we went into Harrison to Uncle Willie's and I called Dr. Kirby. He said, "Meet me at the office."

I took her down there and when he examined her and saw the skin burn on her leg he said, "What's this?" We told him she skinned it skating at Diamond Cove. He said, "It's infected. That's the trouble." We supposed the water at the lake was contaminated. How relieved I was. Some antibiotics were all it took to get her back in tip-top shape.

The kids soon got too old to want to go up there, much to my disappointment. I asked them why they didn't want to go. They said, "Well everyone says, 'look how much they have grown!' 'Why, that little girl looks just like her mother!" Have you noticed how much Bette looks like Aunt Vina Wasson?' 'Let me look at you, you look just like your daddy!'" They felt like they were on display. It was embarrassing to them. Too, there were activities in Conway they didn't want to miss.

The Conway friends, Mary and J. S. Rogers, Dr. and Mrs. Ferguson, Margurite and Priddy Westmoreland, Mamma Jewel and Daddy Ed Anderson and our cousins, Berlin and Ardatha Henderson, all helped me through those years of adjustment as I keep repeating.

I didn't get to go the sewing club very often, but those ladies continued to be a bulwark of strength. God ministered to me through them.

The red tape from the government, after Merrill's death, kept me upset. The papers continued to come for my signature, or pertaining to insurance, pension, etc. His personal effects came months after his death. There were grimy shirt collars, dirty underwear and socks, plus his pictures and a few things he had with him. The hardest thing that came was papers to be filled out saying, "Yes, I want his body returned," or "No, I do not want his body returned but buried in a Military Cemetery in Europe." If I could have just made application that I wanted it brought home, it would have been easier.

They allowed me thirty days to make the decision. I did not discuss it with anyone. I wanted it to be my decision. I thought about it and prayed about it, but to save my life I could not see meeting a train with his body on it. This would have torn us all apart again. On the thirtieth day, I wrote, "No." It nearly tore my heart out. The paper had to be notarized, so I took it to the bank and asked Tom Wilson, the president and my good friend, to notarize it for me. I told him what the papers were. He said, "Now Helen, I am going to notarize this without looking to see what your decision was because I do not want to influence you." He signed his name, then opened to read my decision. Then he said, "Helen, I am so proud of you. This is the decision I feel you should have made for your children's sake." I felt better because Tom was a wise man.

Years later, a letter and map came from the Department of the Army, showing us exactly where Merrill was buried. **(***See Appendices 4 and 5***)**

One summer when Bill was in Washington working, he was on his way to work and an Army officer got on the bus and sat down beside him. Recognizing the insignia, Bill remarked to the man that his father was in the Division he was in. Then Bill pulled out a picture of his dad and showed it to the officer. The fellow took one look at the picture and said, "That's Lt. Cole. I knew him. Where is he now?" Bill told him his father had been killed in Germany. Then the officer told Bill that he was with Lt. Cole in a little town in Germany when he was shot by a sniper. He said he was wounded in the stomach. The medics came and carried him away, and he never saw him again. Bill was so excited, he let the officer leave the bus without getting his name. Two or three years later, a communiqué came from the Army saying that they had been trying to trace the cause of death of each soldier, and their findings confirmed the officer's account.

General [George] Patton's Army was in France, near the Saar River. In November, 1944, a regiment of foot soldiers moved across the Saar into Germany, the first penetration of American forces into German soil. Because of the weather conditions and flooding of the river, tanks and other heavy equipment were unable to get across to help them, so the regiment was pushed back across the river after three days. It was on the second day that Merrill was killed, only two weeks after he was brought in as a replacement in General Patton's Army. *(See "The Fighting Tigers" by William D. Downs, Jr., Phoenix International, Inc., pp 22-26.)*

General [Dwight] Eisenhower, commanding general of the European Theater of Operations and later President, wrote about this siege in his book, *Crusade in Europe.* I am including the reproduction of the first page of the book. You may be interested in more. *(See Appendices 6 and 7)*

This may show the position of the U. S. Third Army. *(See Appendix 8)* This spot is a very strategic spot for the descendants of Merrill Cole and needs to be pointed out in these "recollections."

As I look back now, I can see why we had not been permitted by God to move back to Harrison. Conway was a good place for me to live and raise my family. The schools were good and by the time Bill was ready for college, the Arkansas Legislature had passed a bill giving full tuition, books and a small allowance to a son or daughter of a man killed in service during World War II. This enabled Bill to go to Arkansas State Teachers College, now the University of Central Arkansas, without it costing us a cent. The allowance was enough for a noon meal ticket at the cafeteria. This was great!

Jerry knew what he wanted to do from the time he finished grade school. He wanted to be a band director. He loved the band. He went to early practice and learned to play every instrument in the band by the time he finished school. When he entered Arkansas State Teachers College, he had to pay some tuition for a music major. We managed to do this and, when he directed the ASTC band in his Senior Recital, I was so proud of him. This was one of the times I wished that his father could see him.

My bank job had one feature I could not live with. The lady who worked with me was a "career" woman. She had no children. She had beautiful, expensive clothes, and not much to do except care for her skin and her hair. Every morning, when I came to work, she "eyed" me up and down and this made me feel very uncomfortable. She "played me down" every chance she got, making me feel like a loser. She blamed me for everything, or anything, that went wrong. A sneer and criticism was all I ever got from her. I kept thinking surely there is something more pleasant to do than this.

One day, a friend who had returned from the war, approached me about working with him. He was opening a bookkeeping firm and he asked me to be his junior partner. He offered me the salary I was receiving at the bank, plus a percentage of the profit. I thought this was my chance. I resigned from my job and we set up an office in the First National Bank building. He taught me what I needed to know to help him.

I enjoyed the work but, as time went on, it became harder and harder to collect my salary. I would have to ask him, sometimes two or three times a month, before I could get full payment. Never once did he figure that there was a profit. Of course, there were machines and office supplies to pay for at the beginning, but this was going on and on. I felt like he was taking advantage of me.

One day, I saw an ad in the paper for a bookkeeper for [a local company] and called the number listed. To my surprise, they offered me twice the salary I was getting. This was a good way out of a bad situation, so I resigned that job and took on a new one.

This didn't work out either. In three months, I was fired and looking for work again. This company was operating as it wanted to. They had a small-appliance shop in addition to their construction work, and not one dime of sales tax had they paid. I mentioned this to the boss about two days before the investigators from the state came to inquire about the situation. I explained that I was getting the information ready to file with payment for back taxes, so they left.

We paid sales tax in October and again in November, but in early January when I figured up the tax for the month of December, when the Christmas sales were good, the man refused to pay it. He figured up what he was going to pay on and said, "Forget the rest!" as he handed it to me. I went to my desk and prepared it as he had directed and took it back for him to sign, telling him that I was not going to sign a false statement. With that, he gave me my "walking papers." I was fired on the spot. But, I had stood up for what I thought was right, and I felt no regret.

I began a search for another job. There seemed to be nothing available. Mary Rogers and Olive Ferguson asked me to Little Rock shopping one day. I went, even though I had no money for shopping. When we returned, Dr. Ferguson called and asked, "Did Dr. Minton get hold of you?" I said, "No." He said, "He will, he wants you to work for him." Dr. Minton was head of the Extension Office at Arkansas State Teachers College.

This was music to my ears! Soon the telephone rang and I heard this gruff voice, "How would you like to work for me?" I trembled, but I managed to say, "I would love to." And so, I started to work in the Extension Office at ASTC. The salary was only $100 per month, but this would buy food for my growing family.

Dr. Minton was an unforgettable, wonderful man, head of the Department of Public Relations and Professor of Geography. His ruddy complexion and bushy hair made him stand out in any crowd. I found that the gruff voice did not reveal the gentle character of this dear man. He was a favorite of the student body. I remember once, when the day was approaching for the big football battle with our biggest rival, Arkansas Tech, the spirit of the student body was very low, as the team was not very good and they knew they would lose the game. The president of the student body came in the office and asked Dr. Minton to give a pep talk at the chapel service. He did. He suggested that each class begin with a cheer for the Bears from then until game time. No sooner had classes convened when we heard a cheer down the hall, another one came from the other direction. We heard cheers in the classroom over our office. Only one teacher, Dr. Sixby, an English professor, "reneged." He said, "When they pause to read a poem on the football field, I'll take time from my class to lead a yell." By game time, the stands were filled with cheering students and we almost won the game.

Dr. Minton spent his life struggling to give poor teachers of Arkansas a chance to earn a degree. He set up classes in small towns miles away so that the teachers could earn credits toward their degree. He established a Correspondence Department and many older teachers earned their degrees in that manner. He was truly the teacher's friend.

When teachers and former students came on the campus, they always came by to see Dr. Minton. He would greet them and, if he didn't know their name, he would say, "I want you to meet Helen Cole." I would "rise to the occasion" and say, "So happy to meet you.

Sorry, I didn't get your name." Then they would tell me their name and this saved the day for Dr. Minton.

Each summer he directed a field course in geography, usually to the West Coast. I cut stencils and prepared workbooks for his tours. How I longed to join these groups just to hear this witty man, full of knowledge, stories and expressions, instruct his class through a huge microphone he carried in the front of the bus.

Working for him gave me a sincere desire to widen my horizons through travel. Years later, I wish I could have told him—I would have had to speak loudly because he became almost totally deaf—that I finally got to go to Gallup, New Mexico and to the Grand Canyon. He would have said to his precious wife who was blind, "Lucy, this is Helen Cole, she's been on a western tour!"

Working in the Extension Office meant much to me. I loved working with the students and the young married girls. Life was still ahead for them and they were looking forward to it with great anticipation. It kept me looking up and enjoying life.

I became an avid Bear fan and sometimes went to games out of town with the wives of players who worked in our office.

The first two years I worked in this office, Bill was in college and he often dropped by for a word or we had a Coke in the bookstore. Annette went to the Training School on the campus. I could look out the window in our office and see her playing during recess.

The following is an interesting article about our office that appeared in the school paper. (*See Appendix 9*). You will notice that the article mentions that Jerry worked in the film library. This picture shows him cheerfully rewinding film.

The campus offered so many activities and they were free. We went to concerts, plays, football and basketball games. There were good

Jerry in film library at ASTC

lectures, demonstrations, etc. that we could attend. I had to buy a ticket to the Community Concerts held in the auditorium. I remember one time Margaret Truman came to sing. Before her arrival, we were swamped with Secret Service men, and we saw what great care they take to protect the family of the President of the United States.

The kids enjoyed swimming in the gym. Carolyn became a good diver—good enough, in fact, to do some exhibition diving for the college.

One summer, Bette attended summer school. She and Jerry were in the same psychology class, taught by Dr. Sands. They had to write a paper and Jerry worked hours writing an original paper. Bette wrote on *Dreams*. She went to the library and took one line out of one book, one from another and very carefully constructed her paper from other writings. Jerry told her this was not what she was supposed to do. Little sister paid no attention and turned in her paper. Much to everyone's surprise, when the graded papers came back, Bette had an A and Jerry a B. This is just a sample of sibling rivalry.

I saw much of that, especially on Saturday mornings when I had to work. Often I was trying to settle an argument over the phone. The kids would call telling on each other, or saying, "It's not my turn to wash the dishes," etc. But, we made it! I would tell them to do certain chores while I was at work. Now they tell me how they played with other kids in the neighborhood until nearly time for me to get home, and then they would break their necks trying to get everything done.

Working at the college was fine, except for the low salary. As it became harder and harder for us to exist and keep our heads above water, I decided to take a Civil Service examination and try for a better paying job. There were no Civil Service jobs available in Conway, where I requested. After a year the chance came to go to Little Rock and work at the Weather Bureau. I did not want to live in the city. After a few days, I returned the papers saying I wasn't interested. After the decision, I wrote Mother and Ruth about it. They called when the letter arrived and said they thought I was foolish to turn down the Civil Service job.

When I explained to Dr. Minton what the phone call was about, he said, "Helen, I think you should go see about it." Very reluctantly, I decided to drive down to Little Rock. I asked Mary Rogers to go with me. All the way, I prayed that the job would not still be available. My prayer was answered, but not as I wished. The job was available and it seemed God was pushing me into it.

With tears in my eyes and a lump in my throat, I bid farewell to my beloved job and those I worked with. I have continued to welcome the chance to go back to the college to visit with my co-workers, and I have always kept in touch with the Minton's. I attended their 50th wedding anniversary in 1970, and Mrs. Minton's 90th birthday party, and with a heavy heart, Dr. Minton's funeral. I can truthfully say he was the most unforgettable character I have ever met.

There were lots of other experiences besides work during those years in Conway that I must tell you about. The First Baptist Church contributed much to these years. We were always there when the doors opened, and the people were always by my side both in the good times and the bad.

Sunday's were special. I woke the kids up and we had breakfast, then went to Sunday school and church. When church was over, we rushed home because the kids were starving. There was always a pot roast or a rolled pork roast on the stove cooking, with potatoes and carrots around it. This was a must with five (or maybe more) hungry mouths to feed.

I was superintendent of the Young Peoples Department in the Sunday school. I remember more about the teachers I worked with than the students. W. C. Ferguson was a young man who taught in our department. One thing I remember happened on Mother's Day. "Dub," as we called him, wore two red roses on his lapel. In those days, we wore a red rose if our mother was still living and a white rose if she were dead. This indicated Dub had two living mothers and he explained, "I have one mother living in Heaven and one on earth." I thought this was one of the best lessons taught in the church. Bette and Carolyn were members of the Girls' Auxiliary, a missionary organization. There were steps the girls attained.

Othar Smith was the pastor for the last years we lived in Conway. He was a dear friend to all the family. He baptized, he married, he loved, he comforted and counseled many in our family. The Thanksgiving service was always very special, too. It was at 6 a.m. before daylight. The church was filled. I remember one Thanksgiving we could not get our car started and we walked through the cold morning air, feeling much like Pilgrims, but we couldn't miss that service. The order of worship consisted of songs and expressions of thanks by the people. It was very inspiring and uplifting. The high school football team attended in mass. Afterward, the Young Peoples' Department had a breakfast and the football players were guests.

The schools had much to offer, too. I remember going to P.T.A. meetings and, during the early Conway years when they asked for parents to stand as their children's room was called, I was popping up and down to the amazement of many around me.

Then there was the Band Boosters Club. With three or four kids in the band, this was a necessary membership for me. We raised money by having a snack bar at the football games. Fathers would carry drinks and food through the stands calling out their wares. One year I was purchasing agent for the project. I bought a large sack of roasted peanuts and they were "best sellers." I ordered the second sack, but the weather grew cold and the rains came and the crowds who braved the storms were not as hungry for peanuts as the earlier crowds were so we had a problem on our hands. Mr. Robinette made a motion that we buy an elephant to eat the peanuts I had bought.

Bette was drum major of the band, Carolyn was a majorette and Jerry was playing either the drum or another instrument, so I was always glad to see them march. I often went with them on out-of-town trips if I could make arrangements to get away.

Money never ceased to be our biggest problem. How I ached to be able to do something to ease our financial crisis. Time came when there was not enough money for piano lessons. I told Mrs. Bolls the children would have to quit. She said, "I understand, but I feel Carolyn has too much talent to stop. I will continue to teach her; if you have money to pay me something that will be okay, but, if you don't that will be fine, too. She must continue to study." And, she did. I usually managed to pay her teacher something.

As hot September turned into a chilly October, our plight worsened. The kids tried on their warm clothes only to find they had outgrown most of them. They were passed down, when possible. It seemed the children always needed shoes. But money was gone down a hole with seemingly no bottom to it. I did my best to hold the food costs down, always remembering that Merrill told me that if the kids were not fed a proper wholesome diet, I would have to pay out the money in dental and doctor bills. I cut corners every way I could, yet it was always the same, our bank account was empty! I would swallow hard and remember what the Bible said, *"My God shall supply all your needs."* I guess He did—not all our wants—but, perhaps we had all we actually needed.

The kids did all they could to help remedy the situation. Not only did the boys work, but they were willing to go on a date with only a nickel for a Coke in their pockets. Bette started babysitting as soon as she was old enough. One summer she worked, saving her money and, before school started, she rode the bus to Little Rock and bought material for her fall clothes. On the way home, she could not resist showing her material to her seatmate. She was so proud of it. She told her about the baby sitting that enabled her to buy her precious material. The next day, when our paper boy came, he knocked on the door and said, "I want to see the seamstress." Then he showed us [an] article on the front page. Evidently, Bette's seatmate was a member of the press and liked her story. Bette was furious. She did not want the publicity.

Bette loved to sew and she learned a lot by the trial and error method. Some things turned out real well and others not so good. We have laughed many times about the time she was working on a red satin dress. It was Sunday afternoon and she was trying to finish it. But, time came for us to go to church for B.T.U. (Baptist Training Union). I insisted that she go. She refused to go without her sewing, so I allowed her to take it along. All the family went to BTU, but Bette sat in the car and worked on her dress. B.T.U. was over and we went into the sanctuary for the evening worship. I could hardly believe my eyes when the youth choir walked in. There was Bette in her red satin dress, unpressed, yes, but she did get it finished and that was important to her.

All these experiences really paid off for Bette and her family. She became a good seamstress and eventually sewed for herself, her daughters and the public. One time I recall going to Jonesboro when Caryn, her daughter, was at A.S.U. and was in a beauty contest. We were rather late arriving, and there was Caryn waiting for her dress. Her friends, who were all dressed, said, "Where is your dress?" She said, "Mother is bringing it." "What if it doesn't fit?" they asked. "Oh, it will, Mother knows exactly how to fit me." And it did! She looked beautiful and her friends were dumfounded that she could wait patiently for a homemade dress.

When Bill returned to Washington for the summer, Jerry went along. He had a summer job working in Uncle Jim's restaurant at Manassas, Virginia. Uncle Jim had married Helen Lundis of Manassas. Of course Jerry was happy to get to spend the summer with Uncle Jim. He was very special to all of us.

With both of the boys gone, this was a chance to make a little money. We rented their room to summer school students. One summer we had two girls, Yocharlesea Martin from Stuggart and Reba Malcolm from DeWitt. They were fun to have in our home. The next summer, we rented to my cousins Elmer Casey and his sweet wife, Helen, from Parthenon. We enjoyed them.

As you would expect, with a bunch of kids, there were illnesses of various kinds. When Bill came down with an attack of appendicitis, we had no doctor. There was a young doctor, Charles Archer, just out of the Army, who had opened an office in Conway, so I chose him. He said Bill must have surgery immediately. For some reason the Conway hospital was closed for a month, so we had to take him to Little Rock by ambulance. Luckily I had paid $2 for an ambulance policy and this was a blessing. Mr. McNutt drove the ambulance and he would not leave me at the hospital until they had moved a cot into Bill's room for me to sleep on. Dr. Elbert Wilkes, Dr. Archer's brother-in-law, assisted with the operation and, since he lived in Little Rock, attended Bill while he was in the hospital.

After a week, Mr. McNutt carried us back home and Dr. Archer came over to the house to see how he stood the trip. He saw Merrill's picture on the mantel and said, "Is that who you are?" I said, "That's my husband, if that's what you mean." He said, "I was in school with him in Ouachita." This made us feel closer to him and he took good care of us as long as we were in Conway.

Dr. Archer removed Carolyn's and Annette's tonsils the same day in the Conway hospital. After I took them home, Carolyn started bleeding. He sent us back to the hospital. Not wanting to operate again if he could help it, he told Carolyn he wanted to use some kind of medication on a swab to see if he could stop the bleeding, but it would hurt. He asked if she was willing to let him try. She said, "If you will let me hug your neck." So after several "huggings" and "swabbings," he got the bleeding stopped.

Bette fell off the monkey ladder at school and ended up having her back X-rayed. Fortunately there were no breaks. Jerry sat down on his thumb and broke it, Bill had a head-on collision playing basketball in college and, because of bleeding, had to wear a pressure bandage for a couple of days. The children had the usual diseases. Often I would sit by their bed and stroke a burning forehead, wondering what was wrong. But, we never had a real tragic illness, for which I am thankful.

Annette needed braces on her teeth. I was told her chin and nose would meet by the time she was eighteen, if I did not have it done. This seemed impossible to me because of the down payment required—until I remembered the $100 bill Uncle Lonnie often showed me in the secret section of his wallet when he visited us. He always said, "This is yours, if you ever need it. Just let me know."

This was the time. I wrote him a letter and soon the $100 was there. I made an appointment with an orthodontist in Little Rock. We had no car, so we rode the commuter bus. I showed Annette how to walk from the bus station at Second and Main to the Boyle Building on Capitol Avenue. We climbed the stairs to the doctor's second floor office where he fitted her with braces and set up a schedule for her future appointments.

For about a year, this little ten-year-old girl rode the bus alone to Little Rock for her adjustments. One day, when I met the bus, she was not on it. I met the next bus and there she was. I asked what happened and she told me she had stopped by Blass' on Fourth and Main to ride the new escalator and didn't notice the time, so she had to catch the next bus.

I had the opportunity to visit Mother a few times while living in Conway. One summer Dr. and Mrs. Ferguson went to Washington, D. C., to visit their son, Hubert, and they invited me and Mary Rogers to ride up with them. We had a great time. The cherry blossoms were in bloom and Mother enjoyed showing Mary and me all the sights. She was a super tour guide and was in her glory when she had a chance to show her beloved city.

Another time I rode up with some college teachers who were going to New York City to summer school. This was an interesting trip, and I returned by train. Ulma stayed with the kids and they were well taken care of. I had called Dr. Archer and told him I was going and asked him to watch after the kids if they got sick or hurt. Wouldn't you know, Bette went to a baseball game at the college and the baseball came into the stands and hit her on the head. Dr. Archer took her to the hospital, ordered an Epsom Salt pack on her head, and kept her overnight for observation. We always laughed about Dr. Archer and his Epsom Salt. If it was a concussion, we put Epsom Salts packs on the head, in addition to a dose "to relieve swelling of the brain." If it was a cut or infection, we soaked it in Epsom Salt, so there was always a huge box in our medicine cabinet.

A special treat we had each summer was a visit from Uncle Lonnie and Aunt Katherine. They lived in Des Moines, Iowa, where he was superintendent of the Coca-Cola Bottling Company. Dad Cole lived with them until he became ill with cancer and had to be put in a nursing home.

Word came from Uncle Lonnie that Dad Cole was losing his battle with the cancer and death was near. I felt I must take the children to see him, so we arranged to go during Christmas vacation. Bill had to stay home because of his job. Jerry drove us. I left with $40 in my purse. We stopped in Kansas City for a visit with Aunt Cassie and Uncle Louis. We heard one afternoon that a blizzard was coming in that night, so we decided we should drive to Des Moines before it reached us. On the way we ran into a narrow band of freezing rain about sixty miles from Des Moines. Jerry was creeping along at ten miles per hour when we came around a curve and there sat a car in our lane. Brakes would not stop us; we slid into the back of the car, ruining our radiator.

The car we hit belonged to an oil company in Oklahoma. The driver was out cleaning the sleet off his windshield so he could see to drive. Lucky for us, the company had good insurance and took care of all our expenses. The man saw that we were housed and fed in a good motel and, the next morning, Lonnie brought us a new radiator down from Des Moines. We did not let this ruin our visit. We could drive during daylight hours. Uncle Lonnie taught Jerry how to drive on ice and we reached home safely.

One day, a letter came from Aunt Ruth. I opened it and read:

"Dear Sister, I just have to tell you the good news. A few weeks ago, Mother and I let our cousin, Veda, have her wedding at our house. She was married to John Burns, a Chief in the Navy. John brought some of his buddies. When we served dinner afterwards, one of the guys got a piece of fried chicken that embarrassed Mother to death. It was the neck. This fellow was so gracious to Mother and got such a kick out of the incident that suddenly we became close friends. I have been seeing Harold often since that night. We are already talking about getting married. He is waiting for his divorce to become final. My life has really changed, so someday I may get rid of this name Howard and take on Mrs. Harold Martin. We will see. I will keep you posted. Love, Ruth."

How happy I was for her. Time passed and they were married. She sent this picture to us before they came for a visit.

I shall never forget taking them out to the Extension Office and introducing Harold to Dr. Minton as "Bill Howard." Dr. Minton extended his hand and Harold took it saying, "Martin's the name." How embarrassed I was.

This year we had a new addition to our family. The Trusler family gave Annette a little black dog. Her name was

Ruth and husband, Hal

Seven, because she had seven white hairs under her chin (so the kids said). She became very dear to all of us. We had fun watching her when we would be talking and say the number seven. She would beat her tail against the floor, thinking we were speaking to her. We often did it for fun, just to see that tail hit the floor.

The girls loved to harmonize as they did the dishes (if they were in the mood). They sang old songs and new songs. I thought they did real well, and it was a joy to listen to them. One Saturday afternoon I was cleaning house and I had the radio on. A local talent show came on the air from the Conway theater. One could audition for the show and, if they were selected, they were admitted free to the movie.

When I heard the announcer say, "Now we have the Cole sisters, Annette and Carolyn, singing *Tell Me Why.* I thought I was hearing things, but it was them all right. "*Tell me why the sun does shine, Tell me why the ivy climb.*" My kids had made the radio show! Better still, they got in free to see the show.

They were wonderful kids, really. They did a lot of fine things. One day I came home from work at noon and found Uncle Willie Moore and a friend there. The girls hurriedly closed the kitchen door where they were busily preparing lunch for us. I wondered what in the world they were fixing, because our pantry shelves were not very full. We only bought enough for one week, so they couldn't have much to work with. But they served us lunch and I know Uncle Willie enjoyed it.

Another time, I remember like it was yesterday. It was my birthday. The girls thought I should have a surprise party. So they called my friend, Lila Barham, who was an excellent cook, and asked her to make me a birthday cake. When we came home from prayer meeting that Wednesday evening, I knew they were excited about something. I couldn't figure out what was going on until the people began to arrive. Then they yelled, "Surprise!" It was a surprise all right. It was a lovely party and, as I remember, my gift from the girls was a red hat and a red purse (charged to my account at Farenthal and Swartz).

I guess the greatest thing they ever did for us was to save our house from burning. One morning, Jerry emptied the trash and set it afire before we left for work. He returned the huge card board trash box to its corner on the back porch. Carolyn and Annette were sick in bed with the flu. About the middle of the morning, I got a call that our house was on fire. Jerry and I jumped in the car and drove home to find the fire trucks there and our yard full of neighbors. We could see only a tiny smoke. The fireman met me and said, "Your girls saved your house." It seemed a corner of the box had caught fire and smoldered on the back porch until it blazed. The girls smelled the smoke and one called the fire department and me (in that order), while the other fought the fire with the garden hose. Their reward was a record player. We were so thankful.

The boys were very helpful, too. They worked in the garden, cared for the lawn and took care of the chickens. Jerry was very apt at wall papering and painting. It took us all working together to get by.

I guess they were pretty normal kids, and so, as normal kids, they fell in love. I remember Bill's first love affair, after he started to college. This was a beautiful girl from Ft. Smith. He wanted to go spend a weekend in her home, so I let him go. When we returned, he said, "Mother, she has the biggest house! It was like a mansion! It had a ballroom on the third floor." They had had a big party, so he thought everything was wonderful. But soon, a dapper young man who happened to be the son of the Governor (Ben Laney) had eyes for the girl and Bill lost out. He was killed, humiliated and distressed. He swore he was not going back to school, instead, he was going to the University of Arkansas. I let him pack his bag and hitchhike to Fayetteville to see about entering school. In a couple of days he returned. He had not been able to find room and board that he could afford. His temper had cooled and he was ready to "face the music," and so he returned to Teachers College.

Mr. Bachelor, who owned the Bachelor Hotel, gave Bill a job working at the hotel. After he did, his brother-in-law, E. Ray Scott, came up from Little Rock to operate the hotel. He had a young daughter, Jo Ann, who was a student at Hendrix College.

Bill and Jo Ann

Bill met her and you know the rest. When they became engaged, Mr. and Mrs. Scott came out to meet Bill's family. Of course, Dab Dab and Mam Maw adopted the whole family. He continued to "grandfather" the family as long as he lived.

When Bill graduated, they moved to Little Rock. In September, their first baby, and my first grandchild, was born. He was named Jon Scott Cole. We though he was great and everyone wanted to have their picture made with him.

Jerry had his love affairs, too. There was Beverly Dickerson, a

Bill, Jo and my first grandchild, Jon

Conway girl—but, the one I remember most was a Pine Bluff girl, La Ruth Jenkins. He brought her over to the house often. We would see them coming down the street and he might be chasing her with a switch. They had a lot of fun. Often a lot of their friends would come over with them. Jim Harris and Harold Hutson, I remember most. We nicknamed La Ruth, "Hester," the Rogers maid's name, because she "pitched in" and helped with the housework.

One day a new girl came to school, Dorothy Elam, from Tennessee. She lived with her aunt, Ruby Chick. The kids took a real interest in Dottie and she went to church and sang in the choir with them. Jerry often drove our car and picked up the kids at the dormitories and Dottie. Soon Jerry began to change his interests from La Ruth to Dottie. When I moved to Little Rock, they were "going steady."

Bette was next in line. I remember her first date. It was with Jimbo Flennigan. They went to a party at Nelson Westmoreland's house. Before the evening was over she called for me to come and get her. When I got in sight of the house, I saw Bette standing outside under the street light waiting for me.

When she was a junior in high school, she had a date for the Senior Prom. They went to the banquet at the Bachelor Hotel then drove to the high school gymnasium for the dance. It was raining and cold. When they stopped in front of the gym, Bette didn't wait for her date to open the door; she opened it, jumped out and slammed it shut, catching her little finger. She looked and the end of her finger was gone. She went into the gym, saw Jerry on the dance floor, and walked over and showed him the bloody stub. He nearly fainted.

They took her to the emergency room at the hospital and called me to meet them there. After an hour or so in the operating room she wanted to go back to the dance. I took her and let her watch a minute. That was enough. She was ready to go home and get in bed.

One of her flames was Stormy Smith, who was part Indian. One evening he came to pick Bette up and she was not ready. This gave Annette the chance to visit a while with him. She said, "Stormy, what Indian tribe are you from?" He said, "Cherokee." She quietly rose to her feet and held her hand up with her palm forward and shouted, "How

Brother!" Annette had heard that way back in her father's ancestry there was a Cherokee woman. This made her feel kin to Stormy.

Soon the right guy appeared on the scene— a young fellow, Darrah Ellis, from Malvern, who was a student at Teachers College. They fell "head over heels" in love. He spent a lot of time at our house playing games with Jerry and La Ruth, helping paint and eating spaghetti and beans from a can (he says, *everyday*). My friends said he was "salting the cow to get the calf." He succeeded. They decided to be married and set the date for Christmas Eve, December 24, 1950.

There was much to be done before the wedding. I only had a half-day off on Saturday. I remember going to Little Rock and shopping at Cohn's for her wedding clothes. Bette was not able to go with me because the band had to be in Stuttgart for the "Wild Duck Festival." She and Darrah dropped me off downtown and later picked me up at Bill and Jo Ann's apartment.

JoAnn Magness, from Western Grove, was the buyer in the ready-to-wear department at Cohn's and she helped me select two Hammacher suits—a blue one for Bette and a burgundy for Carolyn. They fit perfectly and the girls were pleased.

Again, my friends showed their love for us. Olive Ferguson gave a rehearsal dinner for her on December 23rd. Christmas Eve was on Sunday. After church, Margurite and Priddy Westmoreland had all of us over at their house for lunch. What a great help.

Bette and Darrah's Wedding

Margurite told me that Othar Smith announced at church that the wedding would be at 4 p. m. "I can see them now," he said, "at home with their hair rolled up getting ready."

Carolyn and Annette had their "puppy love" experiences, too. I guess Jerry Nichols was Carolyn's first love. Annette was so angry because I was going to move her away from Conway and Hank Hawk. This picture was made during the Homecoming Parade the last year we lived in Conway.

Homecoming parade

You can see the girls on the float. Annette was just coming into her glory, and it was a traumatic thing to be moved away from all her friends

I have often thought of how the life of our family was affected by life in Conway. Bill joined the National Guard and, when he graduated from college, he had to wait until he was old enough to receive his commission he had earned through the Guard. Bill was waiting an assignment as teacher in the Pulaski County school system and working at National Shirt Shop. Due to the Korean conflict, the superintendent of schools decided he should not risk having a teacher who belonged to the National Guard, as they might be called up any day. He started working for Franke's Bakery in desperation.

In the summer he went to camp at Ft. Benning, GA. Dab Dab and Mam Maw took Jo Ann and Jon down to see him. They invited me to go along. Aunt Ruth and Uncle Hal lived in Key West and they had invited Carolyn to visit them, so she rode down with us, and I put her on a bus to Key West. I had no idea how far Key West was, but she made it fine, in fact, she had a ball. She returned to Conway on the bus a few weeks later, as brown as a gingerbread man and full of tales to tell.

When Bill returned from camp, he decided that he wanted to go into the Army full time. So, before we hardly knew it, he started his career in Camp Roberts, California. His career ended twenty-nine years later when he retired as a Colonel.

Jerry was different from Bill. He wanted no part of the military. I remember when he had his eighteenth birthday, he waited until the last afternoon of the last day to register for the draft. As I remember it, we pulled up in front of our house for lunch and, before getting out of the car, I said, "Jerry, this is your last day to register. You must do that this afternoon." He asked, "Do I have to?" I told him that was the law and he must. Before time for him to be drafted, he auditioned for the Navy Band, was accepted and all his years in service were with a band. Afterwards, he settled in Virginia Beach, Virginia, near where he had been stationed and has been there ever since.

Col. Bill Cole, (Ret.)

Bette and Jo Ann were expecting babies about the same time. Bette's was due first and Jo Ann came up from Little Rock to await the arrival. One night I dreamed I was trying to get Jo Ann to the doctor and she had her baby by the side of the road. I woke up frightened to death. The dream was so real. The next morning, I made her go home. I know her feelings were hurt, but not for long, because the second day after she left, I got a telephone call from Dab Dab, saying Jo Ann had had a baby boy. Complications had arisen and the baby had been put in an Air Lock, an iron lung for babies, to help his breathing. The sisters at St. Vincent's thought the child would die so they baptized him, but he fought for his life and won. He was named Stephen Merrill Cole. I was sure the Lord had given me a dream that saved his life.

A few nights later, Bette had to go to the hospital. Darrah and I sat with her several hours before the baby came. This was a new experience for me, and I suffered with her as she had contractions. After the baby boy was born and she was back in her room, I went in. She said, "Mother have you been working today?" There I had suffered along with her all day and she couldn't even remember I was there. Thanks to the spinals, she had no memory of the pain.

Darrah and I were at the window of the nursery, trying to get a peek at the baby. Darrah said, "There he is, see his black head." About that time a nurse walked in and picked up the bald headed baby to show us. Darrah had mistaken a black syringe for the baby's head. We had a big laugh. The baby was named Michael Darrah Ellis.

Soon after Christmas Bette and Darrah moved to Little Rock. Bill was sent to Germany and Jo Ann soon followed. It was quite a task for her to go that far with two babies.

I started to work at Little Rock in the fall and rode with some other commuters. When the days grew cold, I knew I would have to move into Little Rock because, when days came that I couldn't drive into the city, those would be the days I

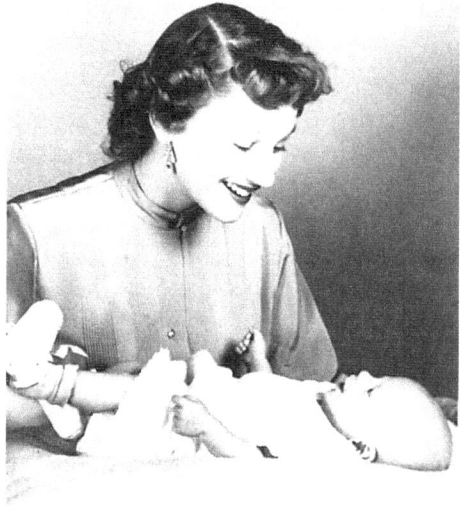

Bette and baby Michael

would be needed most at the Weather Bureau.

I began looking for a place to move. I could not find a house I could afford to rent, so I decided to rent a small apartment in the Riverside

Apartments where Bette and Darrah lived. And so, in mid December, it came to pass that we moved from this dear old house at 625 Donaghey in Conway to Little Rock.

Jerry remained in Conway. He moved into the dormitory. Carolyn was in Washington with Mother, so there was only Annette and me to move.

Well, I went to Conway with a husband, a grandmother, five children and a Jersey cow. I left there a widow, a mother-in-law, a grandmother and a lot wiser than when I came.

Part 5: 1952-1956

Moving to Little Rock was a traumatic thing for me, as well as for Annette. Since it was the Christmas season, we were so homesick for our friends. I could imagine what they were doing and I was missing it all. Annette cried every day. I wanted to but I tried to control my emotions and not let anyone know how I was suffering.

Jerry came home to spend the holidays. I did not have the heart to cook a Christmas dinner for the three of us so I said, "We will eat out." That was a big mistake. We drove and drove from one restaurant to another, only to find them closed. Finally we found one open out Arch Street Pike. By then Jerry and Annette had fussed so much no one was in the mood for a Christmas dinner. But, we had turkey with all the trimmings.

Annette started to school at Pulaski Heights Junior High School. She was in the ninth grade. She liked nothing about it. In fact, she hated every minute of it. We went to Immanuel Baptist Church the first Sunday to Sunday school and church. This was the church I thought we would attend. That Sunday afternoon, I took Annette out to the Heights Theater to see a movie. When I picked her up, she said, "Mother, I want to go to Pulaski Heights Church tonight." I said, "No, I think we better go back to Immanuel. Maybe next Sunday we will visit Pulaski Heights." I had been told Pulaski Heights church was called the "silk stocking church," and I certainly did not want to go where the rich people went.

Annette begged to go to Pulaski Heights because some girls from school were at the movie and she had promised them she would come to B.T.U. Reluctantly, I took her to Pulaski Heights. When I walked in the door, different ones began to greet me. There was Martha Jean Nunnaly, J. S. Rogers' sister, and her husband, Frank. There was Harold Neathery, whose mother, father and sister were neighbors in Conway. His wife, Marie, was so friendly. A sister of Clarence Day, a merchant in Conway, was there. I have never been so welcomed. Needless to say, we never went back to Immanuel.

My work was difficult at the Weather Bureau. It was hard to learn to operate the business machines that were necessary for me to use. I knew nothing of the lingo—everything seemed hard. I wished a thousand times I was back in the Extension Office in Conway. Othar Smith knew what a hard time I was having and he came by and had lunch with me a couple of times when he was in Little Rock. It seemed he was the one I could talk to. He was a good counselor.

Darrah and Bette soon moved to Lonoke to his grandfather's house and Annette and I were alone. Darrah commuted to Little Rock to work each day. I continued to look for a house, but none was to be found that I could afford in the neighborhoods where I wanted to live. Mr. Hickman said I better move into the Highland Courts, a low-rent government development for poor people. I took one look and vowed I would never move there.

The car I had gave me so much trouble. It was a constant pain in the neck. It had a habit of dying when I stopped at a stop light. There were several lights on the way to the Weather Bureau. Often I could not get it to start again and would end up having to ask someone to give me a push. Of course, they dared not refuse because they needed to get through the light themselves, so they would give me a push to get me out of their way.

Finally, I located a duplex for rent that suited me. It was on Crystal Court, an excellent area for us, as it was within walking distance of our church, Annette's school, the Stifft Station Shopping area and, most important, the city bus line. I was thrilled to learn the rent was low enough that I could afford it. So, we moved to 120 Crystal. Now that I was near the bus line, I began riding the bus rather than fooling with the car. I just parked it against the curb and left it there. This meant I had to leave home early because I had to transfer downtown to get a bus out to the airport where the Weather Bureau was.

One day, I remember I was strolling along Main Street waiting for the Pulaski Heights bus to come. I stopped at Kempners and was looking in the windows. I became aware that a man was standing beside me. Every time I would move, he would move along with me. I could not get away from him, and I could not see higher than his belt buckle without looking up. Finally I could stand it no longer. I looked up and, to my surprise, it was Dr. Hicks, our pastor. We had a big laugh.

Dr. Hicks became a close friend. He was quiet and gentle, but had an enormous sense of humor. I met so many fine people in Pulaski Heights Baptist Church, I can't believe I was nervous about going there.

Every summer we had a youth revival. Othar Smith had moved from Conway to Lebanon, Tennessee. I told the Evangelism Committee about how wonderful he was, and they took my recommendation and asked him to come and preach for the revival. Before he came, I became nervous. Was Othar really as good as I thought he was? Or did he help me through so many difficulties that I had a feeling that he was outstanding? I was not disappointed. Everyone in the church was pleased. Our theme was, *Turn Your Eyes Upon Jesus*. That week was very inspirational to me.

One thing that happened in that church that helped me through that era of my life was a sermon Dr. Ralph Phelps, president of Ouachita University, preached. His subject was, "How to Worry." He used Jesus' instructions found in Matthew. A story he told stuck with me. It was about a little clock that got to figuring how many times it would have to tick in a minute, and hour, a day, a month, a year, etc. The number became so astronomical that facing it caused the clock to have a nervous breakdown. A psychiatrist was called in and he mended the broken main spring. He asked the little clock how many times it ticked at a time. The clock said, "One." So the psychiatrist said, "Well, I'm going to set you back on the mantle and you tick one tick, then if you feel like ticking the next tick, do so and go on and on like that without thinking too far ahead." And, you know, that clock has been sitting on that mantle for forty years ticking one tick at a time.

I decided that lesson was for me. I needed to learn to live one tick at a time.

A young German student, named Fred Alkofer, came to Teachers College during the time I worked there. He was a nice looking young man, and I was determined that the kids and I were going to get to know a real live German to try to take away the bitterness we had toward the Germans who killed our dad. I invited Fred to come to our home in Conway and we felt very close to him. Now that I had moved to Little Rock, I asked Jerry to bring Fred down for a weekend. I was able to get tickets for a show at the auditorium that weekend and we had a good time.

When the school year was nearing the end in May, I went to Conway to hear Fred speak to the faculty and student body in Chapel. He made a very impressive talk. I remember he told about how frightened he had been to come to America to study. He said his grandparents had been killed in an American air raid over his hometown. Here he had become close friends with his English professor, Dr. Behrens, who was a bombardier during the war. He said, "How do I know he was not the one who dropped the bomb that killed my grandparents?" Then he added that he had learned that there were just two kinds of people in the world, "Those you loved and those you didn't know." There was not a dry eye in that auditorium, and I felt he did a lot to remold the relationships between the Americans and the German people.

For years Fred and I corresponded. I wish we had continued. I expect I became too busy and it was my fault. While Bill was in Germany, Fred found them and they became friends—so, it is a small world after all.

School was ending and Jerry graduated from ASTC. How proud I was of him. We went up for the big occasion. He knew that he would soon be called into service, so he decided to go into the Navy rather than waiting to be drafted. He auditioned for the Naval School of Music and was accepted.

Another big decision he made was to get married before leaving. So, on June 21st, Betty and Darrah came up and we all attended the wed-

Jerry and Dorothy's wedding day

ding, which took place just after the worship service at the First Baptist Church of Conway.

Jerry had no money for a wedding trip, so I told him Annette and I would go to Bette and Darrah's and he could honeymoon at our apartment. Another thing was our old car—it looked so awful and was so undependable, so Darrah told Jerry he could use his car to leave the church and we would drive our old wreck back to Little Rock. Of course, the kids painted "Just Married," etc. all over Darrah's car and tied tin cans to the axles. This was fun until we got to Little Rock and had to exchange cars. I wanted to go by a car wash and have Darrah's car cleaned, but he said, "No." Bette insisted that I ride in the front seat with Darrah. So we drove through town and into Lonoke with Darrah and me in the front seat. Bette, Annette and Mike ducked down between the seats. One thing about it, we were a happy pair, or so it would have appeared. We were dying laughing.

I believe only one day passed before Jerry called and said he had received orders to report immediately to Great Lakes, Illinois. From there, they went to Washington, D.C.

Jerry in uniform

In 1951 I was invited to the Ouachita College campus for the dedication of a memorial to graduates killed in World War II. The memorial had three sections. On the two outside sections were listed the names of those who had made the supreme sacrifice. On the middle section, there was engraved a praying soldier and the words of his prayer, as follows: *Almighty God, Merciful Father of all mankind. Hear my dying petition. Inspire those who shall live in the world to see the futility and tragedy of war. Fill their hearts with love of Thee and their fellowman. Grant unto them courage and wisdom to guide our world into a lasting peace. May my supreme sacrifice help those who shall come after to remember the terrible cost of war and then I shall not have died in vain but in the service of Thy Son, The Prince of Peace. Amen"*

OBU memorial – *Photo by Bill Down*

Carolyn returned home and entered the University of Arkansas at Fayetteville that fall. Our dear friends, Bill and Jean Holeman, drove up to Fayetteville with me to carry her things.

Mr. Ellis operated a commuter plane called Skyways from Fayetteville to Little Rock. He often invited me to fly with them, since he learned I had never been in an airplane. After Carolyn went up there, I told him I would take him up on his offer. He said, "Fine, if there's an empty seat, it is yours."

When I had a couple of days off, I packed a bag and went out to the airport. There was no one except me and the pilot on the flight to Fayetteville. I spent the night and returned the next day. This was an experience I will never forget. When we were airborne, I felt like I was in a rocking chair, high in the air, seeing my beloved Ozarks from an interesting angle.

Another thing, I had the opportunity of attending a seminar Blake Smith was conducting on the campus. I remember it was on prayer. He was asked by a student, "How can you tell what is God's will for your life?" He answered, "To be honest with you, I have never known beyond the shadow of a doubt God's will for me when I have reached points of decision. But, I have always prayed that God would never let me get too far away from His will and then I did the best I could." This was an inspiration for me to hear, because I had often wrestled with the same question.

Carolyn dated Leon Fields from Little Rock. She was elected one of the dream girls for his fraternity, Pi Kappa Alpha. Soon after this, he was killed in a car wreck.

While Bill was in Germany, he had the opportunity to visit his father's grave.

Mike Ellis grew up fast and was a cute little boy. One day Bette and Mike came out to the Weather Bureau. Bette was pregnant and was having labor pains. Mr. Rink couldn't get us out of there fast enough. We took Mike by a baby sitter and we went on to our apartment. Before long, we had to go to the hospital. Darrah met us there. I went then and picked up Mike and we waited for the news, "A new baby girl!" Caryn was her name. She was a beautiful child and got lots of loving from her family, her aunts and uncles and her grandmother Cole.

We had a chance to get a picture of four generations when Mom came to see us. I don't know what the occasion was to bring on the orchids, but it must be Mother's Day.

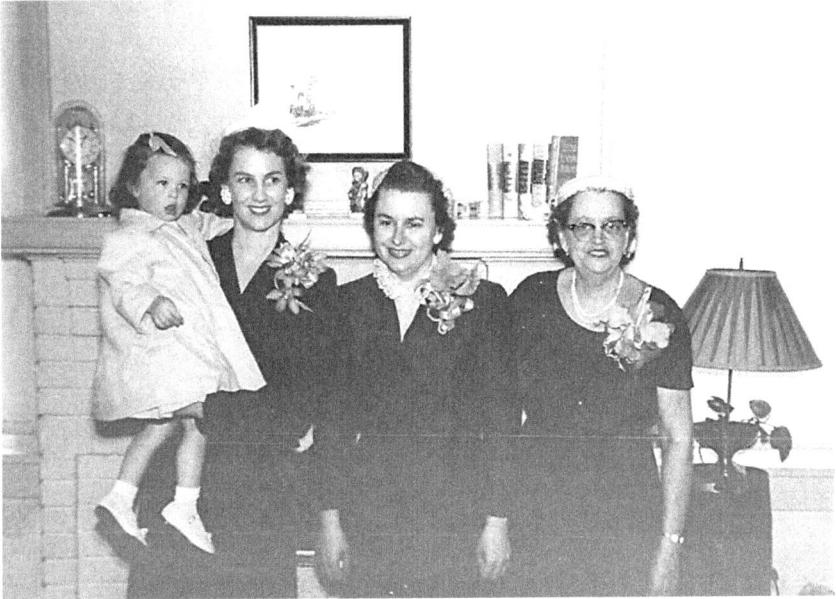

Four generations: Caryn, Bette, Helen and Mother

In the early 1950's when the slogan "*I like Ike*" was sweeping the country, I failed to get into the spirit of it. Even though he had achieved the highest rank in the Army, I was not willing to elevate him to the presidency. But, despite my vote, he was elected and took office in 1953. He soon started his Reduction in Force—a process of eliminating government programs that he thought were not needed. When a government employee or civil service worker's job was wiped out, that person had the right to bump an employee of lower status in another office. Finally, this hit me. I was bumped by an employee who had eleven years of service. I was given a thirty-day notice. My world was shaken again. Had I not followed God's Will when I moved to Little Rock? Here I was with no job! I felt like God and my government, too, had treated me unjustly. The lady who bumped me was not married, had no children, and my husband had given his life for his country and the Lord knew I needed a job.

On the twenty-eighth day after my notice, I had not been able to find another job. Knowing my predicament, Mr. Rink, the assistant meteorologist, called the U. S. Corps of Engineers and asked them if they had a place for me. I had talked with them once and nothing was available. But the personnel manager asked that I come for an interview that afternoon. This presented another problem. I had no car and I was not dressed properly to go for an interview. Mr. Rink took care of this. He sent Mr. Wheeler to drive me home in the Weather Bureau car and wait for me to get dressed then drive me to Third and Broadway to the engineers office and wait while I had my interview.

After talking with Butter Jones in the personnel office, he took me in to meet Harrison Green, head of the Program Development Branch. While in this section, my eyes fell on a nice looking man behind a desk with plaque hanging above his head, saying, Col. Somebody. I thought this was the gentleman's name. When I returned to the Weather Bureau, they said, "Well, how was it?" I said, "I saw the best looking Colonel I ever saw." A few days later, when I went to work in that section, I learned this man was not a Colonel, but J. W. Littleton, and the plaque was a signing board. In other words, it told who was signing letters going out that day.

I hated the work. It was difficult and besides I had had to take a grade reduction, and that meant less money than I had been receiving. My job was getting out the Daily Log for the District. This meant going from one office to another gathering news announcements, etc. to be put together, stenciled, reproduced and distributed before the end of each day.

My boss was an old "Scrooge." He would give me letters to type or work to do and say, "Now there can absolutely be no erasures on this." I could not make a half dozen carbon copies after hearing this without making a mistake. If I made an error in the Log, he was real unhappy with me. I liked the people I met as I gathered news, but I dreaded working at my desk.

One glorious day, the news came that my boss was being transferred to another state. What joy this was to my ears! Then the announcement came that Mr. Littleton, or Lit as he was called in the office, would be given the job. Not many days passed until I made a mistake in the Log. When I found it after it had been reproduced, I took it to Mr. Littleton and told him I had made a mistake, expecting a reprimand. Instead, he calmly said, "Let me tell you something, Helen, the person who doesn't make a mistake never does any work." From that minute on, he was my friend and I felt I could do my work.

The second grandbaby was born to Jerry and Dotty. They sent us these pictures made at Mother's house in Arlington.

Jerry and second grandchild, Suzie

They named her Suzanne Marie, my first namesake. We thought she was so pretty. One day I got a call from Jerry and he was at the Memphis airport. He was sobbing—he had received orders for overseas shipment and he said, "I can't go. I can't leave Dottie and Suzie."

What do you say in a case like that? I knew his heart was breaking, and I could understand why. I said, "Son, you have to go. There is nothing else you can do." Not much encouragement, I would say, but about two hours later, the telephone rang again. It was Jerry. He was at the Little Rock airport and feeling better. He said, "I'll be all right." That made me feel better.

Dotty brought Suzie to visit us and she loved to look at her daddy's picture, and kiss it. She also loved to play the piano and climb the stairs.

News came that the sixth grandchild had been born in Germany. This

Carol Ann, sixth grandchild

was Carol Ann when she was eight weeks old, made by her brother, Jon. Doesn't she have a lot of hair?

Holidays were always special in our household. Easter, 1955, was a big day for us. Jerry was back from the Pacific and Mom came for a visit. This was a family picture made after church.

From left to right: Jerry, Dottie, Bette, Helen, Suzie, Annette, Mother, Darrah, Carolyn and Mike

Jerry and Dottie moved to Charleston, South Carolina, after this. Carolyn was attending Little Rock Junior College this year. There she met young Ferrell McEwen.

Carolyn and fiancé Ferrell

After a few months of courtship, they planned to be married. Aunt Ruth made Carolyn a beautiful wedding dress, and I made dresses for the bridesmaids, Bette, Annette and Sandra, Ferrell's sister. All the plans were made, date set and everything, when Ferrell's father died. The wedding was postponed for about a month. Before the date arrived, I had to adjust all three dresses. They had to be skin tight and each one had changed in some way.

Ferrell belonged to the Westover Hills Presbyterian church, the same church Mr. Littleton belonged to. He was very interested in this marriage and attended the wedding. Mr. Littleton's wife was a heart patient and she was not able to be out of bed very much. He always called her as soon as he got to work and then would go home at noon to see about her. He asked me to remind him 10:30 a.m. each day to call her. I would hear him say, "Hello Lucille, this is your Lucky Strike extra." This kind man! I marveled at his devotion to his wife. She grew continuously worse, and I watched him as her life ebbed away. How I wished there was something I could do to relieve the hurt I knew he was feeling.

The job in our office was a temporary one for him, as they waited for something to open up. He had been working out of the District on a special assignment and had returned to the Little Rock office just before I went to work there. Soon after Lucille died, Lit was moved upstairs to the Engineering Department to a job more suitable for his training and experience. I still got to say hello when I gathered news for the Daily Log. Occasionally, he would go to lunch with some of us in our office.

Bill's tour of duty in Germany was ending. He was coming home. I could hardly wait to see those darling children. Bill suggested that I meet them at Mother's in Arlington, Va. I made arrangements to get off, bought a plane ticket and got ready to go.

The last afternoon before my leave started, I took the Daily Log up to Col. Hesselberger to sign, and he said, "Helen, could I get you to do something special for me tomorrow?" I said, "Sir, I won't be here tomorrow. I'm taking some time off." Then he said, "But this is very important. I need you to do this." My heart fell. I guess my face showed the distress I felt because the Colonel said, "I'm just teasing. Someone put me up to this." Then I said, "You have been talking to E. Ray Scott, haven't you?" He admitted it and I was relieved.

I flew to Washington, but on the way I stopped by Nashville, Tenn. to visit Othar Smith. I needed to talk with him. I found myself more and more drawn to Lit. He was coming down to the office more often and we were eating lunch together most every day. I kept recalling the way I seemed to be drawn to him the first time I saw him. Looking back, it was almost as if the Lord said to me, "That's the one for you." Could this have been a revelation from the Lord? It bothered me that someone had to die to make this possible.

He was well educated, a GS 12, and I was only a GS 2, but when we were together, I had no feeling of inferiority. Could I be falling in love again after twelve years of widowhood? What would the kids think? I needed to talk this over with Othar, even though it was too soon after his wife's death for him to be thinking about remarrying.

Othar assured me that God had plans for our lives. He reminded me of a Scripture passage in Jeremiah 29, where the Lord spoke to His people in exile through his prophet, saying, *"I know the plans I have for you," says the Lord, "plans for good and not for evil, to give you a future, and a hope."* He told me that he believed God's good plans for me went beyond past disappointments, and he asked me to remember that God opened and closed doors for the purpose of guiding us into His plan for our lives. We prayed and I went on my way fully intending to leave my life in God's hands and wait for doors to open and doors to close.

Bill called from New York to tell Mother and me that they had arrived. We could hardly wait for them to get their car and their luggage together and drive down to Arlington. Jon was four years old, Steve three and Carol Ann less than a year. I could hardly believe my ears—that lingo with German accent was my grandchildren speaking. After three years in Germany, what else could I expect?

Luggage, luggage, three children, plus Granny. What a problem. How would we ever get home? Bill bought a luggage carrier to go on top of the car and, with all the bags up there, we found room for all of us in the car—but not much room. Bill soon found that, when he reached a nice traveling speed, the weight of the luggage caused the car to vibrate terribly. Helpful Steve said, "Dadda, don't let de kar wobble out into de woods." On the trip home, I recall a mixture of German and English creeping out. When we passed near a zoo, Jon said, "Look, Mommie, there's a terragarten." A bus passed us in a city and it was a "strassonbaum."

When we reached Little Rock and my apartment, Jon noticed there was something lacking at Granny's house that he found other places, so he asked, "Granny, don't you have any daddy?" This seemed to worry him very much and one day, he announced, "Granny, when I get to be a big boy, I'll come and be your daddy."

On December 16th, I got a call from Farrell saying he was at the hospital with Carolyn. She was seven months pregnant and, due to severe bronchitis, she had gone into labor and the doctor had told her to meet him at St. Vincent's. The baby came and they put the tiny girl in an incubator. Her life was in danger, but we prayed and hoped for the best.

The next morning when I got to work, I called Lit and asked him to meet me at the bottom of the stairs. I told him about the baby and asked him to call his church office and tell Preacher Dick. That evening, when I was standing at the nursery window, watching the little doll fighting for her life, I looked toward the elevator door and there came Mr. Littleton. He said he just had to come out to see about them. My heart beat fast as we stood together looking in the window.

Things went well and after several days, they were able to take Mary Ellen home. This was my seventh grandchild to "ooh and goo" over.

Helen, Carolyn and seventh grandchild Mary Ellen

Bette brought the children to see me every week. This was one of the highlights of my life. When the time came for them to go home to "Nokey," Mike would leave saying, "I joyed it!" I always got a kick out of his blessing at the table. He would say, "Thank you for the eatin." If we drove up Broadway, he would say, "Dar's where Granny works."

"Where?" I would ask. He would point to the old building and say, "In that garage." I guess because a used car lot was by one side of the building and he thought it was a garage.

This used car lot was a blessing to me. When I thought I was going to have to pay someone to tow my old car away from the curb, I stopped by and asked them about it. They said they would pay me $75 for the car. I felt like I had struck oil. $75 was a real fortune.

When Christmas season arrived, my close friend in the office, Jackie Short, asked Lit and me over to her house to see her Christmas tree. So, after dinner, Lit came by and we were off to the Rivercliff Apartments together. After a couple of hours visiting around her beautiful tree, we said, "goodnight" and left for home. As we came down Crystal Court, a couple of rabbits jumped out in front of our headlights. They ran ahead of our car around the curves and down the hill. We left them as we stopped in front of my house.

Lit walked me to the front door. I turned to thank him for a nice evening and he put his arm around me and gave me a goodnight kiss. I couldn't believe it. I quickly opened the door, and he was gone. I pulled myself up the stairs and soon was in bed, trying to forget and go to sleep.

Before dawn, I woke up. In the fog of my half-waking state, it took me a few moments to recall the night before. Then I remembered—the Christmas tree...the drive home....the rabbits.....the security of his arms around me...his lips on mine. There would be no more sleep for me this morning. I lay there knowing there was no hurry about getting up. This kiss at the door changed everything. It seemed for months, two minds and two hearts had been reaching for each other. At that kiss, they merged.

Lit had held off saying the words, but his love had actually been around me for weeks through his tenderness, thoughtful deeds and, finally, the look in his eyes. I loved him as I never thought I could love anyone again.

When the morning light brought the room and its furnishings into focus, I thought, "Have I been dreaming?" No! How suddenly life can enter a completely new phase. Before the night before, there had been loneliness, insecurity, anxiety, wishfulness, searching for a way to show my interest without making a fool of myself, wondering if he would ever want to be more than my best friend. Now this all seemed behind me.

Suddenly, I stopped my daydreaming to face a fact. A solemn one indeed! He hadn't said a word. A bunch of questions whirled through my head. *Was he serious? What would my kids say? Would he want to take on a big family like I had? Would he ever want to marry again? Marry?* No one had mentioned marriage—those were questions that might never need to be answered. The only thing I knew at this point was, I loved him.

Hearing Annette moving around in her bedroom, I slipped out of bed and into the real world. Breakfast had to be prepared. I had to dress for work and walk the half block to Markham Street to wait for my ride to work. One of the girls in the office came down Markham and was glad to have me ride with her. Things went easier that morning, and I was anxious to get to work because there I would see Lit again.

My heart beat so fast when he walked into my office, Coke in hand. What would he say? What would I see in his eyes? His quick warm smile reassured me. Now I could face anything. From that day on, we ate lunch together but never went out together again until after Valentine's Day. After an exchange of Valentines, he asked me and Annette to eat dinner with him at Franke's Cafeteria. Annette thought this was great, so did I.

It was wonderful to discover all the little things two people have in common, the excitement of being together. In truth, I felt like dancing, twirling, skipping and singing. How good to be in love again.

One night I dreamed I had something bad wrong with me. I was so frightened that I called early the next morning and made an appointment with Dr. Dean Wallace, a gynecologist. He said I must have surgery immediately. This was Friday, so I made arrangements to go into the hospital on Monday.

Lit went to Louisiana for a week's vacation, but he put a card in the mail before he left, and it reached the hospital and was delivered to my room just before I went into surgery. When I came back from the recovery room, the girls asked me if I got any mail. I would make a silly reply about getting a card from Lit. They had a lot of fun, but I was too groggy to care.

I have been told that God always hears Lit's prayers. Many say he has an inroad with the Lord. He may have, because the doctor thought I was eaten up with cancer, but the report came back "benign."

Some new neighbors moved in across the street, Bill and Margie Fogleman. Bill was a Presbyterian minister. He had been pastor of the church in Lonoke and had baptized Mike and Caryn. When Lit began picking me up for work each morning, Bill became curious as to what was going on. He was a big tease and a lot of fun.

One time Lit asked me to go to his church to hear a theologian who was lecturing there. I went, but I did not hear one word. Everyone seemed to be looking at me—they were wondering, "Who in the world is that?" We were in the little chapel near the front. As soon as the last amen was said, I heard a deep voice in the back say, "Phew, I smell a Baptist in the house." It was that Bill Fogleman! I was so embarrassed, but I managed to get out of there. The next afternoon when I got home from work, Margie came over and told me that a dozen women from the church had called her to ask, "Who was that woman with J. W.?" You know, I never have been able to get one of those women to admit calling Margie.

Not long after this, we began to talk of marriage sometime in the fall after Annette had gone to college. She was a senior in high school. I had worried how I would ever be able to live alone. It seemed, as Othar Smith had told me, doors were opening and God had a plan for my future. I was so grateful.

The next thing that happened was receiving a ring. I had never had a diamond ring and this was beyond my dreams. Lit said, "Don't wear it or show it until I have a chance to tell Mrs. Calhoun, Lucille's mother." So, off to Louisiana he went to tell her family. That night he called me and said, "You can ring the line and tell people now." They had received the news real well and, in years to come, accepted me as one of the family. When Mrs. Calhoun wrote us letters, she would begin, "Dear Children." What a blessing this was.

I decided I would ride the bus to Ft. Smith where Bill and Jo Ann lived and tell them. I asked Bette to let Mike ride up with me. We had a big time. The evening before, at the dinner table, Jon said, "I know what would make Gran happy, if we could find a man who would marry her, and be her daddy." What the grandson didn't know was that Granny had found her one who really was going to marry her.

When Jo Ann picked us up at the bus station, I kept flashing my ring around. I rubbed my nose, I shook my hand, I used it to emphasize everything I was saying, but she didn't notice the ring for a long time. When she did, she pulled to the curb and stopped. She "ooh-ed and aah-ed" and then hurried home to tell the rest of the family.

The main topic of conversation that weekend was Lit. That afternoon, when we were resting, I was lying beside Jon and I was telling him that he would have to come to see me now so he could meet my new "daddy." I told him he was a big man, "bigger than your daddy." This ruffled Jon and he said, "Granny, don't talk like that." Not knowing what I had done or said, I asked, "Don't talk like what?" He said, "Well, don't say my daddy is bigger than your daddy. That's like little kids do."

Nothing more was said about size until Lit had to go to Ft. Smith for the district and he went out to see Bill and his family, carrying gifts for each of the children in "sure nuff" grandfather fashion. During the evening, Jon sidled up to him and said, "I was going to get Granny a man if she hadn't found you." Lit inquired, "Well, what do you think about the one she found?" After looking him up and down from head to foot, Jon said, "Think I would have picked a bigger one."

Annette had a problem. What was she going to call Lit? She talked to her friends at school and one day Jane Brockman came up with an idea, "Why don't you call him Daddy Lit?" That was it!

Mike and Caryn were very fond of Daddy Lit. He enjoyed their affection and thought it was wonderful to be taking on a family, having never had any children. They tell a joke on him at the church. They say he prayed that the Lord would not let him get lonesome. But, as the family increased, he cried out to the Lord, "That's enough! That's enough!" But, we know that isn't so.

We became more and more excited about getting married and one night, Lit said, "Why are we waiting until fall? Why don't we get married now?" We felt so old then. We thought probably we would not have more than another ten years to live. So we set up our date, not once, but twice. Finally, the date was set for April 21. I invited Mary and T. S. Rogers down for dinner and to meet Lit. I fixed broiled chicken and I can remember practicing and practicing on that. It was real important that I broil it just right. Lit came over a little early and we watched the Lawrence Welk Show. That was one of our favorites.

Every one of my friends and family approved of Lit. He wanted his friends to meet me, so one Sunday afternoon, he took me to meet a couple of elderly ladies that were very dear to him. The first stop was at Mrs. Goodnight's. She was a real aristocrat who lived in a big home on Gaines Street, filled with antiques like I had never seen before. Lit rang the doorbell and we waited for her to come to the door. My heart was pounding. Lit greeted her with a kiss and she motioned for me to sit on the love seat next to her.

"How many children do you have, my dear?"

"Five."

"Are they married?"

"No, Annette is a senior in high school."

"I see, Is she planning on going to college?"

"I hope so. At the moment, I don't see how I can send her, but Lit says we will work that out."

"How many grandchildren do you have?"

"Seven."

"That's quite a family."

The line of questioning was making me increasingly uneasy. I had a strange feeling in the pit of my stomach.

"J. W.," she said, "You will be taking on a big job. Never having children, do you think you can handle this?"

"I'm looking forward to it," Lit replied.

"Where did you go to college?" she asked, turning back to me.

"Arkansas State Teachers College at Conway," I answered.

"Did you graduate?"

"No, I only went half a semester. You see, my husband was killed in World War II and I had to go to college to get a license to teach kindergarten."

"J. W. is a very well-educated person, he likes people, but sometimes he is too soft hearted. I want to know that this is real love and not just a marriage to help you, whom he admires, or for convenience. You know he just lost a lovely wife."

"Yes, I know."

Lit took over the conversation and was able to convince the dear soul that we really were in love. We started to go after a while and when we got up she ushered me over to the window and pulled the drape so she could see my face. I felt like my upper lip was curling up. Honestly, I felt like a fool. She said, "You're a pretty lady." With that we were gone. As we drove away, Lit reached over and squeezed my hand. "I can tell, Helen, that our visit with Mrs. Goodnight was not very pleasant," he said.

"I'm afraid not."

"She is different from us. She is interested in financially and socially prominent people. She probably had one of her well-to-do friends picked out for me. Don't let it worry you, she will be all right when she knows how much "Jamie" loves you. She will love you, too. O.K.?"

We laughed a bit, to ease the tension.

"I will try to learn to sit, talk and eat properly. That would please her," I promised.

"She grilled you too hard," Lit said.

"Let's forget it—I had rather think about us," I said.

He squeezed my hand and said nothing more until we pulled up in front of Miss Grace's house, across the street from Lit's home. "This will be different. You will love Miss Grace," Lit told me. No words could have been truer. This gracious old lady met us at the door with the warmest welcome I had ever received. We sat and talked and laughed for more than an hour. I loved this woman. She loved Lit, too. When we started to leave, she went to the door with us, then sheepishly grinned and half whispered, "You don't have anything to worry about. I'm not supposed to tell it, but Mrs. Goodnight called me after you left and..... you passed!"

With this secret, we parted with a promise to see each other often when I moved in across the street. Our friendship grew and grew. She called Lit "Our husband," and I loved it.

The next place we went to was to the Baptist Hospital where Mae Fuller was a patient. Lit and Lucille had rented a small house just back of the Fuller's large home and they were good friends.

We went in the room and Lit broke the news to her. She said, "Well, I had someone in mind had I known you were ready to get married again." Then she looked up at me and said, "You have some mighty big shoes to fill." By this time, I had had it, so I answered, "I won't be trying to fill anybody's shoes. I have some of my own." Then I softened up and explained, "Lit and I know that both of us have had happy marriages. We each have respect for the other's first mate. There will be no competition or jealousy."

There was another friend I had to meet. This was Lit's fishing partner's wife, Marion Holder. I had met Fred one time and he advised me never to marry Lit until I saw him in his fishing clothes. Marion invited us over for dinner a few nights before the wedding. I dreaded this, as Marion was Lucille's best friend. I soon learned that I had nothing to fear. Through the years that have passed, Marion and I have been bosom friends.

I chose Jackie Short, who worked with me in the office and who invited Lit and me over to see her Christmas tree and "got the ball rolling," to be my Matron of Honor. Lit chose Cooksey Fuller as his best man.

The girls in the office were all excited abut our wedding. They gave me a lovely luncheon and nice gifts, at the Sam Peck Hotel, a few days before the wedding. This is Jackie in the picture.

Helen and Jackie Short

Since I would be retiring, I would not be getting out the Daily Log anymore. On my last working day, a Special Daily Log was printed.

The Foglemans gave a tea for us on Sunday afternoon before we were married. It was such a nice party, and I got to meet many of Lit's friends from Westover Hills and elsewhere. Our plans were just about all finished.

Bill and his family came down a few days early to help with the moving, etc. One evening we were sitting on the sofa, Steve on one side of me and Lit on the other. Suddenly, Steve leaned over me, interrupting the conversation, and said, "Daddy Lit, are you really gonna marry Granny?" It was almost unbelievable!

Jerry came from Charleston, South Carolina, for the wedding. He and Bill moved our furniture from the apartment to Lit's house. Lit helped with the move and the three decided that they would go fishing as soon as everything was moved. This made them work faster and, in spite of complications, they did get to go. In the rush to get on the lake, Jerry dropped Lit's motor in the lake, and they had to fish it out.

Lit's brother, Rassie, came to help with the wedding service. His wife, Fay, and their children, John and Alice, came also. They stayed at the house with Lit. His sister, Jewel, came and was guest of the Fuller's.

We had a big surprise when Cassie knocked on the door. She rode the bus from Kansas City. She found a bed at Dab Dab's.

Many of our friends gathered at the church for the wedding. It was a simple, sweet wedding. Thurman Watson sang *Always*. There was no procession. We walked in the side door and sat on the front seat until time for the ceremony. We had a lovely reception in the Fellowship Hall.

Helen and Daddy Lit on their wedding day

Off to Niagara Falls

It comes to my mind what Berlin Henderson said to me soon after Merrill was killed. He said, "Helen, it is like you are traveling a road, and it turns. Sometimes a quick turn and sometimes a long curve, but, someday you will find yourself on a new road, an interesting road, a different road, but a good road."

Here I was heading down that new road, and it was not a disappointment. It has been a wonderful one for more than thirty years--and the road goes on. Thanks be to God!

Postscript

My book really ends with the new road, but I must give you a glimpse of what it has been like. Right quick, I became a fisherman, and Lit taught all the kids and grandkids to fish. What fun! Many new faces have been seen—new grandchildren from the first year of our marriage until we totaled twenty-two. Annette was married a couple of years later to a high school classmate, Terry Watson. He has been our friend, dentist and fishing partner throughout the years—also, the father of two of our grandchildren, Dan and Missy. Thanks be to God!

The grandchildren have married and had babies and now we have eighteen *great*-grandchildren and more on the way. I could tell you why they call them great, but that would make another book. All have been a real source of joy to us. Daddy Lit says his best investment is in grandchildren, and he has helped them in many ways.

Now, don't believe everything along the road has been free of worries or problems. We had to see Bill go to war in Vietnam. We grieved with him and Jo when little Jody died. We are thankful this has been the only grandchild we have lost. Divorces have come—Jerry first, after four children. Then Bill, after twenty-five years of marriage. Farrell had a cardiac arrest and died in 1982. Mom had a stroke, and for nine and one half years was an invalid. Daddy Lit's brother, Rassie, died and Uncle Jim, too. Daddy Lit had a heart attack. I had a triple bypass, plus a knee replacement. The grandchildren have had problems of various kinds, but always there had been the love of family that keeps us all together.

When an S.O.S. is sounded, all respond with love and encouragement. We pray and hope, remembering the quote, "God isn't finished with them yet." Jerry, Bill and Carolyn have all remarried, and now we have Beverly, Elaine and Dick to bring joy to our family. Beverly is the mother of three of our grandsons. Elaine is a great hostess. The Cole's have played the Littletons in games of bridge. (Daddy Lit has to have help!—that's all right.) Our family gets together at the "drop of a hat." Dick is attending his first family Christmas with us.

This new road has been interesting and different, as promised. Just think:

- I have had high tea at the Empress Hotel in Victoria;
- Looked at the sampan boats in Hong King;
- Walked the Boardwalk in Atlantic City;
- Stood breathless beside Niagara Falls;
- Watched the changing of the guards at Buckingham Palace;
- Rode an elephant in Thailand;
- Walked the rim of the Grand Canyon;
- Ooh-ed and aah-ed at Lake Louise in Canada;
- Eaten on the riverside at San Antonio;
- Shopped in the French Market in New Orleans;
- Watched Arkansas beat Oklahoma in the Orange Bowl;
- Went to a "sure 'nough" Luau in Hawaii;
- Fished off the shores of Monterey, California;
- Shelled the beaches of Sanibel;
- Toured Glacier Park in Montana;
- Listened to the St. Louis Symphony Orchestra;
- Sat in on the General Assembly in Edinburg, Scotland;
- Painted on location in Prescott, Arizona;
- Sailed from Victoria to Seattle aboard the Princess Marguerite;
- Was a kid for a day at Disneyland;
- Cheered for the Cardinals at the World Series in St. Louis;
- Panned for gold in Arizona;

- Gazed at the Golden Gate Bridge in San Francisco;
- Shopped the Galleria in Houston;
- Followed the Freedom Walk in Boston;
- Celebrated the Bicentennial in Philadelphia;
- Trolled the waters of Chesapeake Bay;
- Hunted for bargains in Gonzales, Mexico;
- Worshiped in Peter Marshall's church in Atlanta;
- Laughed at tall tales in West Virginia;
- Felt the healing waters at Hot Springs;
- Flew around Arkansas in Mrs. Rockefeller's private plane;
- Had breakfast in Shakertown, KY;
- Smelled the rhododendrons in the mountains of North Carolina;
- Plied the canals to the Floating Market in Bangkok;
- Thrilled to the sights and sounds of Ireland;
- Celebrated Uncle Willie Moore's 109th birthday;
- Climbed the Washington Monument;
- Wintered with the Kansas City Royals in Southwest Florida;
- Weathered a hurricane at Littleton, New Hampshire;
- Fished for rainbow trout at Calico Rock;
- Ridden the Amtrak across Northwest part of the United States;
- Enjoyed the fall foliage in Vermont;
- Eaten lobster on Bailey's Island in Maine; and
- Attended Expo '86 in Vancouver, British Columbia.

You probably are saying, "What a road!" Instead of time hanging heavy on our hands, we are unable to find enough of it to do all the things we want to do. Someone said, "Some have the gift of laughter, some the gift of love." My children and their families have enhanced both gifts a hundred-fold. When they get together, it is such fun to hear tales about things that have happened.

I can identify a little with Job who after all his suffering, the Scripture says, *"lived long enough to see his grandchildren and great grandchildren."* For this I am thankful!

We have not been a perfect family. We have made many messes, many mistakes, gone off in the wrong direction many times, but it seems God keeps drawing us back, and we have always been given a second chance.

And so, I leave you now with the challenge to pass it on and, "*tell the next generation about the Lord's power and His great deeds and the wonderful things He has done, so the next generation might learn them and, in turn, should tell their children, even the children yet to be born. In this way, they also will put their trust in God and not forget what He has done, but always obey His commandments.*" Psalms 78: 4, 6, 7.

Thanks for letting me reminisce.

Gran

Epilogue

"Sometimes bumpings are blessings in disguise…you cannot know one without knowing the other" - Jon Cole

Helen Marie White Cole Littleton, lovingly known as Granny, passed away on June 30, 1994, at the age of 80. Similar to her life, her death occurred in a manner that demonstrated the divine choreography that occurs around us each day, but of which we are often unaware. After suffering a severe heart attack followed by a massive stroke, Helen lived for four days in a coma at St. Vincent Hospital in Little Rock, Arkansas. Throughout this time she was continually surrounded by no fewer than six, and sometimes as many as fifteen children and grandchildren holding her hands, stroking her face or hair, or just silently praying over her. A tape recorder was placed on her pillow, and her favorite hymns were played and sung. As friends and family would form a circle around her bed to pray, often the nurses and doctors would join that circle.

Family members from around the country continued to arrive daily. On the fourth day, the last of her grandchildren arrived. They spent a few moments praying with her and saying their goodbyes. Within two hours of their arrival, with all of her children and grandchildren gathered around, singing *"Amazing Grace",* Helen Marie gently passed away.

The publishing of Helen's "Remembrance Book" is one of the ways that we, her children and grandchildren, are taking up the final challenge with which she charged us. In the telling and retelling of the stories our Granny passed down to us, stories of the faith, love, and courage of those who have gone before us, we have been encouraged and strengthened through our own "bumpings and blessings". We will all be forever grateful for our amazing grandmother, whose greatest gift to each of us was her living testimony of the unfathomable love and faithfulness of God.

The Cole Family

Biographical Sketch

Helen Marie Cole Littleton was born in 1914 on a farm near Valley Springs, Ark. She attended Union Grammar School and graduated from Valley Springs Training School in 1932. Before graduation, Helen married her classmate and sweetheart, Merrill Cole.

Helen and Merrill had five children: Billie Jon, 1930; Jerry, 1932; Bettelyn, 1934; Carolyn, 1935; and Annette, 1938.

After Merrill was called to active duty in 1941, the Cole family moved to Conway, Ark., while he was stationed at Camp Robinson. In November 1944 she was notified that Merrill had been killed in action in Germany, leaving her a widow with five children. In Conway, she opened Cole's kindergarten, attended and worked for Arkansas State Teachers College (now UCA). She became employed by the Weather Bureau in Little Rock and moved there in 1951. She became an active member of Pulaski Heights Baptist Church.

In 1954 she was employed by the U. S. Corps of Engineers. There she met James W. Littleton, who was a member of Westover Hills Presbyterian Church and they were married in 1956. She became a member there and was elected as the first female elder in that church. She was active in various civic organizations and was a member of Little Rock's "Panel of Americans," during the 1957 integration crisis. She and "Daddy Lit" moved to Presbyterian Village. He died in 1987 and Helen died on June 30, 1994

Acknowledgements

It is time to say thank you.

- To Helen Marie for leaving this beautiful collection of memories.
- To her son Bill, now deceased, for getting the manuscript in our hands.
- To Carolyn Hardie, Annette Watson, and Jerry Cole, the three surviving children, and other members of the extended Cole family who contributed so much to the completion of this project.
- To Dr. Dan Watson, her grandson, who made all of this possible by directing us to his sister, Michele.
- And especially to Michele, who we lovingly refer to as "Missy." She has tirelessly and enthusiastically given us her love, support and prayers while never missing a beat in taking care of her marvelous family. By telephone, by e-mail, Missy was always there, ready to gather and provide any information that we needed. We will be forever grateful for your warm welcome into the Cole family.

Sincerely,
Bill and Vera Downs

Appendix 1:

My Son
By Merrill Cole

As I am lying here upon my pillow, tossing uneasily in a vain attempt to sleep, suddenly your tousled hair and laughing face appear transfigured in the room. But this time your dancing blue eyes seem to be challenging me, inquiring about what future lies before you, what dreams are planned, what ambitions will be inspired. My answer to your questioning look is this:

For long years, we shall journey hand in hand. We will follow Goldilocks and Little Red Riding Hood into the woods. We will climb Jack's beanstalk and adventure with Robinson Crusoe. Then we will sit at the campfire of hundreds of people, and lie with the Shepherds of Syrian hills, listening, as each recites the legends of his race.

Gradually, step by step, we shall venture into the halls of knowledge where you shall meet the immortal teachers of man. They will teach you how to live with yourself and others. Sometimes "others" will crowd out the personal pronoun and you will learn the deeper meaning of sacrifice. You will know the high joy of having friends, and greater still of being one. You will be taught the proper attitudes towards your body and how to use and care for it. You will be encouraged to play sports—tennis and golf—to swim, run and enjoy life. History will open the past and show you the kingdoms of the world. You will see man's persistent struggle for light. You will discover that all who wore purple silks were not kings nor all who were persecuted, felons.

Science will teach you to trace the paths of electrons, to analyze compounds, to overcome diseases, and chart a universe of a million whirling galaxies. It will lead you to seek the soul of earth in rock and flower. You will plot the laws of fleeting thoughts and move mountains with figures. The arts will teach you the beauty of line, color and sound. These will be the eyes and ears of your mind to a world essentially invisible. At the same time, you will learn to apply your skill to the world's work. Literature will transport you on its magic carpet to distant (places) and introduce you to strange and beautiful truths.

Philosophy will help you take the long look. It will teach you to think, though no man will be wise enough to tell you what to think. Finally, religion will take your hand and lead you into the temple. There your spirit will be lifted up in worship. Let devout wisdom be the acid by which you test every gem of faith. But above all, find HIM who whispers in the stillness of night, who draws back the curtains for the dawn, and guides the birds in their migrations. Be sure that the essence of your religion is this: to find God and befriend man. Follow that gleam to the new day!!! Gradually you will grow beyond me. The time will come when you will choose your life work and your life companion. You will assume your place of responsibility among new leaders. Then one day you will take your son and show him a still greater day for mankind. By that time we will no longer be walking together. You will have pushed out into a world unknown to me and will be leading a people I shall never see. It will be your day and your generation. Such is my dream for you, my son.

Good night.

*"The Fighting Tigers" by William D. Downs Jr., pp. 28-30. Phoenix Intl, Inc. Fayetteville, Arkansas, 2004.

Appendix 2:

Government letter confirming Merrill Cole's death

319

VETERANS ADMINISTRATION

WASHINGTON 25, D. C.

4 - 2 - 45

Mrs. Helen M. Cole
625 Donaghey Street
Conway, Arkansas

YOUR FILE REFERENCE

IN REPLY REFER TO. MBAB -9

COLE, Merrill
XC-3,788,869

Dear Madam:

You are hereby notified that as the   unremarried widow of

Merrill Cole   whose death was   due to service, an award
of death pension   has been made to you under the provisions of the act of
3-20-33 as amended   at the monthly rate of $100.00 commencing 11-30-44; $91.00
from 7-12-50; $78.00 4-20-52; $65.00 from 11-24-53; and $50.00 from 12-15-56.

A check covering the initial amount due you under this award will be
mailed within the near future.

Payments of compensation or pension to or for a widow will be discontinued upon her remarriage or death. Payments of compensation or pension to or for
a child will be discontinued upon reaching the age of 18   , marriage, or death.
Payment of compensation or pension to or for a dependent parent will be discontinued upon death, or when actual dependency ceases to exist, and may be discontinued in the event of remarriage. Payments of compensation or pension to a
guardian or other fiduciary will be discontinued upon his discharge.

Upon the death, marriage or the CHANGE OF ADDRESS of any person receiving compensation or pension the Veterans Administration must be immediately
notified. Severe penalties involving fines and imprisonment are provided by
the laws of the United States when a person fraudulently accepts any payment
to which not entitled or obtains or receives money with intent to defraud the
United States.

Any correspondence with reference to this case must show the veteran's
name and the XC-number given above.

Respectfully,

R. J. HINTON,
Director,
Dependents Claims Service.

Enc. 1099

Form P-31
Revised Sept. 1943
16—99353-1

Appendix 3

End of World War II *Sandy Grady story in Arkansas Gazette*

August '45 stands out as time of unity, joy, hope for world

—WASHINGTON.

There's never been an August like that one, never a time since then when the country felt all in one piece.

And there's never been a moment like that hot August night 40 years ago, never so much laughter and hope and cockiness that the world would be okay.

What we heard first were foghorns. Every tugboat and ship in New York harbor had gone crazy, hooting and bellowing.

Then through the open window we heard taxis blaring and people yelling in the streets. A radio clicked on. " I repeat, the Japanese have surrendered," a man was saying.

My cousin and best pal, Joe, looked at me and grinned. "I knew when they heard we were coming," he said, "they'd give up."

We were trying to act cool. But we were stunned.

Both of us were 17 — this was my birthday — and we were going into the Navy the next week. We had driven up from our hometown, Charlotte, N.C., in Joe's '36 Chevy to have a bash in New York before going away to war.

Just a couple of Southern boys, barely shaving and drinking beer, playing warriors-to-be in the big city — except now there would be no more war.

"Hey," said Joe, "where's this here Times Square?"

That's where we went. Joe, his older brother, his wife and I rattled on the subway to 42nd Street and 8th Avenue. It was like falling into a volcano.

In the next four decades, I'd cover a lot of mob scenes in sports and politics. But this thing in Times Square on V-J night wasn't a crowd. It was a beast of a half-million people, a beast that roared, swayed, whooped, sweated,

Sandy Grady

Philadelphia Daily News

hugged, cheered and never stopped laughing.

Through the Broadway haze you could see the movie marquees — Joan Crawford in "Mildred Pierce" and Ray Milland in "The Lost Weekend" — and the New York Times lights flashing: "TRUMAN SAYS JAPS SURRENDER." Down below in the orgiastic mob, there was one rule: If you wore a uniform, you could grab any girl and give her a Grade-A, passion-

Watching the newsreels on TV, I thought again of that night the country was in one piece, together, proud, cocky in the neon glow.

ate, Gable-style kiss.

Joe and I felt like hollow spectators. We walked miles that night. The bars were jammed, the jukeboxes poured out "Sentimental Journey" and "I'll Never Smile Again" and you couldn't pay for a beer.

Nobody argued about the strange new bombs that had blown away Hiroshima and Nagasaki.

Emotions were primitive: Our side had won. The four-year horror and intensity was over. Nei-

ther we nor anybody we loved was going to get killed. We fell asleep at dawn, knowing there'd be a future.

By late winter 1945, though, I'd see the other side. I would be a seaman on the seaplane tender Rehoboth, steaming into mountain-rimmed Sasebo on the southern tip of Japan.

It seemed incredible that this devastated, rotting country had attacked the United States. The rusted-steel naval works was out of the 19th Century. The people looked worn, servile, not like the Rising Sun juggernaut of the newsreels.

One winter morning we sank the last of the Japanese navy. A row of subs, destroyers and cruisers was towed into the China Sea. It took all day for our planes and bombers to sink them in target practice.

"That's the end of the Japanese empire," said our C.O., a man who probably drives a Datsun 280Z and watches a Sony today.

I didn't get to Hiroshima. My own education came on a slow train ride from Yokahama to Tokyo. I saw mile after mile of shattered landscape where American fire bombs had lit flaming winds that killed 130,000 in a night.

Nothing moved. There was only the gray, still bleakness of death. That 1945 train ride across Tokyo has always colored the way I think about high-tech wars.

So life got more complex. Back home, I worked on papers again and raised kids. When Joe and I got together over a bottle of Old Crow, he'd say, "Hey, remember V-J night in Times Square?"

And in the last week, with the grainy newsreels flickering on TV, I thought again of that night: the country was in one piece, together, proud, cocky in the neon glow.

Maybe we'll never feel that good again.

Appendix 4

Department of the Army letter *Merrill Cole's* burial in St. Avold Military Cemetery

DEPARTMENT OF THE ARMY
OFFICE OF THE QUARTERMASTER GENERAL
WASHINGTON 25, D. C.

IN REPLY REFER TO

21 April 1949

1st/Lt. Merrill Cole, ASN O 305 994
Plot B, Row 18, Grave 43
Headstone: Cross
St. Avold (France) U. S. Military Cemetery

Mrs. Helen M. Cole
625 Donaghey Avenue
Conway, Arkansas

Dear Mrs. Cole:

This is to inform you that the remains of your loved one have been permanently interred, as recorded above, side by side with comrades who also gave their lives for their country. Customary military funeral services were conducted over the grave at the time of burial.

After the Department of the Army has completed all final interments, the cemetery will be transferred, as authorized by the Congress, to the care and supervision of the American Battle Monuments Commission. The Commission also will have the responsibility for permanent construction and beautification of the cemetery, including erection of the permanent headstone. The headstone will be inscribed with the name exactly as recorded above, the rank or rating where appropriate, organization, State, and date of death. Any inquiries relative to the type of headstone or the spelling of the name to be inscribed thereon, should be addressed to the American Battle Monuments Commission, Washington 25, D. C. Your letter should include the full name, rank, serial number, grave location, and name of the cemetery.

While interments are in progress, the cemetery will not be open to visitors. You may rest assured that this final interment was conducted with fitting dignity and solemnity and that the grave-site will be carefully and conscientiously maintained in perpetuity by the United States Government.

Sincerely yours,

H. FELDMAN
Major General
The Quartermaster General

Appendix 5

Map location of St. Avold Military Cemetery

THE HAGUE
ROTTERDAM
Rhine River
ARNHEM
NIJMEGEN
Waal River
Maas River
ANTWERP

H O L L A N D

Ruhr River

WAREGEM
AUDENARDE
BRUSSELS
MAASTRICHT
MARGRATEN
AACHEN
COLOGNE
BONN
G E R M A N Y

B E L G I U M
HENRI-CHAPELLE
LIÈGE
NEUVILLE-EN-CONDROZ
EUPEN
VERVIERS
REMAGEN
NAMUR
Roer River
KOBLENZ

A R D E N N E S

BONY
BELLICOURT
MAINZ

SEDAN
LUXEMBOURG
LUXEMBOURG
HAMM
TRIER
Moselle River

Aisne River
SOMMEPY
ROMAGNE
MONTFAUCON
Meuse River
Saar R
SAARLAUTERN
SAARBRÜCKEN

REIMS
FÈRE-EN-TARDENOIS
VERDUN
METZ
ST. AVOLD

BELLEAU
Marne River
THIAUCOURT
MONTSEC
Rhine River
STRASBOURG

NANCY

V O S G E S

VITTEL
ÉPINAL

Appendix 6

"Crusade in Europe" book cover

DWIGHT D. EISENHOWER

Crusade
in Europe

DOUBLEDAY & COMPANY, INC.   1948

GARDEN CITY, NEW YORK

Appendix 7

Prelude to War

Chapter 1

PRELUDE TO WAR

IN THE ALLIED HEADQUARTERS AT REIMS, Field Marshal Jodl signed the instrument of German surrender on May 7, 1945. At midnight of the next day there ended, in Europe, a conflict that had been raging since September 1, 1939.

Between these two dates millions of Europeans had been killed. All Europe west of the Rhine had, with minor exceptions, lived for more than four years under the domination of an occupying army. Free institutions and free speech had disappeared. Economies were broken and industry prostrated. In Germany itself, after years of seeming invincibility, a carpet of destruction and desolation had spread over the land. Her bridges were down, her cities in ruins, and her great industrial capacity practically paralyzed. Great Britain had exhausted herself economically and financially to carry on her part of the war; the nation was almost entirely mobilized, with everybody of useful age, men and women alike, either in the armed forces or engaged in some type of production for war. Russian industry west of the Volga had been almost obliterated.

America had not been spared: by V-J Day in the Pacific, 322,188 of her youth had been lost in battle or had died in the service and approximately 700,000 more had been wounded.[1] The nation had poured forth resources in unstinted measure not only to support her own armies and navies and air forces but also to give her Allies equipment and weapons with which to operate effectively against the common enemy. Each of the Allies had, according to its means, contributed to the common cause but America had stood pre-eminent as the arsenal of democracy. We were the nation which, from the war's beginning to its end, had achieved the greatest transformation from

Appendix 8

Position of Third Army

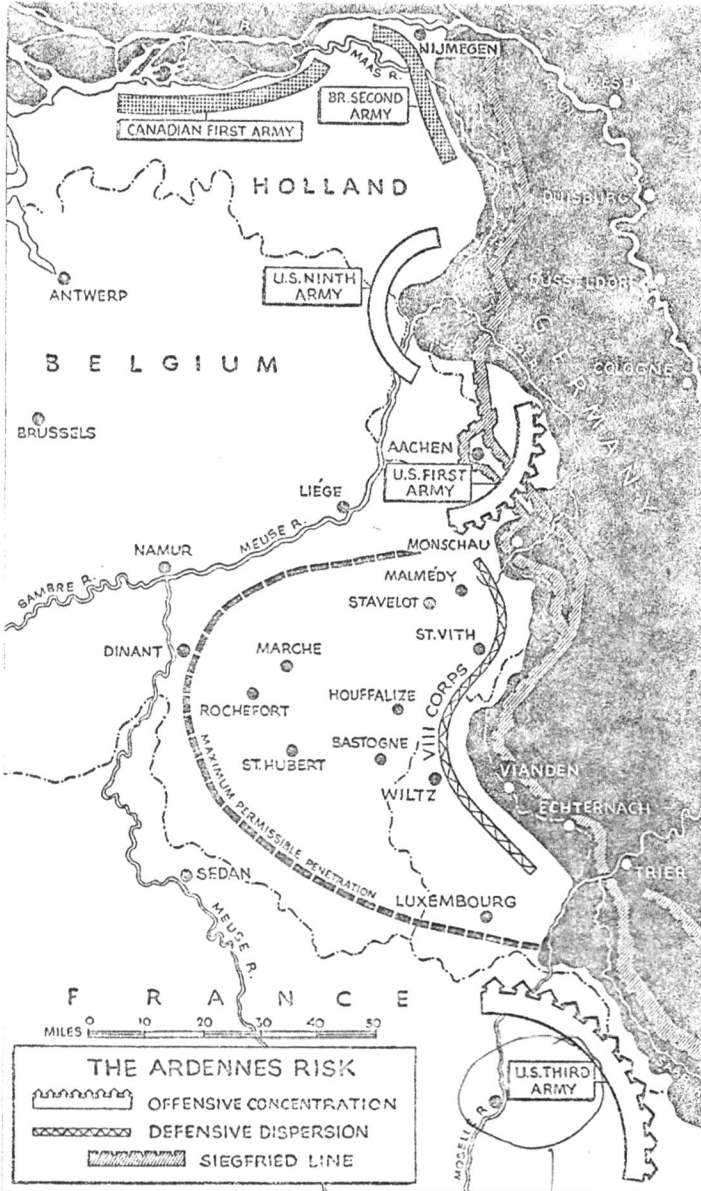

Appendix 9

Newspaper article on Helen Cole

Extension Office a Lively Spot; Jobs and Jargon All Its Own

By Doris Thompson

Receiving everything from canned fruit to human fruits, the extension office is one of the liveliest places on the campus.

Mrs. Helen Cole, who has been with the office for five years, can tell many unusual stories about the constant stream of mail, lessons, instructors and students.

For instance, one correspondent wrote claiming that he had ordered the flying saucers to come to earth.

Another student sent a box of canned fruits to the teacher. The instructor distributed the goods among the extension workers.

Mrs. Cole has charge of the alumni files and oversees the film library workers. Billy Hoggard is runner-up for oldest employee. He has worked in the office during his entire four years at college.

He and Jimmy Hone are employed for the dirty work—mimeographing, wrapping books for shipping and handling the mail. Four student office workers are Lanelle Watkins, Mrs. Tommy Smith, Miss Mary Woodyard and Miss Louise Taylor. They handle the clerical work for the correspondence courses.

Mrs. J. E. Griner, Dr. Minton's secretary, keeps payrolls. She is in direct charge of the files for correspondence and extension work, and is the only full-time secretary other than Mrs. Cole.

Incidentally, the proper name of the office is "Department of Public Relations," and Dr. H. L. Minton is director. He is assisted by Mr. Graham Nixon, who directs the publicity office.

Miss Koletta Jenkins, student worker, is in charge of the film library desk. Three boys operate the projectors—Jerry Cole, Harold Stiverson and Carl Ham.

Mrs. Cole characterizes the workers thus: "Some of our students take a full course and work all the hours they aren't in class. Some of them are married and earn money while their husbands go to school."

"They cope with the public temperament without losing their tempers; they open, unfold, sort and answer mountains of mail." Other duties include "answering a million questions, hunting the teacher who disappears completely when an urgent call comes for a grade, speeding the boss (Dr. Minton) to class or getting him off for a speaking engagement at night, producing an aspirin, calling a taxi or showing a film."

The workers have a particular jargon of their own, which sometimes causes difficulties. In the office vernacular, the moistening machine for envelopes is called the "licker."

One day some visitors to the college heard Mrs. Cole say, "Bring the licker over here, Billy." They were quite shocked, as they had received entirely the wrong impression.

Another office expression is "ditto" for persons who continue to come back on the same business every day for a week. Dr. Minton summons workers to his desk by calling out "Front and center!" in the approved military manner.

An "extracurricular" project in the extension office is a scrapbook for Dr. Minton. It contains the pictures of all the workers, past and present, and their babies. It is referred to as "The Old Family Album."

The department checks correspondence courses to students in Louisiana, Missouri and Tennessee, as well as some other states. Lessons even come in from foreign countries, from soldiers who are studying while in service. The office does a thriving business, and completely pays its own way.

Faculty members often write notes to correspondence students in the margins of their papers. This may lead to an exchange of letters. The student and the teacher sometimes form a lasting friendship in this way.

Thus the department, without too much fuss, serves a great variety of needs. It is a friendly, busy place, with a great many interesting machines and personable workers.

CPSIA information can be obtained at www.ICGtesting.com
Printed in the USA
LVOW011249071212

310180LV00003B/12/P